THE FINNS

AND THEIR COUNTRY

THE FINNS
AND THEIR COUNTRY

Wendy Hall

MAX PARRISH · LONDON

MAX PARRISH & CO LTD
2 PORTMAN STREET, LONDON W1

Printed in Great Britain by
Hazell Watson & Viney Ltd,
Aylesbury, Bucks

Preface

This book is in great part a continuation, and in smaller part a revision, of my previous book about Finland, *Green Gold and Granite*, which was completed in 1952. At that time the future, political and economic, of Finland still remained uncertain, and Finnish experts were themselves divided in their forecasts of the country's lines of development. In retrospect, the year 1952 appears as a watershed in time, marking the final separation of the old Finland from the prosperous and highly modern state of today. Rapid economic progress and the favourable evolution of Finland's political status have so changed the character of this small northern democracy that a mere revision of a book written in 1952 would be inadequate. So, although I have used my previous book as a starting point, and incorporated a small amount of material from it, this book is in the main a new work. In it I have tried to give a picture both of Finland's traditional background and of her emergence as a modern state and one of the most prosperous countries of the world today.

I cannot adequately express my gratitude to all the Finns who, during my many visits to Finland, have helped me in countless ways to learn more about their country. They are far too numerous to mention by name, so I can only hope that they will accept my thanks in anonymity, and forgive the book's shortcomings, for which they are in no way responsible.

WENDY HALL
London, November 1966.

For

KATHARINA

my Finnish goddaughter

and

ANTHONY

my English godson

Contents

I

THE NORTHERN SCENE

1 Land of Challenge 13
2 The Natural Background 22
3 The Capital City 32
4 The People of Finland 43
5 Daily Life and Society 56
6 The Arts and Entertainment 72

II

HISTORY AND POLITICS

7 Under Swedish Rule 85
8 From Russian Tsar to Finnish President 96
9 The Stormy Years 110
10 New Bearings 125
11 Political Life 138

III

INTO THE MODERN WORLD

12 The Vanishing Idyll 151
13 Farm and Forest 160
14 Setting for a New Society 171
15 Designing for the World 184
16 Industry Today 196
17 The Nordic Family 205
Bibliography 212
Index 217

List of Plates

between pages 40 and 41

I Among the lakes and forests

II Helsinki: the market place

III Helsinki: the President's Palace

IV Tavasts from central Finland

V A Karelian girl

VI Mid-winter in the forest

VII Mid-winter in Helsinki

VIII A lakeside sauna

between pages 184 and 185

IX Vuoksenniska Church, Imatra

X A Finnish factory

XI A power station in the north

XII The home of an industrial worker

XIII Tapiola town centre

XIV Bust of Sibelius by Väinö Aaltonen
'A la Russe' by Eila Hiltunen

XV Table mats by Dora Jung
Double decanter and 'Kilta' ware by Kaj Franck

XVI Ceramic bird by Birger Kaipiainen
Crystal bowls by Nanny Still

The photographs are by: Arabia Wärtsilä (XV), Finnish Society of Crafts and Design (XVI), H. Havas and the Museum of Finnish Architecture (IX), Kanerva (VII), Lehtikuva (V, XIII), Pietinen (IV, VI, XI, XIV, XV), Roos (X), Chris Ware & Keystone (II, III) and A. Ylanen (XII).

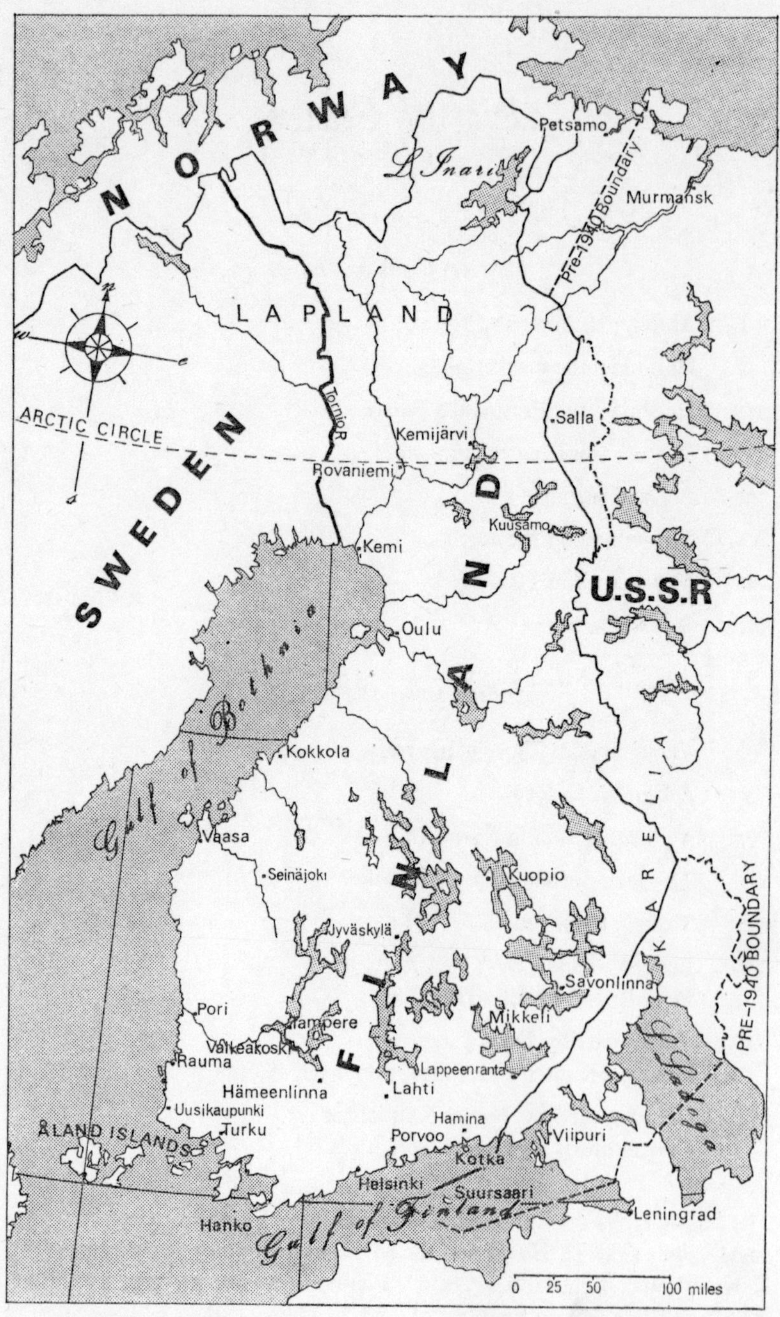
NORWAY
L. Inari
Petsamo
Pre-1940 Boundary
Murmansk
LAPLAND
Tornio R.
ARCTIC CIRCLE
SWEDEN
Kemijärvi
Salla
Rovaniemi
Kuusamo
Kemi
U.S.S.R
Oulu
Gulf of Bothnia
Kokkola
FINLAND
KARELIA
Vaasa
Seinäjoki
Kuopio
Jyväskylä
PRE-1940 BOUNDARY
Savonlinna
Pori
Tampere
Mikkeli
Valkeakoski
Rauma
Lappeenranta
Hämeenlinna
Lahti
Uusikaupunki
Hamina
ÅLAND ISLANDS
Turku
Porvoo
Viipuri
Kotka
Helsinki
Suursaari
Leningrad
Hanko
Gulf of Finland
0 25 50 100 miles

Part One

THE NORTHERN SCENE

CHAPTER ONE

Land of Challenge

When the Finns became independent in 1917, they had already been living in Finland for close on two thousand years. For much of that time a perverse destiny seemed to control them. They were men of a fierce personal independence, yet national independence eluded them until this century. They were men without designs on their neighbours; instead, for nearly seven hundred years, they were dominated by the countries on their borders. They were a peace-loving people, but they were driven into many wars, in which they gained little and lost much. Their country, for all its beauty, was harsh and inhospitable, yielding them often less than a bare subsistence; yet they clung to it with an extraordinary devotion. Isolation increased both their own hardships, and the sense of mystery with which the outside world regarded them for several centuries. Who were the Finns? Where had they come from? What was the origin of their language, which is neither Germanic nor Slav nor Latin, and belonged to a group outside the Indo-European family?

History, with its own perversity, could give no easy answers to these questions. The Finns themselves have been so baffled by their past that they term as 'prehistory' all that happened to them before A.D. 1100, the date of their earliest written records. The most controversial period of their prehistory lies far behind the time, at the beginning of the Christian era, when they arrived in Finland. It is generally thought that in some remote past, possibly four thousand or more years ago, all the Finno-Ugrians – that is, the ancestors of the Finns, Lapps, Estonians, Hungarians, and some groups still in the Soviet Union – were living together in a primordial homeland. Where that homeland was has not yet been conclusively proved. The earliest theories situated it far away in Central Asia. Later, philologists made what then seemed a reasonable case for a home in South Central Russia. The most recent archæological researches have thrown doubt on this philological thesis, and suggest that the original homeland may have been as close to Finland as Estonia, where the Finns certainly lived for several hundred years before they crossed the Baltic to its wilder northern shores. Finno-Ugrian tribes were the earliest known inhabitants of Central Russia. According to the older theories, they belonged to a great westward migratory movement which ultimately took the Finns and the Estonians to the southern Baltic and the Hungarians to Hungary. The newer theories hold that, if the southern Baltic was the original homeland of the Finno-Ugrians, they fanned out from there northwards to Finland, eastwards to Russia and southwards to Hungary. Many experts, however, still await more conclusive archæological and other evidence from inside Russia in support of these recent views. Should they be proved correct, the existence within Europe of a group speaking a non-Indo-European language would still pose a fascinating and baffling problem. The Finns' closest linguistic relations are the Estonians, whose language is so similar to Finnish that the two peoples understand each other fairly easily. The more distantly related Hungarians speak a language which also belongs to the Finno-Ugrian group, as do also Lappish and some dialects spoken in the U.S.S.R. This group is part of the Ural-Altaic family of languages, which also includes Turkish, Mongolian and Samoyed, and so has an extraordinarily wide, though scattered, spread from the edge of Western Europe to the Far East.

The tribes who settled in Finland nearly two thousand years ago led, for much of the time, the nomadic life of hunters and fishermen. They traded the pelts of the wild animals they caught in their vast forests with men of other lands who came to their shores. They raised such few crops as they could in their brief summers. They remained for hundreds of years without any coherent political or social organization to connect their sparse and widely separated settlements, although their western neighbours were already progressing towards a more unified state. Thus, in the Middle Ages, their country could be easily annexed by Sweden, and gradually swallowed, administratively, into the kingdom of Sweden-Finland.

The chances of independent development disappeared. As time went on, the ancient language of the Finns was displaced by Swedish for almost all official, educational and literary purposes. They heard Finnish only from the pulpit and from the lips of their families and neighbours. Their country became both pawn and battlefield in the recurrent wars between Sweden and Russia, and was eventually ceded by the Swedes to the Russians in 1809. Not until the eighteen-thirties was the vigorous national spirit of the Finns crystallized in the cry of independence: 'We are not Swedes, we will not become Russians, so let us be Finns!' But at that time the Finns in Finland numbered less than a million and a half, thinly and inaccessibly scattered over a country whose vast lakes and forests defied human communication. Nevertheless, they had created, perhaps almost unconsciously, a unity of unspoken resistance to absorption by Swedes or Russians, and created it in circumstances which should have been highly favourable to gradual and painless absorption. They had used their characteristic tenacity to develop an identity whose most powerful expression was the Finnish language.

But they had evolved no political organization of their own, and compared with their western neighbours, they had created only a limited culture. Thus they lagged behind the nineteenth-century wave of nationalism, and even came near to being submerged by it when pan-Slavism brought to Finland attempts at russification and oppression. They had to wait until revolution, also, came to them from the east, and in 1917 they seized the opportunity to be rid of their tsarist masters. Finland was the last country but one in Europe to become independent.

What can one make of a people which is, in the end, pushed into nationhood largely by the course of external events? Certainly the Finns lacked the aggressive instincts which might have made them independent far earlier. While the Vikings foraged and forayed their way through Europe, the Finns, who had little inclination to explore and attack, stayed peaceably in their own homes. Certainly they lacked, too, the natural gift for social and political organization which their Scandinavian neighbours had shown from the earliest times. Without either militancy or political sense, the barest national survival would seem improbable. How then did the Finns survive, and survive as a compact, highly self-conscious entity?

An answer is to be found in the theory of challenge and response which A. J. Toynbee develops in *A Study of History*, and in his austere thesis: 'Ease is inimical to civilization.' Toynbee lists five stimuli which have, singly and individually, fostered the growth of viable and sturdy civilizations. The five stimuli of new ground, of hard countries, of penalization, of blows, and of the pressures of the marchland, have all been simultaneously present in Finland.

Not only was Finland new ground to the early settlers; much of it has remained so right up to this century, as men have left their old farmsteads to clear with a struggle another patch of land, or stubbornly pushed the frontier of human habitation farther and farther northwards. Right up to this century, too, Finland has been a hard, often harsh cradle. It has brought, as well as the long darkness of winter, the long deep frosts which might reach into summer, killing the sparse crops yielded by the poor soil, and heralding a year of near-famine when tree bark was ground down and mixed with flour. Today the Finns, by ancient endurance and modern technical skills, have tamed their wilderness, lit their darkness, defeated the cold, and even made themselves agriculturally more or less self-sufficient. Of the people of the world who live above latitude 60° (which cuts through the southernmost tip of Finland) more than one-third are Finns, who have managed to surround themselves with many more comforts than the other two-thirds at the same latitude. But memories of frost and famine, poverty and struggle, never lie far below the surface sophistication of the often elegant city-dweller.

From the Middle Ages until 1917 penalization, though often in a mild form, was the recurrent lot of the Finns. The Swedes who governed them for six hundred years were benevolent overlords, who brought them learning and industry, and married their own political and legal organization to the native Finnish instinct for social democracy. The Finns welcomed the western civilization which the Swedes brought to them, and showed little resentment against their rulers. They were represented in the Swedish Estates, and probably had few aspirations to political independence. But they insisted on remaining Finnish, on speaking Finnish, while the Swedes made Swedish the language of the schools, the courts, and all official life. The only way to social and educational advance lay through the Swedish language, but the mass of Finns refused to give up Finnish. At the zenith of Swedish power, not more than twenty per cent of Finns spoke Swedish as either their mother or their adopted tongue.

Then, during the century when Finland was a Grand Duchy of Russia, the pendulum swung between extremes of permissive benevolence and penal russification. At one time Russia acquiesced to a degree of Finnish self-government far greater than the Swedes had ever allowed. At another, she pursued a policy of persecution and oppression of which the Swedes would have been wholly incapable. But the Finns needed persecution to goad them into a more militant mood. The gentler policy of the Swedes would have brought no such reaction from a fundamentally conservative and agricultural people. The tsars did for the Finns what the Swedes could not do: they made them into a nation born out of opposition.

The blows of war, which began in the thirteenth century and continued to this century, were far more cruel than the penalization of the overlords. During the period when Sweden was a great power, constantly at war with Russia, Finland was always Sweden's front line, and Russia's coveted 'window to the west': the land that was the bargain, to be demanded and ceded without regard for its people. Twelve major wars were fought between Sweden and Russia on Finnish soil. Seven times before 1809 and twice after, the eastern boundary was re-drawn, and the Karelians on the marches tossed from one master to another. The most savage of blows were inflicted by the military defeats of the Second World War and the crushing conditions of the peace treaty. Yet such blows 'nerved the community to purposeful action' as, according to Toynbee's thesis, they had done in defeated countries throughout history.

Today only the pressures of the marchland remain. The geopolitical border imposes its limitations. If, internally, freedom is more complete in Finland than in some other countries in Western Europe, in foreign affairs she has to accept the neutrality imposed on her by her geographical position alongside the Soviet Union, while attempting to make it as constructive a neutrality as possible. Finland is also a climatic and an agricultural marchland, with the limit of cultivation and the line of 'economic zero' running through the far north and presenting a constant challenge to a country still obtusely determined to wrest self-sufficiency out of highly unfavourable conditions.

Not all the pressures of the political marchland have been hard or cruel. The cross-play of the cultures of east and west, of the religions of Byzantium and Rome, have stimulated and enriched the native culture of Finland. To both her neighbours Finland stands in great debt. Sweden gave her political cohesion, law and order; Russia opened the windows of the rich cosmopolitan culture of the nineteenth century, offering her a view of a wider world than she had known before. The heritages of the Swedish and the Russian periods, immediately visible and sensible to the visitor of today, still make Finland both like and unlike the rest of Scandinavia. They have complicated the national personality and contributed to the peculiar individuality of Finland in the context of Western Europe.

It is a wayward, stubborn, often enigmatic individuality, as much thrust on the Finns by their circumstances as created by them, and resistant to easy classification. Turn which way they will, tidy-minded observers of Finland find only an impasse where they look for a pigeon-hole. The Finns' uncertain parentage and racial eccentricity have earned for them the description 'the orphans of history'. Their language is a fascinating freak that has strayed, as an interloper, into the totally unrelated family of European tongues, and there survived while native-born languages have died. Their social structure, into which feudalism never entered, has a historical parallel only in Sweden. From the earliest times the Finns have been free men and yeomen, masters of their own patch of land, owing neither rent nor service to another. Meanwhile, on the other side of an invisible border, unmarked by rivers or mountains, the Russians lived in serfdom until mid-nineteenth century.

Geographers up to the present day have failed to place the country of Finland in any single regional grouping. It is not part of the Scandinavian peninsula formed by Sweden and Norway; geologically it has to be considered, together with Eastern Karelia on the far side of the Russian border, as part of Fennoscandia. Only in recent years has the comprehensive shorthand term 'Scandinavia' become generally used to indicate Finland, Norway, Sweden, Denmark, and even Iceland which has, geographically, no claim to inclusion. Previously many Finns had insisted on the expression 'Finland and Scandinavia' in order to underline the racial and linguistic differences between Finland and the other four countries.

Nevertheless, Finland's institutions are not all identical with those of her Scandinavian neighbours. She has more in common with Sweden than with any other country, and it might have been expected that, with her long inheritance of Swedish rule, political life in independent Finland would develop on much the same lines as it has done in Sweden and the rest of Scandinavia. Instead, the Finns evolved their own different system, with a president instead of the monarchs of Sweden, Norway and Denmark, and a single-chamber Parliament instead of the two Houses of Sweden and Denmark. While political life in the neighbouring Scandinavian countries has grown into a stable and monotonous adherence to the middle way, in Finland governments have fallen like ninepins, and between 1917 and 1967 Finland had fifty changes of government. Both Sweden and Finland elect by proportional representation; in Sweden the same party could remain in power for thirty-five years; in Finland a number of parties, at times semi-circling from extreme right to extreme left, have rarely been able to find sufficient common ground for any one government to hold its own for more than a year. Only recently have the Finns begun to emulate the long-standing Scandinavian interest in social experiment. It is not that a social conscience is lacking in Finland; there are historical reasons here for the state being less active in social affairs. But the Finns, like the British, are noticeably more dedicated to liberty than to equality, while their Swedish and Soviet neighbours have both, in their totally different ways, sought theoretical equality above all else.

In external affairs, Finland has been prevented repeatedly, and often mercifully, from fitting into well-defined patterns. Since independence she has sometimes chosen the lonely way, but more often been forced to take it. In the Second World War Finland was the only belligerent country, other than the United Kingdom, which was never occupied, and which maintained its existing form of democratic government throughout the war. She emerged from the war as the only country on Russia's European border to escape a Communist government. For years after the war, when other European countries were organizing themselves into alliances and blocs, Finland remained in isolation, unable to join even the United Nations, yet evoking both admiration and bewilderment by her determination to stand firm and alone.

But in the one great respect which overrides and absorbs all these varied differences and distinctions, Finland is clearly and immediately classified – as part of western Christendom, sharing western democratic institutions and western respect for the rule of law. A nation on the marchlands can choose which way it will turn its face, and

Finland has steadfastly and at all times turned to the west, even when this attitude has needed all the courage and determination she could muster. Today the Finns know with certainty that they have found their place in the modern world – not only as part of Western Europe, but as part of the Scandinavian family.

This certainty of belonging to Scandinavia is only recent, and can be associated particularly with the new Finland which began to take shape in 1952, when the Finns freed themselves from the heavy charge of war reparations to the Soviet Union. That year was a turning-point. The major challenges of two thousand years had been largely overcome. The way out of isolation and into the European community was open, even if it sometimes seemed more like a tightrope than a high road. Unrealized by most Finns, the old agricultural way of life had begun to yield fully to industry. Most dramatic of all, in terms of daily life, was the soft-footed arrival of affluence. By the early 'sixties, the words of the national anthem, 'Poor we shall always remain', had been proved wrong for the first time since they were written in 1846.

The new challenges of prosperity and of the man-made world had come to confuse the Finns: to divide them in mind and spirit between eagerness for ease, novelty and experiment, and nostalgia for the hard and simple life that still lies among the forests and in the islands; between the standardization of a shrinking world and their own sharply-defined Finnishness. How are they to prevent the erosion of this Finnishness, to preserve all the distinctive qualities and characteristics which have served them well throughout their history and brought them through the bad days into the good? Hitherto the Finns, though always subject to foreign influences, have exercised an almost unconscious selection and rejected those influences which did not accord with their own character. The 'juniper country', as they sometimes call Finland, has bent but never broken. This selection has been aided by remoteness, by the barriers of forest and lake, frost and snowfall. Today all are pierced by radio and television, icebreaker and aircraft. The highly individual Finn is beginning to turn into a variation of Standard Western Man.

Still more demanding and confusing is the sudden challenge of the man-made world. Every country has to face the problems of transition from the natural world, in which man lived in obedience to the pattern of nature, to the man-made world, in which man must, by his own decisions, create his own pattern of life. Farther west, where nature has been less exacting and industrialization has come earlier, this transition has been more gradual, extending over a century or more. The Finns have been rocketed, in little more than a score of years, out of subjection to a nature more imperious and imperative than the West has known and into a technical mastery of their surroundings greater than they dreamed possible. Sometimes they seem to grope and stumble, unsure of their direction and uncertain how to react to the new man-made world around them. Decisions still come hard to these people, for whom nature has decided so much and so fiercely. But as President Kekkonen once observed, with an eye on history: 'Finland has a way of falling on her feet like a cat.' She will probably fall on her feet in the man-made world.

Chapter Two

The Natural Background

Finland stands on some of the most ancient rocks in Europe. The oldest among them date back twenty-nine million years, the youngest about eighteen million. Here is a landscape rooted in time, owing its serenity and spaciousness to the erosion of those millions of years, which wore smooth the sharper peaks and made the rough places plain. This had already been brought about before the Ice Age of ten thousand years ago spread a sheet of ice over the whole country, and created in the peneplain beneath it the low hills and hollows of the Finland of today. As the weight and pressure of the ice cap lifted and the ice melted away, the land rose above the waters, and the thousands of lakes and the islands of both coast and lakeland were born. Still today the land continues to rise, the sea to recede; the land slowly triumphs over the sea and new skerries emerge in the island-girdle of the south and west. The maps of the last four centuries show a constantly changing coastline and distribution of land and water. Yet, paradoxically, the fundamental character of landscape, lakescape and seascape remains unchanged. They preserve their mysterious sense of the primeval and eternal: the sense that the forests, the lakes, and the great granite boulders that form both a natural line of defence between land and sea and a stern ornament to the inland scene, have all looked as they do now for century upon century, and that their total composition cannot be modified by the hand of man.

These three elements – forest, water and rock – form the perpetual basis of the Finnish scene, varying in their proportions from region to region, but always, except in the farthest north, creating a type of landscape distinct from any other in Europe. The dark forests cover nearly three-quarters of the country. In southern and central Finland the deciduous trees common elsewhere in Europe – oak, lime, maple, alder, aspen and willow – are still to be found, but wholly dominated by the pine, spruce and birch which stretch far beyond the Arctic Circle, there to grow ever more slowly and dwindle in size and strength as the tundra approaches. Everywhere else the woodlands stretch into the towns even to the doorsteps of homes and offices, and always the distant horizon wears the nearly imperceptible saw-tooth edge of the vast forests of pine and spruce.

The pines and spruces are austere, uniform and unbending, altering only when their branches are whitened and bowed by snow cover. In their regimentation they look as if grown with intent for industry and mass production – dark, deliberate and utilitarian. The more frivolous and wayward birch gives a feminine grace to the forest – a grace once puritanically scorned, but now discovered to have its practical value. For in spring its still-bare branches allow the sunlight to penetrate more fully to the floor of the forest, and dry the soil left moist or boggy as the snow carpet melts. And gradually, more important industrial uses are being found for the birch, which reproduces itself so liberally and rapidly, filling the old clearings which farmers of former times made by burn-beating. One of the most frequently-quoted proverbs is 'Finland without forests would be like a bear without a skin.' The forests clothe a landscape which would otherwise often be bare and uninteresting; and without them Finland would lack a means of livelihood in the world, and might long ago have died like an animal deprived of the protection of its fur.

Finland's sixty thousand lakes cover almost one-tenth of the country, breaking it up as if by countless sparkling mirrors which throw off the light and compensate for the gloom of the forests. Many of these lakes, particularly those in central and eastern Finland, are immense and apparently limitless, and so connected by streams and channels that they make up labyrinthine waterways, an almost artfully contrived means of transport for the timber from the great forests. Yet only rarely is one aware of their vast size, for the lakes of Finland are not simple in shape, but irregular in their shores, broken by promontories and studded by hundreds of islands. Their winding rocky shores, concealing their farther reaches behind the forests that slope down to the water's edge, often give them a small, intimate feeling which belies their real size.

This inland pattern of forest and water, islands and headlands, is repeated along the coastline, and in its greatest beauty in the archipelago in the south-west, which forms a series of stepping-stones across the Baltic to the Åland Islands. The land stretches its fingers into the sea in numberless narrow, rocky and tree-clad promontories; the sea invades the land in thousands of creeks, inlets and bays. Here sea and soil are rarely divided by a no-man's-land of sand and sedge; they join hands so harmoniously that the pattern does no more than change from land studded with lakes to water studded with islands. So quietly and imperceptibly does it change that it is impossible to know where the cartographer would draw the coastline. He has himself admitted defeat, and condensed it to an estimated length of about three thousand miles. But if every tiny indentation and promontory, and every inch of coast round the sixty-two thousand islands were added, the total length of coastline in Finland would be almost fifteen thousand miles – and some authorities make it considerably more.

The island is an essential part of life and landscape. Wherever the Finn looks on to water, whether from the coast or from the shores of an inland lake, he looks, too, on to islands. For him they signify places of refuge and retreat, whose ownership is coveted as a pearl of great price; they signify, too, the mysterious and the unknown. Thousands of the smaller, unnamed islands in the lakes have never been inhabited by man; they lie there within sight and reach, yet totally uncivilized, wild, dark and archaic. Many round the coast, once inhabited, have been abandoned as the small means of livelihood they offer has dwindled, and the rising comforts of the mainland have drawn away their people. Thus the islands, lonely and wild, leave the Finn for many years to come with the hope of escape into an Arcadia of solitude and the natural world of the near past.

This landscape of mingled land and water is a horizontal one, gaining beauty from its spaciousness, yet eluding total appreciation from the lower ground. Always the eye is drawn to the far horizon, and always against the skyline lie the same forests, the same gently undulating silhouette of distant blue hills. In many countries of great scenic beauty one has to lift one's eyes to the high mountains; in Finland it is the view from above that reveals the charm and character of the horizontal landscape. But the heights in southern and central Finland are few and rarely rise above 600 feet; the highest mountains are in north Lapland, where the pattern of lake and forest gives way to that of fell and turbulent river. From one of the few ridges in central and southern Finland, but far more clearly from the air, one can grasp the harmony of pattern of landscape and seascape, the balance of land and water, the variety of shapes of lake and forest, or of islands and skerries lying in the sea. Viewed only from a vantage point in Helsinki, the islands which lie before the city take on a new outline; from the air the country is transformed and seen in all its spaciousness and detail.

The pattern is for the most part so repetitive as to suggest an overall similarity. Yet north and south, east and west, each has its distinctive character. The landscape of the south and south-west is more smiling and comely than elsewhere in Finland. The low hills roll gently away, and leafy birch-fringed lakes shimmer under brilliant summer skies or brood in autumn greyness. The Finnish landscape is commonly thought of as Sibelian, and so it is in many of its wilder, more rugged aspects. But here in the south it has something of the lyricism and chromatic melancholy of Mozart; an impression heightened when, on a still summer day, his piano music is played in a lonely country house, and the birds gather round the windows to sing in concert.

In the centre and the east the scene changes. The smaller, scattered lakes are exchanged for wider waters, separated only by jagged ridges of pines. Here, almost a third of the area may be water. Then the eye is dazzled by the extent of lakes studded with small islands, stretching far beyond its reach. The lakes brood placidly, the forests savagely, in those twin intensities of calm and drama, lyricism and harshness, which stamp both Finnish landscape and Finnish character. Only with difficulty does the eye catch sight of cultivated field and small dwelling, to provoke the mind to wonder who these people are who live surrounded by the mighty forces of lake and forest, bare rocks and gnarled and windswept trees. This, perhaps the most typically Finnish of all regions, is the landscape more readily associated with the music of Sibelius, with its majesty of conception and power of orchestration.

To the west the flat and dreary plains of Ostrobothnia bring the traveller a sense of realism which disappears again with the approach to Lapland. The scale of central and eastern Finland is vast; in Lapland it is vaster still. Lakes are fewer, swamps more frequent, fells and moorland less broken by forest; mountains are higher, rivers wider and swifter. The summer greens and blues of the meadows and lakes of the south are exchanged for the purples of the distant fells and the sharp turquoise of the rushing rivers. The signs of life grow even more rare, the solitude more intense. Yet neither here, nor anywhere else in Finland does loneliness evoke fear. Man has not triumphed over nature, as he has farther west. Generations of loving care have not subdued it and shaped it to his will. But the Finn feels for it awe, rather than terror, and is conscious of its elementary harmony rather than of its remote cruelty.

The Finnish landscape is often described as monotonous, generally by those who have spent only a limited time in Finland and probably driven at high speed along the splendid motorways which cut depressingly and unswervingly through field and forest. Finland has few rewards for the restless tourist, who can justifiably complain if he finds little but a repetition of the same pattern at the end of a journey of a couple of hundred miles. Its delights are for those who are willing to stay quietly in one small patch of land, by sea or lake, and watch it under the changing light of sunrise and sunset, of the brilliant noonday and the white midnight of summer; for those who will hear and feel the deep, total peace of the countryside far from the motorways, where the loudest continuous sound is the song of the grasshopper. This peace, so rare elsewhere in Europe, is already threatened in parts of southern Finland; but in the east and the north it retains its complete and compelling quality, and restores to the half-deafened and blunted ear some of its original sensitivity.

The charge of monotony is rarely made by those who have seen Finland through the round of the year, when the landscape changes, and changes again, with a drama and suddenness unknown in more temperate lands. Greenness, in varying degrees, is the constant of the temperate country; intensified by spring and summer, dimmed by autumn and winter, but always present. In Finland the colours of the landscape change dramatically from season to season; and, with the colours, the shapes and patterns as well. So, with every change of season, the same scene becomes new, different, even challenging to the eye. In the clear, sparkling light of summer the countryside is endlessly green, the lakes and the sea are vividly blue, both contrasting with the red granite boulders of landscape and seascape. In the autumn all is dominated by the flame and yellow of the deciduous trees, themselves pale if compared to the treeless Lapland fells at this time which the Finns call *ruska.* Then the small berry plants which creep all over the slopes seem to catch fire, and the fells which in summer were blue and purple are now entirely rust and orange. And now, anywhere in Finland, the seasons may take each other by surprise. An Indian summer, after a few days of frost early in September, turns the sea to a sparkling blue again, and out of it the islands, with their covering of flame-leafed trees, rise like patches of fire. Or the first sparse snows fall before the leaves, and in the forests the birches, turned that sharp and brilliant yellow typical of the North, grow out of a white carpet; then this combination of yellow and white, of the silver bark of the birch and the green-black of the pines, looks, to the innocent eye, as if created by art rather than nature.

By November, autumn has come in all its greyness; the low, heavy skies drain all the colour out of the land, the sea and the towns; damp and darkness take hold of body and mind, and the whole country longs for one thing above all: the arrival of the snow that will lie until the spring. Then the landscape turns into an endless world in which sea and land, forest and lake are all united by a blanket of snow. Whiteness gives a similarity of look to the whole country, and makes a colour photograph almost identical with a monochrome. Lakes and sea freeze and hold a weight of snow which makes them barely distinguishable from the land. Roads and fields, lakes and sea, rivers and meadows disappear; on darker days, the sky too turns as grey-white as the land, and the horizon loses itself in the middle distance. Sky, land and water become one. Against this cosmic whiteness only the pines and spruce etch out their cruel blackness, only the birch trees show their naked, wintry grace. The immobility of the scene is broken only by the dark outline of horse, sleigh and man moving silently across the landscape, silhouetted against their white background like a symbol of the northern soil and the northern winter. Had the Greeks lived in this Arctic land, the picture would have been perpetuated in relief on stone or in terra cotta. In Finland it is slowly vanishing as the machine age takes over.

Suddenly, out of this grey-white winter, springs the most spectacular and unbelievable moment of the year. It may come in late February or early March, as the days lengthen, the sun gains strength, and skies grow steadily brighter and clearer. The Finnish name for February is *helmikuu*, 'the pearl month', which so aptly describes the time when brightness and warmth begin to creep into the snow cover. The sun plays in its sharp brilliance on white snow and dark trees, until, as it sets, it casts pale gilded shadows over the snow and gives the trees a new depth of blackness. This splendid world of gold and black and pearl, without any hint of green, bears not the slightest relation to the Finland of midsummer. Who can be surprised that these extremes of climate have their counterpart in the extremes of the Finnish character?

When the snows melt and the ice layer on lake and sea breaks up into all its myriad shapes, there comes a brief period when the country seems to stand still and waiting on the brink of spring. Suddenly, again, an almost magic transformation takes place. Overnight, it seems, the trees burst into leaf. The spring flowers that farther south would dawdle into bloom one by one, all begin to blossom at once here, and the flowers of six more southerly months crowd themselves into the three of northern spring and summer. At last the fragrance of scented birch and lilac enfolds the land, and high summer reigns. The lilac tree that John Tradescant brought from Persia to Britain was taken thence to Finland, it is said, by a British army officer, who planted only one tree on the fortress island that guards Helsinki. From there it spread as far as the Arctic Circle, thriving better in the intense cold than in the mild British climate, and offering in summer its immense profusion of blossom in garden, avenue and mid-countryside alike.

A surprising number of the flowers, wild and cultivated, of the more temperate zones are to be found in Finland. But more typical of the northlands are the fruits of the forest, the undergrowth and sometimes of the fell. Here are the wild strawberries and blueberries of other countries, but also the raspberry-like but low-growing Arctic bramble, and the amber-coloured cloudberry, which conceals a multitude of woody pips under a thin layer of luscious-looking flesh. And among the small plants, the moss and the pine needles of the forest, there are mushrooms and an endless variety of fungi. About a hundred of these are safe to eat, but most eagerly sought after is the graceful golden chanterelle, which has inspired the designer as well as the gourmet.

The forest hides, too, the wild beasts that roamed the whole country when the Finns first reached it. In those early days the Finns traded the skins of the animals they had trapped, and so their present-day word for money, *raha*, comes from an old word meaning 'fur'. Still today there are elks within a few miles of Helsinki; and the tiny red squirrels that live in the woods and islands on the edge of the capital have been tamed by their appetites to a friendliness almost embarrassing. It is to the north and the east, towards the borders of Russian Karelia, that the wilder animals have gradually been pushed by advancing civilization. Here are to be found the lynx and marten, bear, wolf and wolverine that, a century ago, might wander all over the country. Then wolves were killed in the southernmost provinces. Now they have retreated to the north and the east, and only rarely there does the news of a wolf in the neighbourhood make it necessary for small children to be escorted on their long walks to and from school. The occasional appearance of bear meat on the menu of an expensive Helsinki restaurant comes as the only current reminder that perhaps a score of bears are killed in a year in the far north. But beyond the areas of human habitation there still exists a natural reserve of wild life, probably larger than any other in Europe.

Steadily man, with his homes and farms, his factories and power stations, is invading more and more of Finland. Yet any journey outside the towns reveals the still enormous disproportion of man to nature and man to land area, and the difficulty he has in coming to terms, physically, with his surroundings. The weight of the population is all to the south-west; eastwards and northwards it disperses and dwindles to three people to the square mile in Lapland, compared with a hundred and fifty in Uusimaa, the province in which Helsinki is situated. The communes and parishes, which usually have common boundaries, stretch over enormous areas of land and water, and the 'church village', which is their centre, is often little more than a straggling collection of small wooden houses, with a church, a school and one or two shops. Farms and dwellings are scattered far and wide, away from the roads, across the lakes, behind the forests, and often on the higher, well-drained ridges away from the lake waters. Water has been, until very recently, the traditional means of communication in the countryside, and even now some places are more easily reached by lake than by the rough tracks of the land. In summer, boats carried goods and men, and on Sundays the many-oared 'church boats' transported several families, wearing the costume of the province, across the lake to the simple wooden church. In winter sleighs speed smoothly over the snow-covered surface of the frozen lake. Only when the spring thaw turned soil to impassable mud, or during the rains of October, in Finnish *lokakuu*, 'the mud month', was the loneliest farmer sometimes completely isolated. So one can still drive for hundreds of miles between one small town and the next, and see only the rarest evidence of human life. The villages of Western Europe, with their history and character, and their role as centres of a community radiating outwards from them, have no counterpart in Finland.

The Finns have taken few of their architectural gifts into their countryside. Though they are today building some of the most beautiful garden cities in Europe, they have also allowed villages unrivalled in ugliness to develop. Their wooden houses are plain and unappealing, often in need of a coat of paint, and, unless happily surrounded by trees, often set in a piece of waste grass or dreary scrubland. Occasionally one sees the charming and graceful old church, or the well-proportioned parsonage or manor house of which timber is capable; these were the buildings destined for relative permanence. Otherwise the buildings of the Finnish countryside are still temporary in style and character, designed in the tradition of mobility which made the farmer and smallholder move to unexploited land when the limited resources of one holding had been exhausted. Where industry has invaded the countryside, it has lifted its ugly factory chimneys to offend the eye in the midst of lakeland and forest, and the cellulose mills have fouled the pure air with the stench of sulphate. Only the generation of architects working since the Second World War have begun to relate their buildings in size and scale to their surroundings. They have been notably successful in the great new power stations in northern Finland, which harmonize worthily with their backgrounds.

Yet in most other respects the Finns stand in closer relationship to the world of nature than do most other Europeans. Until recent times the forest has supplied the whole framework of their lives: not only their houses and furniture, but their boats, wagons and sleighs; their plates and tankards and all the implements of home and farm which they could fashion out of wood; and even, from the plaited birch bark, their rucksacks and sabot-like slippers. Today the forest earns Finland's living in the world; and one may doubt whether the Finns would have taken so readily to industries which had grown less naturally out of their woodlands and water.

The Finns of the pre-Christian era found their religion in the natural world. They endowed trees and birds and animals with human characteristics to form a link between man and his surroundings. They peopled their solitary country with spirits: the spirits of the forest; the spirits of the mountains; the spirits who inhabited the water and were credited with the gifts of music and poetry; the spirits who supplied squirrels from the woods and the spirits who guarded the oats. Their houses, their barns, their bath-houses and their cattle sheds all had their own *genius loci*; and so little was their influence diminished by the advent of Christianity that even *kirkonhaltija* – the churchyard spirit – came to take its place in their lore. The forest god, Tapio, is today commemorated in Sibelius' tone poem *Tapiola* (the dwelling of Tapio), and in the beautiful town of the same name near Helsinki. And still there are atavistic moments, one suspects, when the Finns revert to a vague half-belief in the spirits of pre-Christian days.

For the Finns of today, the countryside which they so much love is the refuge that soothes and tranquillizes, and at the same time the stimulus to creative imagination and the source of inspiration of their modern design. But above all, it is their link with the past, their history, the element which makes them conscious of the centuries behind them. The Finns have few old buildings, few great exploits of past days to celebrate, and no cavalcade of great men marching through their history books. But the ancient bedrock of Finland, the often archaic and untouched countryside, relate them, through feeling rather than thought, to a past more distant than any described in their own history.

Chapter Three

The Capital City

The first sight of Helsinki should be from the sea, the time should be late spring or early summer. Then eye and mind can encompass, in one broad vista, the whole of the life of Finland; for the South Harbour and its surroundings form a microcosm not only of the capital, but of all Finland. Early in the morning the overnight boat from Stockholm reaches the islands that fringe the coast in the region of Helsinki, and as it turns landward, the capital rises out of the Baltic, white and gleaming in the clear northern light. Its skyline is dominated from afar by the dome of the Great Church, or Lutheran Cathedral, built on one of Helsinki's many small hills, and looking as if lifted above the whole city. As the ship docks in the harbour, the white cathedral still dominates the scene, but below and before it there appears more clearly a sequence of gracious neo-classical buildings. They include the Palace of the President of the Republic, the Courts of Justice, and the Town Hall which is part of the legacy to Helsinki of the early nineteenth-century architect, Carl Ludvig Engel. To the east of the harbour the ornate Greek Orthodox Cathedral stands as a reminder of the Byzantine and eastern influences in Finland's history; but clustered round it are the more powerful symbols of the Finland of the present day. Behind it, a factory chimney points to industrialization; cranes along the shoreline indicate Helsinki's role as a major port; and, in front of the Orthodox Cathedral, the most recent building of all stands as witness to Finland's architectural distinction. This is a great woodworking concern's head office, designed by Alvar Aalto. It is wholly modern, yet harmonizes perfectly in size, style and scale with its neo-classical neighbours built by Engel – the humble homage of this great architect to a forerunner whom he has outshone.

All these buildings form the background to the colourful and crowded market place which stretches to the very edge of the water, and which will always remain, in an emotional sense, the heart of the city, although the town-planner must, of necessity, make its real centre elsewhere. For here the sea, the islands and the countryside meet the modern industrial and commercial capital, and here farmers and fishermen trade, unawed by the complicated apparatus of government housed in nearby buildings. A sprawling market in Parliament Square in London, outside the White House in Washington, or in the Place de la Concorde in Paris would be unthinkable. It is a measure of Helsinki's humanity and lack of self-importance that the market stays where it is, hindering traffic and making its mess and untidiness, but always reminding the President, the administrators and the citizens of the world outside the capital. It is also a measure of an essential difference between the civilizations of the Mediterranean and the North. The Mediterranean genius flowered in cities; the men of the North, from Norway to Russia, are at heart countrymen on a visit to their cities.

To this market, covered wagons drawn by the small, wiry Finnish horses bring from the countryside fruit, flowers, vegetables and also the products of hand and loom – rag rugs, baskets, wooden utensils. From the islands the fishermen chug in, their boats piled high with fish. Some sell their catch as they ride at their moorings, with the rough-and-ready equipment of rusty scales and newspaper; others, more advanced, unload and sell from stalls covered by gay striped awnings. The seasons bring their specialities. There is the crayfish time of August and September, when the housewife must be in the market by seven in the morning to pick the best of the catch. There are the few days in October, when from the Åland Islands come smoked and spiced sprats and other small Baltic fish. The arrival of the Åland boats is unheralded, but somehow sensed by half the town; and in the restaurant of one of Helsinki's most elegant hotels, one may eat these delicious fish and look, at the same time, across the harbour to the stall where they are being sold.

So naturally do market place, harbour and government buildings merge that one could believe that here was the original nucleus from which the city had developed. It was, in fact, quite otherwise. Helsinki has had a strange and chequered history. It did not grow, at some point where men learnt that it was fitting to live and trade, but was artificially created at the whim of Gustavus Vasa of Sweden. In 1550 he ordered the unfortunate citizens of Rauma and Ulvila, on the west coast, and Tammisaari and Porvoo on the south coast, to leave house and home and colonize the new town as a trading rival to the Hansa port of Tallinn, across the Gulf of Finland. (Turku, on the west coast, and nearer to Stockholm, was the capital of Finland during the period of Swedish rule.) The new town was not built on the site of the present city, but to the north-east, at the mouth of the Vantaa River. It took its Swedish name of Helsingfors from the rapids by which it was situated. (Swedish *fors* = rapids, waterfall.) But it had little of its intended commercial success, and nearly a century later the town was moved to a site by a better harbour – the North Harbour of today – and from there the present Helsinki grew, after years of difficulties and troubles.

All the timber-built Finnish towns of the past were subject to the constant danger of fire, and epic 'Great Fires' recur in most of their annals. They account both for the relative absence of buildings predating the late eighteenth century, and for the proverb which the Finns have had so many opportunities of testing: 'Rebuilding is more important than life'. The young town of Helsinki was burnt out in 1713, when Russians troops swept across Finland in the Great Northern War. Three years earlier it had suffered cruelly from an outbreak of plague, and so this fire, like the Great Fire of London, had some positive value.

The town was slowly, if unpromisingly, rebuilt. Then war again changed its fortunes, this time for the better. The conflict of 1741–43 between Sweden and Russia left Swedish power at its lowest ebb, and the Finns in a state of defensive apprehension of Russia, whose new boundaries cut deeper still into their country and took into Russian territory the eastern frontier fortresses of Sweden-Finland at Hamina and Lappeenranta. The Russian border now approached Helsinki more nearly than ever before or since, and Helsinki was the place chosen for a new system of fortifications. A great plan, based on the principles of Vauban, was drawn up. Though never completed, it made Helsinki into a strongly fortified city, and created on the outlying islands the fortress-base of Sveaborg. (Its Swedish name, meaning Fortress of Sweden, was changed, after Finland became independent, to Suomenlinna, or Fortress of Finland, although this 'Gibraltar of the North', as it was sometimes exaggeratedly called, had then ceased to have any military importance.)

The fortification of the mainland and the islands did more than restore confidence to the citizens of Helsinki; the naval and military garrisons brought them prosperity and culture. The officers who lived on Sveaborg possessed some of the largest libraries in Finland, and the fortress became a social and cultural centre which stimulated the intellectual life of Helsinki. Thus, ironically, the Swedes created, in defending themselves against Russia, a city ripening for the capital status which the Russians were to give to it half a century later.

The last war between Sweden and Russia in 1808–9 brought yet another upheaval to Helsinki. A fire in 1808 destroyed a quarter of the town and made urgent a plan of reconstruction. The following year, at the Peace of Hamina, Finland was formally surrendered by Sweden and became an autonomous Grand Duchy of Russia. The Tsar Alexander I deemed the old capital of Turku, on the west coast, too close to Sweden and too far from St Petersburg, and in 1812 the seat of government was moved to Helsinki. He commanded that this town of only 4,000 souls should be rebuilt in accordance with its new status as a capital, and himself inspected every detail of the plans. The execution of the project was entrusted to a native of Helsinki, J. A. Ehrenström, and to the German-born architect Carl Ludvig Engel. These men used the neo-classical style of the time with great felicity and sense of proportion, and gave to the city a dignity of which it can still be proud, while avoiding the pomposity and excesses of scale of later architects. Engel's most important and distinguished contribution was Senate Square, flanked on three sides by noble terraces housing the university and government buildings, and on the fourth by the white, copper-domed cathedral, raised on a high flight of steps. This is a square which, in a less remote part of Europe, would have become justly celebrated; so also would Ehrenström's town-plan which, despite its modest scale, gave Helsinki what J. M. Richards has described as 'a consistent and monumental official area rivalled in few European capitals'.

The work of present-day Finnish architects is more closely related to this neo-classical core than are most of the buildings put up since Engel's day. The most pleasing relic of the late nineteenth century is the Esplanade, which leads down to the South Harbour and is one of Helsinki's most characteristic streets. Its uniform neo-Renaissance façades, Paris-inspired, escape pretentiousness and the broad street is given a natural air by the pleasant informal gardens running through its centre. Until a few years ago, there were droshkis to be hired at one end of the Esplanade; these decrepit conveyances, and their even more decrepit drivers, were the last survivals of the Helsinki of tsarist days, when the Esplanade was the fashionable thoroughfare along which the upper classes drove in their carriages.

By the beginning of this century Finnish architects had thrown off the restraints of neo-classicism and uniformity, and the national romantic movement of the time expressed itself in massive buildings of rough-hewn native granite and residential areas whose large blocks of flats had more than a hint of Scottish baronial. To this period belongs Eliel Saarinen's imposing railway station. Though famous as a pioneer among buildings of this type, it remained for decades ludicrously disproportionate to the few small, wood-fired engines which performed the daily miracle of puffing in and out of this gigantic home, until they were recently pensioned off and replaced by modern diesel engines. Today it seems an extravagant anachronism when compared with the almost non-existent bus station, from which an impressive service operates, or the temporary-looking wooden buildings of Helsinki Airport. The enormous yellow General Post Office close to the railway station is, though of later date, equally disproportionate to the few letters the unepistolary Finns manage to write, but its vast main hall is for that reason wonderfully queue-free. The last of the great granite buildings was J. S. Sirén's Parliament House of 1930, an attempt to wed Finland's own granite with the neo-classical style. The result – a rugged, outsize Greek temple – finds few admirers today, and its paternoster lifts remain the terror of all who use them.

Within a stone's throw of some of these massive piles (and 'piles' they often are, rather than buildings) can still be found the occasional timber town house of the late nineteenth century, with its fretted cornices and decorated window surrounds. These charming and typically northern dwellings are disappearing fast from the capital, but remain, in greater numbers and in a better state of preservation, in some country towns. Like the cobblestones of Helsinki, so hard on feet and car-springs, they are reminders of the small space of time which separates the past from the future in Finland.

The future – or at least a forward-looking present – is represented in Helsinki by the many new buildings which have gone up since 1952. These, by Aalto and the younger generation of architects, many of them his pupils, make no attempt at the sensational. They are basically honest, muscular and functional buildings, conceived with the regard for purpose and for the people who will use them which distinguishes all Finnish design. The incidence of these new buildings is haphazard and unplanned, but they generally merge successfully into their surroundings. This is partly because the city's regulations prevent the building of towers. Architects are compensating for the limitation on height by excavating more deeply into Helsinki's granite foundations and planning for as many as four storeys below ground to the maximum of ten allowed above ground.

As Helsinki has grown, the problems of town-planning have multiplied fast, on the two levels of public buildings and private dwellings. Public buildings have sprawled over different parts of the city, and suburbs have sprawled over the islands and headlands round the city. Years ago Helsinki burst out of its old traditional centre of market place and Senate Square, but failed to settle anywhere else. Eventually Alvar Aalto produced a plan for a new centre, which will be realized at least in part during the decades to come.

Ehrenström's masterly plan of a hundred and fifty years ago was made for a city whose population of four thousand could easily be contained within its peninsular site. The Helsinki of today, with a population of more than half a million, has had to extend northwards from the tip of the peninsula towards the hinterland, and as this happened, the city became divided by a pleasant lake and by railway lines and a goods yard situated in a wide depression. The division was accentuated as Kallio, to the east, became a working-class area, and Töölö, to the west, a middle-class district with the Parliament buildings on its edge. Aalto's plan aims, in the first place, to link these two areas, now physically and psychologically separated. The goods yard will be removed and the wide depression roofed over to provide a large parking area, while over it a Central Place will be built on several levels. Here, and along a water-front walk which will continue out of the Central Place and alongside the lake, various public buildings will be erected. These will include a 'Congress Building', which Aalto sees as a national and city hall for entertainment rather than administrative purposes; a concert hall, a theatre or an opera house, an art gallery and a public library.

The whole plan thus corresponds to Aalto's conviction that, the more a city grows, the more important it is that in their leisure time its people should be able to meet in a single, fairly compact central area. His hope is to give to Helsinki a modern, northern equivalent of St Mark's Square, Venice – a place where all the citizens can meet and talk, eat and drink and enjoy themselves. If this hope is realized, Helsinki will probably be the only capital in Europe with this type of centre designed for leisure. Some years ago Aalto showed the direction of his thought, on a much smaller scale, when he built an indoor piazza in his *Rautatalo*, a large block of offices and shops in the centre of the town. The piazza, with its fountains and green plants, is on the first floor, surrounded by galleries leading to the offices on this, and higher floors. In this piazza is a café, arranged much as it would be if out of doors, and with twice the amount of space of a normal indoor cafe. This the young people of Helsinki have adopted as their own meeting place, and one that gives them the same sense of freedom as the outdoor cafés of more southerly towns. It exemplifies Aalto's shorthand philosophy of architecture: 'H is more important than S' (H = the human element; S = the system) – a philosophy voiced with just a hint of a hiss in the S.

Aalto's plan also links up with the development of the city northward and landward – the only way it can now continue to grow. Already Helsinki has hopped as far as it can from island to island and from one side of a bay to the other. This has made it possible for a great number of people to live within about twenty minutes' journey from their work, and yet also in idyllic wooded surroundings by the edge of the sea. Helsinki is sometimes called 'the daughter of the Baltic' – a name earned, in the first place, by its site on a narrow peninsula, surrounded by islands. The constant closeness of rocky shore and sea not only gives the city a feeling of great spaciousness; it gives its inhabitants the opportunity to limit its urbanization. This they have seized eagerly, refusing to build concrete promenades and the like along the sea front. Rough paths still wind round the town through the pines and the granite rocks at the water's edge; there are still pleasant bays for bathing within ten minutes' walk of the Parliament building. And while the bigger islands have become suburbs, some of the smaller ones, easily accessible, have been kept as places for pleasure and leisure. Suomenlinna, the fortress island, is now a museum-piece with an excellent restaurant in its ramparts; Korkeasaari is the Helsinki zoo; Seurasaari is a charming open-air folk museum, consisting of old buildings from the different provinces of Finland and relics of peasant life of the past. Yacht clubs extend over other small islands; a restaurant dominates another. Islands and mainland are linked sometimes by bridges, sometimes by ferries which operate in summer; for in winter, when the sea freezes, communications cease to be a problem, and anyone with a pair of skis can visit the islands more easily than in summer. (In the severe winter of 1965–66, a half-hourly bus service ran over the ice from the mainland to some of the outlying islands.) The frozen sea is Helsinki's winter playground; not only for the skiers, but also for the ardent bathers, for whom a hole is hacked out of the ice; for the anglers, who delight in the change in technique that again requires a hole in the ice; and even for the gliding enthusiasts, whose machines are drawn by lorries and vans appearing incongruously on the frozen sea.

Helsinki is also called 'the white city of the North' – a name less fully justified than 'the daughter of the Baltic'. It is true that, from the sea, Helsinki looks almost startlingly white. On closer view, one sees this whiteness is deceptive; only the cathedral, which is entirely repainted at least every fifteen years, retains this dazzling look. Helsinki's dominant colour is the warm golden yellow of the facings of the neo-classical buildings and terraces. This yellow is so exactly the colour of the birch trees of Helsinki in autumn that one is almost persuaded that nature is bent on imitating art, particularly when one observes the same colour in the yellow postboxes, the yellow and green tramcars, and even the yellow General Post Office.

This is the colour that lifts the city out of its mid-winter greyness, though that greyness, too, is often deceptive. Two colours predominate in the Finnish granite used for building – a rose-red-brown and a blue-grey. In both, the subtle gradations of colour disappear in many lights and, in midwinter especially, only drabness remains. Yet concentration on a single cobblestone (a dangerous occupation) reveals all the varied and beautiful shades contained in one small piece of granite. Recently architects have begun to exploit the colour possibilities of granite, building walls from irregularly shaped pieces of red and blue-grey, juxtaposed to set each other off, so that even under grey skies their colours are not lost.

The citizens of Helsinki, however, rarely note in detail the colours around them, because the city revolves at a steady tempo which rules out loitering and dawdling. In winter, when the streets are covered with knobbly ice, Helsinkians proceed purposefully towards their goal: not too fast, lest they should slip and break a limb; not too slowly, lest the cold should take too firm a grip on them. On the coldest of days they dare hardly pause in the street to greet their closest friends; and certainly not to gaze at shop-windows, where displays, understandably, rarely reach the high standard of indoor exhibitions. The winter sets the steady, even tempo for the whole year, and the tempo belies the nervosity of the Finns. Yet in Stockholm, where the winter is only slightly less harsh and where the inhabitants are far less highly-strung, the tempo is much more nervous, governed less by the climate than by the pursuit of business.

In summer, Helsinkians have little more inclination to loiter than in winter; sometimes even less, if they are hastening through their work in town in order to escape to the country, where they often stop overnight throughout the summer months. For Helsinki has its two sharply contrasting moods of winter and summer. From October to May there is the incessant round of entertaining to which the hospitable Finns devote themselves so wholeheartedly: the opera, the theatres, the concerts, the exhibitions; the ski-ing and ski-jumping on one of the city's several jumping hills, and the skating on the innumerable open-air rinks, lively with youngsters and music. In summer almost all forms of entertainment are shut down, and the Helsinkians depart to the countryside. Their city is abandoned to the tourists, spiritual descendants of the upper-class Russians of the nineteenth century for whom the Finnish capital, with its sunshine, bracing air and beautiful surroundings, was a favourite holiday place.

Helsinki is a fast-growing city which, between 1948 and 1965, had increased its population by about 200,000, and is expected to top 700,000 by 1980. When it reached the half-million mark in 1965, it reached, too, the point of diminishing humanity. Until then it had been – and it still remains, if to a lesser extent – a city where people live rather than a place where they earn a living. But now, as more

PLATE I. *Among the lakes and forests of eastern Finland.*

AVALL
H. SINKKO
K-VI № 5

PLATE II (left). *Seagulls are customers in the market by the South Harbour in Helsinki.*
PLATE III (above). *Junior citizens stop and gaze at the President's Palace.*

PLATE IV (above). *A placid face and a stocky figure are typical of the Tavasts from central Finland.*
PLATE V (right). *Karelians from eastern Finland can be recognised by their lively faces and slender figures.*

PLATE VI (left). *Mid-winter in the forests is the time for felling.*
PLATE VII (above). *Mid-winter in Helsinki: ships and harbour are ice-bound.*

people move out to the new suburbs, friends begin to be separated by distance, fewer children play in the gardens around the Parliament House or in the little square in front of the Foreign Ministry, and the village shops that had come to town are being replaced by more sophisticated enterprises. Narrow streets are becoming clogged with cars which they can never contain, and bridges between the islands and the mainland are turning into abominable bottlenecks. Talk of decentralization is always in the air, but before it began to be taken seriously the pressure of the population towards Helsinki and the south-west had already become established and irreversible.

This pressure of population does not mean that Finland lacks other towns where it is pleasant to live. Historic Turku, the old capital, looks on to the most beautiful of Finland's archipelagos. In the days of Swedish rule Turku was the second city in the Swedish realm, and in summer it was nearer to Stockholm by sea than Gothenburg was by land. Its university, founded in 1640 and moved to Helsinki in 1828, was at one time held in as high esteem as Uppsala's, and the inhabitants of Turku acquired a civic pride which made their city's reduction from capital status in 1812 an insufferable insult. Even people living today have heard in Turku the scornfully uttered words: 'Helsinki, the *new* capital.' Today, Turku has its own two universities, one Swedish, one Finnish, which put their stamp on this leisurely city and give it something of the feeling of Oxford or Cambridge. This feeling is accentuated by the devotion of the two universities to the annual boat-race, rowed in the manner of its more famous originators, on the river which divides the city. Then there is Tampere, the second town in Finland, heavily industrialized yet admirably situated on a wooded isthmus dividing two great lakes. Tampere is the adventurous theatre town of Finland, to which special trains are run for the people of Helsinki, who readily make the two-hour journey and return home after the evening performance. Lahti is younger, newer, but already known as a centre for international ski-ing competitions and for furniture-making. Oulu, on the north-west coast, boasts the most northerly university in the world, the first of a group planned to relieve the pressure on the University of Helsinki, with its 15,000 students.

The towns of Finland, even when small and remote, have unexpected vigour and vitality. They have hotels and restaurants as

PLATE VIII. *The ideal place for a sauna is on the edge of a tranquil lake.*

modern and elegant as those of Helsinki, but able to provide excellent food at half the Helsinki prices. They have theatres and orchestras, both partly manned by local amateurs. Their manufacturers are frequently also exporters, and there is a certain amount of coming and going between some of these small places and larger cities elsewhere in Europe. Moreover, these towns are highly ambitious. Most of those with more than 20,000 inhabitants have clamoured for a university of their own; and many of them, including very small places, are obsessed with plans to build bigger and more modern civic centres. Some of Aalto's most original building was done for the civic centre of Säynätsalo, a country town in central Finland, with a population of only 3,000. More recently, he has rescued the down-at-heel town of Seinäjoki, in the north-west, with a new town plan and group of civic buildings, which includes a town hall, a church and a theatre. The town's decision to spend the large sum involved could be viewed as either far-sighted or foolhardy; but its population is growing as manufacturers, impressed with Seinäjoki's leap into the modern world, open factories there.

So the paradox persists and gains strength – the paradox of the people who build beautiful and modern towns, only to escape from them into the countryside at every opportunity; the people with great gifts for making urban life comfortable and enjoyable, yet who long always for the discomforts of their primitive homes in the country. Perhaps both kinds of life are necessary to their complicated temperament.

CHAPTER FOUR

The People of Finland

Until recent times, few Finns travelled abroad and few people from other countries found their way to Finland. As a result, the unknown Finns have been credited, for close on two thousand years, with various outlandish characteristics, some invented, some merely exaggerated. Tacitus, in a less reliable moment, observed that 'the Finns are extremely wild'; later research has suggested that he was really speaking of the Lapps, but the Finns insist on perpetuating his now classic statement. In the far-off days when the British Merchant Navy recruited foreign hands at its ports of call, Finns were often to be found in its crews. But so firmly rooted was the belief that all the sons of Finland were adept in witchcraft that the officers took the propitiatory precaution of inviting them to eat at their table, while all other nationalities remained at their proper station below deck. Even today, one of the last legends persists. Still a civil servant in an office in Helsinki is obliged to spend a good part of the month of December kindly answering letters from all parts of the world addressed to 'Father Christmas, Finland'.

Small wonder, then, that the traveller arriving in Finland may sometimes be surprised to find how normal the Finns look, how easily and naturally they fit into the European family. He may be more justifiably surprised, if his first view is of Helsinki or one of the bigger towns, by the apparent absence of a single dominant national type. In this country of less than five million people, there is a diversity of looks and temper greater than in many lands ten times as populated; the spectrum includes not only the dark and lively Karelians from the east, the stocky and impassive Tavasts from the centre, and the taller and more slender Nordic types from the west, but also the many strains which intermarriage has made less easily identifiable.

The core of each of these three main groups, however, is still distinct and well defined. Each group reached Finland by a different route, settled in a different area, and there remained through the centuries in which forests, lakes and long winters prevented any regular communication between the thinly scattered peoples of a spacious land. When the Finns left the southern shores of the Baltic early in the Christian era, one tribe, the Tavasts, crossed the sea and settled in central Finland. Another, the Karelians, came by land from the region of Lake Ladoga, and made their homes in the east. Already, for several hundred years, there had been a steady trickle of Scandinavian immigrants into west and south Finland, and their numbers were reinforced from the thirteenth century onwards, when Sweden annexed Finland and Swedes began to settle there as colonizers and administrators.

The characteristics of each of these three groups are thrown into sharper relief by the differences between them. The people of Finland, Tavasts and Karelians especially, act as foils to each other; and pure Finns* and Swedo-Finns sometimes differ in temperament as much as the languages they speak. The Tavast is often viewed, and with some justification, as the typical Finn; certainly he is more distinctively, obviously Finnish than either the Karelian or the Swedo-Finn. The short stocky figure, the light fair hair, the pale round face, with short, slightly upturned nose, and pale blue or blue-grey eyes identify him inside and outside Finland. He may have an open face which his frank smile furrows deeply in later years; or he may be taciturn and immobile as to feature, concealing his emotions beneath a deep mask of impassivity, and betraying only the tenacity characteristic of most Finns, but of the Tavasts above all.

The people of eastern Finland, whether Karelians or Savolaks (from the province of Savo, which broke off from Karelia in the later Middle Ages) could well belong to a different country from the Tavasts. Many Karelians still think of themselves first as Karelians, and secondly and more remotely as Finns. They devotedly nurture the Karelian *mystique* which has gained strength since a large part of the province was ceded to the Soviet Union after the Second

* The expression 'pure Finn' is a misnomer which is used throughout this book because no adequate term exists to indicate a member of the Finnish-speaking majority of the population, as opposed to the Swedish-speaking minority. Members of this minority can be described with greater, though not complete accuracy, as Swedo-Finns. The word 'Finn', as used in this book, refers to all Finnish citizens, whether Finnish- or Swedish-speaking.

World War. Here, in the east, one meets a more lithe and slightly-built type, with dark hair, steady grey eyes and finely chiselled features. True good looks are not common among the Tavasts; but they are so frequent in eastern Finland that, even in some petrol station beyond an unending stretch of woodland and water, one may look at the young mechanics and wonder if one has strayed into a film set; or one may admire the elegance at the Saturday hop of the farm girl who, earlier in the day, was wading in the mire or washing down the cows.

These are the lively voluble talkers who more than make up for the silence of the Tavasts, the ready wits, the people who combine gaiety and unquenchable optimism with a strain of eastern melancholy, the people who have produced so many of both the poets and pedlars of Finland. Some say that they have a streak of laziness, that they have always preferred to drop their work and yarn to each other rather than struggle to master a difficult job, as the Tavasts would. Certainly all the traditions of rune-singing and folk poetry have been preserved in eastern Finland; and if the Karelians' devotion to work is occasionally less than total, they make up for it by the liveliness of their imagination, their warmth and their goodwill. Here is a people whose land has been a battlefield over the centuries, who have been regularly dispossessed and disinherited, transferred *en bloc* from Finland to Russia and back again. Yet they remain without grudge or resentment, and with nostalgia for their lost homes their only backward-looking emotion.

It is generally assumed that the Swedo-Finns stand temperamentally midway between the two extremes of the pure Finns and the Swedes of Sweden. The Finns, whether Tavast or Karelian, are primarily people of emotion and imagination; in this they are closer to the Russians than to the Swedes, who are primarily people of intellect and practical realism. Often the Swedo-Finns seem to partake of something of the character of both Sweden and Finland: with a keener intellectual grasp than the pure Finns, but with less imagination and sensitivity; less highly-strung than the pure Finns, a little more formal, a little less immediately warm and welcoming. But any attempts to assess such differences are dangerous. The Swedo-Finns ceased long ago to be a purely racial group and became primarily a linguistic group, which includes the descendants of Swedish settlers, of immigrants from Germany and the Baltic who chose to learn the easier and more familiar Swedish, and also of pure Finns who, through choice or circumstance, at some time became absorbed in the Swedish-speaking community. (There are also Finnish families to whom Finnishness is nothing short of an article of faith, but who can nevertheless trace their descent from a pure Swedish administrator of the seventeenth or eighteenth centuries.) Thus any characteristics attributed particularly to the Swedo-Finns must be bred largely by circumstances. The centuries in which the Swedish-speaking Finns formed the educated *élite*, the upper class which felt itself superior to the pure Finns, have inevitably left their mark. The feeling that they are separate and different from the Finnish majority remains, although it is far less evident than formerly. And while the Swedo-Finns have a lively culture of their own, their numbers are so relatively small (350,000 approximately) they are bound to be influenced by the culture of Sweden. The differences between the Swedish and Finnish tongues are greater than the differences between, for instance, French and German, and must come into play in that largely uncharted psychological region where language and temperament interact on each other. Equally, the existence of two official languages fosters a duality of temperament, with its ensuing tensions, among intellectuals, and the country's leaders and administrators, who must be able to move with ease in both languages and in both communities, whether their mother tongue is Finnish or Swedish.

The differences between Tavasts and Karelians, pure Finns and Swedo-Finns are, however, far fewer than the common traits which make the generalized national character, based on inherited and innate characteristics, but also influenced, over the centuries, by climate, geography and economic and political conditions.

Certain Finnish qualities must have been present since the earliest times, acting on events and, in turn, being influenced by events and circumstances. First and foremost, the universally known *sisu*, without which the Finns could never have survived all the hardships of history and climate. Its nearest translation is 'guts', but this fails to convey exactly the stubborn fierceness of this reserve of inner moral strength on which the Finns draw when physical and nervous resources are used. *Sisu*, combined with the violence which is the counterpoint of the loving-kindness of the Finn, has always made him a dangerous adversary in war, and it accounts to a great extent for his extraordinary resistance to the far stronger Soviet armies during the Winter War of 1939–40.

Closely related to *sisu* is the equally characteristic tenacity – admirable in the form of a determination to overcome all difficulties and obstacles, exasperating in the form of downright cussedness – ally and enemy of the Finns. It has been the ally which has helped them to surmount and survive the obstacles they have met in history and geography; still today it is the motive force in making Finland economically viable in the modern world. It has been the enemy which has blinded them to the realities of a situation and led them to entanglement in hopeless causes, as in the Second War of 1941–44. It underlines and emphasizes their virtues and failings alike, making them steadfastly loyal, overwhelming in kindness, brooking no refusal of their generosity; but also, when unscrupulous, determinedly and brazenly thus, and when submerged in confusion, determined to remain so rather than yield to the easy and obvious way to clear it up.

Sisu provokes admiration, even when put to foolhardy ends; tenacity provokes admiration and exasperation. But it is by their deep, simple gift for human relationships that the Finns touch the heart and command devotion. They are without pretence or pretentiousness; they have a sincere, direct and confident approach to others, respecting them and considering their needs as equal human beings, not as people who may be richer or poorer, employers or employed. The humblest of smallholders will invite you into his neat and spotless two-roomed cottage with as much ease as the managing director into his splendid home. The wooden cottage and the land round it are his own; he is a free man, independent of others; it is not for him to make excuses because his property may be smaller than others in the village; it is sufficient that he owns it.

On the basis of an equality which is sympathetic and without truculence, it is easy to establish a *rapport* with the Finns. There are no layers of formality, prejudice or tradition to be stripped away. At the first or second meeting the Finn may share with you many of his deeper thoughts – particularly if he is of the introspective nature so common in Finland. But his confidence is not given lightly nor temporarily. Few people in the world are more steadfast and generous in their friendship, more quick to help in times of difficulty and trouble. Nor is his introspection exclusively egotistic. He subjects others as well as himself to the same honest but tolerant analysis, sharing their feelings and looking for the opportunity to show sympathy in some practical way. Many Finns still retain something of the simple countryman's sensitivity and instinctive understanding; but in a few individuals, materialism and mechanization have blunted or killed this gift. The result, then, is tragic, because the real core of Finnishness seems to disappear. One of the hallmarks of the Finn, however simple, is that he cares about both art and life. But there are philistines in Finland, and men and women who lose their sincerity in pursuit of money and position. Probably their numbers are smaller than in most other European countries, but they stand out more sharply in their divergence from the norm, and are more scorned and derided than their counterparts elsewhere.

Climate and latitude provide the key to some characteristics of the Finns. Geographers attribute to the people of this northern latitude, in Scandinavia and elsewhere in the world, physical, mental and nervous energy; psychologists take it for granted that the long darkness of the long winters will set up tensions of some kind; and here, as in the north of Scotland, instances of second sight are too well authenticated for scepticism. (On the other hand, many Finns like to think that they can foretell the future when they can, in reality, see little beyond their noses, and their hair-raising prognostications of approaching disaster are not to be taken too seriously.)

But of the tensions, there can be no doubt, although they are often belied by calm, poise and quietness of movement, and would probably come more quickly to the surface were the Finns not protected by the family feeling which exists among them. They are creatures of extremes, and their tensions take extreme forms. Their most splendid products are the wealth and distinction of Finnish achievement in music, architecture and industrial design; their most unhappy result is a violence which is occasionally responsible for a crude murder with none of the carefully calculated quality of the crimes of Anglo-Saxon fact and fiction. (For this reason, the Finns adore British and American crime novels, but seem incapable of producing them themselves.)

More often the Finn tries to cure himself of violence by a homœopathic dose of violent spirits, in the shape of an entire bottle of the roughest and most potent *schnapps* that the State Alcohol Monopoly allows him to lay hands on. When a British cleric returned from a brief official visit to Finland, he began his report with the pronouncement: 'The Finns are either extremely drunk or extremely religious.' It is their tendency to empty a whole bottle, if not several, at a sitting, that gives them their reputation for drunkenness. A couple of drinks, and no more, means to them moderation, that most elusive of virtues. There are statistics to prove that the Finns consume considerably less alcohol per head, per year, than many other nations, including the Americans, the Germans, the Swedes and the Italians. No statistics exist to show which nationality consumes the most per man-hour, but the Finns must be near the top of the table, and often with disastrous results to career and character.

More fortunately, the highly-strung Finns also seek release from tension in order and harmony, quiet and solitude. Although their frequent parties may become uproarious, the Finns in ordinary life speak and move quietly, and live in neat, clean and well-ordered homes. Their passion for solitude and quiet is such that they repeat as proverbial the story of the countryman who learnt that another human being was building himself a home no more than fifty miles away. Without hesitation, he picked up his knife, and went out to kill his would-be neighbour.

The twentieth-century Finn has to accept less drastic solutions. In the towns, he has to live cheek by jowl with his fellows, and the gregarious half of his nature lets him enjoy fully the life of the community for a part of the time. But not for the whole time. He must be able to escape to the country, or to the creeks and islands of the coast, even if his refuge there is no more than a shack. His house must be as far as possible from other habitations, and he buys as much land as he can to surround himself with solitude, or finds a place where lake and forest will safeguard his peace. If a road is built within ten minutes' walk of his home, he moves, if he can, to a less civilized place. The Russians protected themselves through the centuries from the limitless spaces of their country by the togetherness which was given a sacred significance in the Orthodox Church. The Americans, when scattered in a boundless land, made togetherness a social virtue and a symptom of psychological health. The Finn will have none of this. Quiet, loneliness and space without end are as essential to him as food and drink.

Finland being a small country in terms of population, many of the Finns' most endearing and human qualities have been nourished, if not bred, by this smallness and remoteness, until recently, from the main highways of the world. They still think of themselves as one family, rather than as a nation divided by hierarchy and class. There are, indeed, times when the stranger begins to wonder whether the whole population is related; the mere mention of a name so often provokes the comment, 'Oh yes, she's my second cousin,' and there follows an exposition of a complicated family tree. The Finns have a discretion and a disinclination to gossip which is unusual in a small country forced by isolation to turn inwards on itself. But they disclaim discretion as a virtue and claim it as a necessity. If they speak ill of X to Y, they say, they are sure to discover that X is Y's second cousin.

The family feeling is also evident in their lack of respect for their rulers, as such. To great presidents, such as Mannerheim and Paasikivi, to great men such as Sibelius, they give unbounded and unqualified admiration and affection. But the lesser men are their second cousins, their old classmates in school and university. Their failings are known to one and all, and they have little hope of success in inflating their public image. They would, in any case, be hard put to it. The Finns have little natural 'presence', and what they have triumphs only with difficulty over the universal mufflers and galoshes of winter, to say nothing of the mild practical jokes which, in this informal country, are still played in the corridors of power.

These corridors are far freer from red tape, files and functionary ritual than their counterparts in larger countries farther west. Right up to the early 'fifties there was a refreshing simplicity in dealings with government and business alike. One man alone could take the initiative or the decision without a word being put on paper; memory and honour looked after the rest. Today the Finns still remain averse to the sort of organization and planning that entails paper work and long-term decisions. They have not yet adjusted themselves to the more complicated operations that demand committees, reference to higher levels, and memoranda in place of memory. Sometimes nothing worse than confusion results; but sometimes those in the outside world who do not know the Finns begin to suspect that confusion might cloak a crooked deal – and this does a startling injustice to a notably honest and honourable people.

The advantage of this attitude – and of the smallness of the country – is that it is extremely easy to make contact with ministers, heads of government departments and leaders in every field. The Finns, though naturally an unprotesting, ungrumbling people, have no need to organize protest marches or similar desperate demonstrations. They can make their views known in the right quarters and the general pressure of public opinion is fairly quickly registered. Besides, they have a propensity to take action and exercise their gifts of management rather than grouse, and this they can often do with outstanding success in a country whose size and relative freedom from complicated regulations leave plenty of room for movement and manœuvre. The large and energetic scale on which individuals and small groups are ready to pioneer is shown in the now famous garden city of Tapiola, a few miles from Helsinki. A number of people, who were dissatisfied with the post-war development of urban and surburban life, did not form an association to proclaim principles and pass resolutions; instead they organized a group of existing voluntary organisations, and, as a practical demonstration, bought a large area of land and there built a new town for 16,000 people. Today Tapiola has become known among town-planners all over the world, and the group that built it has gone on to create other communities of different types in various parts of Finland.

When the Finns succeed in ventures such as this, they are properly proud: and national pride, largely the consequence of belonging to a young nation, is one of their marked characteristics. They love their country with a devotion which has nothing to do with chauvinism; but overlaid on this devotion is a pride in achievement which sometimes develops into a *folie de grandeur*. Happily, the ability to laugh heartily at themselves generally saves the Finns from succumbing further to the more characteristically eastern preoccupation with size for its own sake. But it is shown in some of their buildings, particularly those of the national romantic period of the early part of this century. It survives in the constantly heard references to the largest industrial complex, ceramic factory, printing works, bookshop, and even laundry in Scandinavia or in Europe, all of which are said to be found in Finland. Every Finn is a public relations officer for his country, not only highly knowledgeable, but delighted to give up his time to act as guide, informant and interpreter to the visitor, and so express simultaneously his national pride, his generosity and hospitality, and his interest in people from other countries.

National pride and self-consciousness are also strongly evidenced in the great interest which the Finns take in their language. This is not confined to the more literary among them, and is surprising in view of their aversion to committing themselves to paper, whether in business documents or private letters. They prefer to use the telephone, at a cost which must be astronomical, judging from the length and distance of their conversations. (They do not, however, equal in suspicion of the written word those Swedes who, when they achieve the feat of a letter, telephone to confirm it.) In Finland, language competitions of one kind and another are frequent and popular; in one, which consisted in finding the largest number of synonyms for any single word, the prize was won by an entrant who had listed more than seven hundred words, all signifying degrees of inebriation. Even when its particular social connotations are put aside, this entry indicates the amazing richness of the Finnish language in both literary and everyday use. The most recent dictionary of present-day literary Finnish contains about 200,000 word-entries. This appears extraordinary when one considers that Finnish has been a literary and an official language for less than a century and a half. In fact, the relative absence of the standardizing influence of the printed word has added to its richness. More than a century ago the Finnish language was little more than a collection of dialects, each of which brought its own distinctive and spontaneously created store to the whole. For the same reason, there are, it is said, more proverbs in Finnish than in any other language, and the folklore archives of the Finnish Literature Society are among the largest in the world.

The Finns' devotion to nature and their unusual sensitivity to minute variations in sound are reflected in the great wealth of the vocabularies of nature and of sound. For instance, when the wind soughs in the pine trees, the verb to be used is *humista*; when the wind soughs in the birch trees, it is *kohista*. Not surprisingly, the Finns remark that Swedish is a meagre language compared with Finnish, and not capable of the vividness and variation of expression so characteristic of Finnish folk poetry. From a distinguished Swedish scholar and authority on Finnish, Professor Björn Collinder, has come the far more surprising statement: 'An old Finnish peasant, speaking only his own parish vernacular, may command more words than are contained in the complete works of Shakespeare.' But he adds a significant comment on a fundamental difference between English and Finnish. The English language, with its weight of classical derivation is, as it were, stratified socially and educationally. The more homespun Finnish is the common property of the whole people, and therefore a levelling factor socially.

The Finnish language is not only made apt for poetry by its wealth and variety; it has a melodic quality surpassed, among the languages of Europe, only by Italian. There are few prepositions to break up the line or the phrase, as these are embodied in fifteen different case endings. No Finnish word begins with the double or triple consonant groupings which often introduce a staccato note. *Ranta*, for instance, meaning 'shore', is a loan word from the Germanic *Strand* which came to Finnish through Swedish and lost the first two consonants in the process of naturalization. Vowels which are frequently doubled or diphthongized give a sonorous length; and Finnish is the only language in Europe in which, in ordinary speech, there are more vowel than consonant sounds. The tonic accent falls regularly and smoothly on the first syllable of each word, and so seems to add a certain fluency and ease to speech. Finnish is a fairly lengthy language; an English passage, when translated into Finnish, can take up one-fifth more space than the original. It has been suggested that the length of words and expressions is the reason for the Finns' natural fluency – they have time to think while they are speaking. But when the Finns are voluble (and some are extremely silent), they are voluble in all the languages they know, and crash boldly through sentence after sentence, often cheerfully breaking every rule of grammar that they meet, but making themselves fully understood.

The Finnish language is above all remarkable for the hold it has over those who speak it, and for its astonishing capacity for survival. When the ancestors of the present-day Finns trekked across Russia in the far distant past, small groups were left behind here and there, and were eventually absorbed into Great Russia and then into the U.S.S.R. But still today some of them speak either a Finnish understood by the Finns of Finland, or the related Karelian and Veps dialects. It would be hard to find a comparable example of linguistic tenacity elsewhere in Europe.

The Lappish dialects, spoken by the 1,500 or so Lapps who live in the far north of Finland, are related to Finnish, although Lapps and Finns do not immediately understand each other's tongues. The Lapps are to be distinguished from the Laplanders, who are Finns living in the province of Lapland. The Lapps of Finland are few compared with the total of those of Sweden (10,000), Norway (20,000) and Russia (1,500); but they add colour and interest to the far north, although, like beefeaters and battlements, their importance is exaggerated in the eyes of travel agents and tourists.

Few of the Lapps are now true nomads. During this century they have lost the habit of following their reindeer and putting up their tents amid snow and ice wherever it suited them. Today they live with their families in modern timber huts in small communities, and some of the menfolk take to their tents only in summer, when the herds move to fresh pastures. All those who know them well and can speak with them in their own language are attached to the Lapps. In their simple way of life they find a natural dignity, as well as a lively intelligence which distinguishes them from many other so-called backward peoples. Some who have wandered across the political borders of the north can speak Swedish, Norwegian, Finnish and Russian as well as Lappish. They read eagerly and write with a graceful, cultivated hand. Much that they know by instinct has had to be relearned by the scientists of less 'backward' races. As an instance, an authority has related how, when margarine first made its way northwards, the Lapps began to buy it because it was cheaper than butter; but they shortly returned to butter with the complaint that margarine was bad for the eyes. This was many years before dieticians discovered that margarine needs to be reinforced with vitamins if it is to nourish the eyes in the same way as butter.

The Lapp needs to buy little from the outside world because his reindeer provides him with almost everything he needs. Its skin makes his clothing, its bones his implements; in summer it gives him milk, which he can dry against the winter; it draws his sleigh; it provides meat which can be eaten or sold; and it reproduces itself so that, at the spring and autumn dividings, young reindeer can be sold to bring money to the herdsman. Many reindeer kings are rich men, but without any desire to spend their wealth on material goods or to leave their remote northern communities. They remain innocently untouched by the material progress which has leap-frogged over several generations in the north. There was an air service to one of the most northerly points in Lapland before more than one good motor road had been made; today it remains uneconomic to carry the railway far beyond Rovaniemi, on the Arctic Circle. And so a Lapp woman, who had come by plane to Helsinki to see a specialist could say: 'The flight was nothing, because we are used to going to Rovaniemi by air; but it was a great experience to ride in a tramcar in Helsinki.'

This almost passive acceptance of such changes that come to them is typical of the Lapps, who take no initiative to alter their circumstances. Their society could thus be endangered by the steady movement northwards of modern industrial civilization, but the Finns are making considerable efforts to preserve the old Lapp culture. They have great sympathy for the Lapps, with whom they share a deep love of nature and the solitary way of life. The Finns feel that if the old Lapp society were to disintegrate, something of their own way of life would disappear with it.

Chapter Five

Daily Life and Society

In the north of Finland the sun never rises above the horizon for six to eight weeks in midwinter; but for the same length of time in summer it never sets. Two or three hours of grey light mark the middle of the day in winter; and in summer night disappears. In the south, in midwinter, there are five or six hours of daylight; at midsummer, only a whitening of the sky proclaims the short hours of night. The temperature can range between the same fierce extremes: from the lowest recorded point of $-49°$ C ($-56°$ F) to the highest of 36° C (97° F). These extremes give a duality to daily, even to national life. The long months which the Finns describe as autumn winter, high winter and spring winter are the time of determination, purposeful activity, and a gritting of the teeth in the battle with snow and ice. Summer is the time of escape, the holiday from reality, when all activity slides into low gear. National problems are shelved until ministers and administrators return to Helsinki; personal problems until the summer cottage is closed up. Political crises have a way of reaching their height in the late autumn. Were they developing unnoticed, one wonders, while all Finland was lying enchanted on the magic carpet of high summer?

Winter is not only reality, but the hardest and most expensive of realities. Its estimated cost is equal to one-quarter of the whole state budget; as much, proportionately, as the cost of defence in many highly armed countries. In a bad winter – and fortunately, all are not equally bad – there is the endless clearing of ice and snow from sea as well as land. Icebreakers must keep open the channels in the Baltic for passenger and cargo ships and tankers to come in and out of Finnish harbours. Snow ploughs must constantly clear roads and railways. Gangs of men must work constantly on the roofs of buildings, chipping away at ice and frozen snow and nonchalantly hurtling it into the road beneath, regardless of passers-by. Citizens are obliged by law to keep clear the pavement in front of their homes, and if they are too old or too frail they must employ someone to do it for them.

Heating increases living costs heavily, but the Finns never cut down on warmth to save money; however low the temperature outside, it is exceptional to feel cold indoors. In the country, houses are still often heated by the ceiling-high decorative porcelain stoves which allow a minimum of wood to give out a maximum of heat. In the towns, central heating is the rule, and district heating is becoming more and more common. At times, one needs a personal oxygen kit to survive the heat and airlessness of hermetically sealed rooms where a group of people have been chain-smoking for several hours. (The Finns are extremely heavy smokers, and although they breathe, out of doors, some of the purest air in Europe, their lung cancer rate is one of the highest in Europe.) Only the elderly, however, now insist on running sticking plaster round the frames of their double windows to prevent any wisp of air from entering; younger people allow some ventilation through a small opening called a 'health window'. But there are still Finns, and not very elderly ones at that, who solemnly warn winter visitors that if they sleep with the window open they will never wake again! Even the continued existence of such dare-devils fails to convince them that cold air is not completely lethal.

The high temperature – up to 25°C (77°F) – in houses, flats, offices and public buildings means that only light clothes are needed indoors. It also means that extremely heavy and numerous additions are required before venturing out into a temperature which can be 50° lower. Men and women alike have to say goodbye to elegance and a good deal of money when they buy winter clothes; and they have to keep on spending. Heavy top-coats must be cast off as soon as one enters a restaurant, for instance. The doormen who look after them must be among the wealthiest men in Finland, as they expect a tip of up to one mark per coat.

The cost of winter continues, indirectly, throughout the year. Buildings must have a certain solidity, although wooden houses, surprisingly, are often as warm as granite or concrete buildings. They must have double windows and heavy double doors; most important, their foundations must reach deep underground so that pipes are well below the frost level. This is one of the reasons why so many Finns live in rather small flats rather than in the individual houses they would often prefer. Deep foundations can physically support several storeys, and cannot economically support fewer than three or four; and expensive thermal installations are better shared by several units. Roads also have to be specially constructed in depth if the annual spring break-up after the frost is to be avoided.

All these things done, the Finns make few further concessions to the winter. They give parties, they go to theatres and concerts, and about two million of them ski, from necessity or for pleasure or both. Small children play out of doors, under the eye of the 'park aunt', until the thermometer registers more than ten degrees of frost. The 'park aunt' (all adults, relatives, friends, teachers or total strangers, are 'aunt' or 'uncle' to the Finnish child) is a Scandinavian institution highly prized by mothers of young children. An 'aunt', paid by the municipality, is installed in parks and green spaces, and mothers can leave their children with her for a few hours each day for a small charge. Only the countryman adjusts his life to the seasons, sleeping as long as fourteen hours in midwinter unless he has acquired a television set, and as little as four hours in midsummer.

The townsman who starts work in a factory at seven or in an office at eight or eight-thirty cannot afford the luxury of fourteen hours' sleep. He must go to work in the dark and watch the sun rise through office or factory windows; then return home, again in the dark, at four or five. In theory, he and his family have a hot dinner about half past five. The evening is then punctuated frequently by cups of coffee, the national addiction, and occasionally by sandwiches or cakes. But these evening arrangements are flexible and unexpected, particularly in more cosmopolitan circles. The guest who is vaguely invited to 'come round at seven-thirty or eight' may be offered coffee and cakes; or he may, after eating a precautionary meal, find himself sitting down at eight o'clock before an excellent steak. In hotels and restaurants it seems possible to eat anything from a sandwich to a full-scale hot meal at any time from four o'clock onwards.

In December, darkness has reached its darkest, and rarely, except in Lapland, has enough snow fallen to lie and reflect what little light there is. In compensation, the Finns throw themselves into a round of junketing which culminates with Christmas. On 13th December the feast of Saint Lucia is celebrated, marking the shortest day of the year according to the old calendar; for weeks before, the press busies itself publishing photographs of beautiful girls who may be elected to represent Lucia, wearing a crown of candles, in the local celebrations. But before that, 'Little Christmases' have begun. Every office, every club, society or group of any kind has its party, and some people find themselves obliged to attend about ten of these 'Little Christmases' in the space of two or three weeks. Once the real Christmas arrives, they are so sated with celebration that they accept without demur the austerity of some of their Christmas fare. For now they deliberately maintain the traditions which belong to the days when all were equal in poverty. Thus the Christmas food which was festive a century or more ago seems almost penal today. But still the Finns insist on eating on Christmas Eve a variety of dried cod whose chief characteristic is an all-pervading and particularly revolting smell, boiled rice, once a rare imported delicacy, and small prune pasties. The meal is fortunately redeemed by the excellent pork, interpolated between cod and rice, from the pig traditionally killed at Christmas. The less traditional side of the festival is represented by the professional Father Christmases, who advertise themselves in the newspapers as 'good' and 'reliable', and able to visit any number of homes on Christmas Eve. The less reliable among them have a tendency to drink deep on all their calls, with the result that by midnight the police stations in the larger towns are said to be full of merry gentlemen, all with long white beards, and all clad in scarlet robes.

In summer, the mood and rhythm of life change dramatically. The people who during the rest of the year demand warmth, comfort, ease and often sophisticated surroundings, now demand, with even greater insistence, a rough and primitive life in the country. The cottage *without* water or electricity becomes as desirable as the most luxurious of town flats. Even the wealthiest and most waited-on of Finns suffer from the nostalgia for the primitive, and men in high places assure you that their only reason for working eleven months of the year is to be able to spend the twelfth in their cottage in the country.

Some consider themselves fortunate if the cottage is within reach of their work. Then the whole family can spend the three months of the school holidays there, and the father can drive to and from town. Offices all shut one hour earlier in the summer months so that everyone can take advantage of the brief period of sun and light. This accounts for one of the requirements of the ideal cottage – that its windows and verandah should face west to catch the long low sun of evening. The other requirements are that it should be as far as possible from any road, even a cart track; that it should be close to the sea or to a lake; and that it should be extremely simple – perhaps only one room, with a couple of alcoves fitted with bunks, and a verandah; no water, only a wood-fired stove for cooking. There are, of course, those who backslide from the primitive goal, and install water, occasionally electricity, and even the telephone, to the accompaniment of excuses and explanations for the benefit of those who view these lapses as decadent. In the unspoiled life of the countryside the Finns look for a release from the tensions of ordinary life; and perhaps, also, from a niggling guilt-complex about the comforts of the rest of the year.

To own a country cottage is not the good fortune of only the few. Factory workers often have their wooden cabins, built by themselves, in the country, although they may not be able to afford the more delectable sites on the edge of sea or lake. Young people who have left their parents' farms to work in the towns may return to build a cottage on a piece of the farm land. Often the Finn starts by building not the cottage, but the sauna or Finnish bath, without which neither life nor home would be complete. In the country, almost every home has its own sauna, either adjoining the house or on the edge of the water, and in the towns blocks of flats have one in the basement, which the tenants use by roster.

For the sauna is the Finns' most characteristic and ancient institution, with close on a thousand years of history behind it. Its principle is dry heat, between 90° and 110°C (195° and 230°F), generated by a stove topped with large stones. From time to time a little water is thrown on the stones, the steam so produced being absorbed in the wooden walls of the sauna room. 'Bathers' sit or lie on wooden platforms, gently beating themselves with birch leaves (not twigs), until the heat becomes too much for them. Then they go out and plunge into sea or lake, or roll in the snow, according to what is available; if none of these is at hand, they take a cold shower. They return to the sauna and repeat the process once or twice more, and then rest quietly, wrapped in their towels, for half an hour or so before dressing. For the Finn, the sauna is a weekly ritual which he often shares with his friends, and one which he treats with respect and even reverence. An old proverb runs: 'Two places are holy – church and sauna.' Today it is still considered offensive to talk loudly or move boisterously in the sauna. Mind and body alike are supposed to emerge cleansed and refreshed. In recent years, so-called saunas have been built in many countries, but few can catch the feeling and atmosphere of the authentic Finnish bath. Some, unforately, are the reverse of authentic, and have given to the name 'sauna' connotations which the Finns have always determinedly avoided.

The sauna is always part of the celebration of midsummer, which has been conveniently fixed on a Saturday so that everyone can spend it in the country. Now birch takes the place of the Christmas fir, and great branches are cut to decorate houses, cars, and even railway engines. After the sauna, there is outdoor dancing, and bonfires are lit on lake and sea shores. Midsummer is a simpler festival than Christmas, but for the Finns it has a greater, if pagan appeal, relating them more closely to the life of the countryside and celebrating the precious gift of twenty to twenty-four hours of daylight, compared with none to six, according to latitude, at Christmas.

Summer, naturally, is the time for all outdoor sports other than ski-ing or skating. The Finns have been, since the end of the last century, among the most sporting of nations, and have today more than three thousand active sports and athletic societies all over the country. Organized athletics, and sports such as football and a local version of baseball proceed much as in other countries – except in frequency. The Finns claim, for instance, that the number of athletic contests held in a year is twice as great in Finland as in the U.S.A. But in addition there is an exercise-for-everyone movement, stimulated by both the precept and the practice of a former sports champion, President Kekkonen. Its chief manifestation is the walking contests, in which about a million and a half people take part each year. Towns challenge each other, their citizens turning out in force, led by their mayors; offices, led by their managing directors, do likewise, and it is rumoured that some government departments have threatened with delayed promotion prospects the staff who fail to do their stint of six to twelve miles in inter-Ministry walks.

Finland's day-to-day life is lived in the context of an open society which appears, on an initial view, to have been achieved without effort. Social democracy is native to the true Finnish character; the Finn not only thinks that he is as good as the next man; he treats the next man as his equal. The open society is a product, not of political theory, but of self-respect and mutual respect.

The absence of hierarchy and horizontal strata is constantly in evidence in Finland; so also is the absence of vertical divisions. Society is open sideways as well as upwards; coteries and circles are rare, and people of widely differing professions and occupations meet and mix to their mutual benefit. Sibelius used to assert, half humourously, half seriously, that he preferred the company of businessmen to that of other artists, because artists always talked about money, while businessmen talked about art. The most distinguished, though exceptional, example of this broad-based mobility was a cleric M.P. (both the clergy and civil servants may sit in the Finnish Parliament) who became Prime Minister and subsequently Archbishop of Finland.

Since Finland's social democracy has so little to do with political theory, it is not built round a striving for material equality. At its best, it simply disregards and views as unimportant differences in income or possessions, family or profession. At its worst, it rarely degenerates into the chip-on-the-shoulder brand of egalitarianism. The farmers and farm-workers who, in terms of money, are often the least favoured of Finns, are also the least envious of people. Social democracy seems to come so naturally that one tends to assume that it has always existed. The native inclination to view all men as equal has certainly always been present; but until the First World War class differences were strongly, sometimes bitterly, marked. Some Finns hold that they did not completely disappear until the Second World War, and are also doubtful whether the present democratic structure can withstand the new social problems caused by rapid industrialization.

During the time when Finland was part of Sweden and until the beginning of this century, the Finns were subject to the hierarchical system of the Four Estates – the nobles, the clergy, the burghers and the peasants. This system had a weakness peculiar to Finland: the burghers formed the least influential group of the four, because they never developed into the wealthy mercantile class that arose in

Western Europe. As a result the Finnish urban middle class remained relatively insignificant right up to the First World War. On the other hand, the name 'peasant' has always had a connotation different from that generally understood farther west and south. The peasants of Finland included crofters and cotters, but they were more often yeomen, the owners of their land, however limited, and, as such, men of a certain independence. They were, in a sense, middle-class, but they lived outside the towns, which were largely occupied by the upper and working classes together with the foreign merchants who monopolized so much of Finland's trade.

The nobles never reached any great social heights, and no castles, and few stately homes exist in Finland to recall their more influential days. The old castles which remain are fortresses, not dwellings. The nobles of the realm of Sweden-Finland were deprived of their fiefs by the king as far back as the seventeenth century, and the Finnish nobles eventually became gentry rather than nobility. Most of them were Swedish-speaking by birth or inclination, and so belonged to the *élite* which was influenced by the more aristocratic society of Sweden, and which tended to regard the pure Finns as little more than hewers of wood and drawers of water. Finland never had a ruling class in the English sense of the term, but the Swedish-speaking Finns, often the descendants of men who had governed and administered Finland on behalf of the Swedish Crown, felt themselves historically as people with the rights and abilities to fill the higher positions in the land. Now former noblemen, who have lost their wealth and their lands, have merged into the middle class, working in the usual run of middle-class jobs. Some have dropped their titles, and those who still use them derive no advantage, socially or otherwise, from their baronial prefixes.

Today, pure Finns and Swedo-Finns work side by side in complete equality. But there is between them the only vertical division of any importance in Finland – a division essentially linguistic, but with its inevitable social consequences. It is entirely natural that those whose mother tongue is Swedish should congregate together from childhood and schooldays onwards, although the division is by no means rigid. Many intellectuals are equally at home among pure Finns and Swedo-Finns; at the same time, there are some pure Finnish bigots whose misguided brand of patriotism forbids them to speak a word of

Swedish or to think well of any Swedo-Finn. Otherwise, rancour has largely disappeared from relations between the two language groups. The proportion of Swedish-speakers (seven per cent of the population) is dwindling as a result of emigration and finnicization through intermarriage, and some people foresee, in the distant future, the almost total disappearance of the Swedish language in Finland.

The class cleavage was accentuated in the early part of this century by the influence of Marxism in Finland. It obtained a hold over the workers, in both town and country, because it represented opposition to the tsarist oppression and persecution from which Finland, at that time, was suffering so bitterly. With revolution and independence it overflowed into civil war, and left memories which had to be gradually wiped out before the democratic society of the present day could be achieved. One of the many paradoxes of Finnish life today is that a large Communist Party can exist and thrive in a country which attaches so little importance to social differences.

Since Finland became independent in 1917, the pull towards a democratic way of life has been strong. From the outset, the pure Finns, who accounted for over ninety per cent of the population, naturally took over a far greater part in government, administrative and public life than before, and a stratified society was foreign to their egalitarian temperament and background. It is interesting to note that, in the discussions of the future constitution which took place after the Declaration of Independence, the Swedo-Finns were strongly in favour of a monarchy, and the pure Finns of a republic. The Swedo-Finns, however, were second to none in their efforts to put the young republic on its feet; many, for instance, undertook the representation of Finland abroad at their own heavy expense, before a diplomatic service was organized.

A small and rapidly developing country cannot, in any case, afford a closed or stratified class structure. If the five million Finns of the present day are to maintain modern systems of government and industry, communications and public services, and diplomatic and commercial representation abroad, they have to make the best use of their available man- and brain-power. Social background cannot be considered where ability is urgently needed. Thus it is easier to get to the top in Finland; and thus life nearer the base of the pyramid is more interesting. Mere drones are an extravagance, and the lower and more junior ranks have to take more responsibility than they would in more heavily-populated countries. One has the impression in Finland that a high proportion of the population is at a fuller stretch than elsewhere – which makes for greater general satisfaction, if also for greater tension.

A desire for education and knowledge is a natural part of this open, full-stretch society; an equally natural part is a democratic education system which has included neither boarding schools, exclusive or not, nor expensive day schools. Since 1921 the State has provided free education for all, in primary and middle schools, from the age of seven to sixteen. The forty per cent of pupils likely to go on to the university have transferred, at the age of eleven, to secondary schools where very modest fees were charged. Since 1965, however, Finland has been moving towards a comprehensive system, similar to that in force in Sweden, in which secondary schools are abolished and all pupils attend one and the same school from seven to sixteen. The clearest measure of this desire for education is to be found in university attendance, which doubled between 1955 and 1965. In relation to the population Finland has more students at its universities than any other Scandinavian country, and more than almost any country in Europe. The percentage of women students, who number about half the total, is the highest in the world.

However, in spite of the extent of equality, there are in Finland a self-evolved hierarchy, a 'pecking order' and some minor snobisms, though none is important or widespread. The limited hierarchy merely reflects the Finnish scale of values which attaches the greatest importance to learning and creative activity. The most respected and admired members of society are university professors and creative artists – whether composers, writers, painters, sculptors, architects or industrial artists. In recent years the success of Finnish design abroad has given the industrial artist a pride of place often a little exaggerated, though probably only temporary. The respect owed to learning is indicated by the fact that the title 'Professor' is not confined to those holding university chairs. It is also awarded by the President of the Republic to those who have distinguished themselves in the arts, though they may never have given a single lecture. Sibelius and Alvar Aalto are among the many to have been made honorary professors. (The equivalent title awarded to industrialists and businessmen is 'Counsellor'; this, and 'Professor', are the only titles current in the Republic, although decorations are generously offered to all and sundry, from the country's leaders to its washerwomen and waitresses.)

The pecking order is most evident in small towns, but even there can sometimes be treated with levity. The coffee party is the most usual form of entertaining in the home, coffee and cakes being set out on a long table from which the guests all serve themselves – in an order predetermined by their social standing. The wife of the parson or the doctor, for instance, will be expected to help herself first. But frequently, in less formal circles, the coffee goes cold while knotty problems of protocol are discussed, and eventually solved, perhaps, by some large and practical lady who observes that she is the heaviest person present, and so will go first to the coffee table.

The Finns' little snobisms, on the other hand, are most evident in Helsinki and the larger towns. For when the Finn has social aspirations, he (or, more often, she) directs them towards the foreign communities in Finland. The vast majority of Finns are sincerely interested in foreigners for their own sakes, and sincerely anxious to show them kindness and hospitality. But a minority invests them with a snob value which they may or may not merit, and the foreign diplomat with the highest value of all. The inclusion of one's name on the invitation list of an embassy (or preferably two or three) is an objective to be pursued unrelentingly. The strangest manifestation of this foreign snobism is to be found in the lavatories of expensive hotels and restaurants. Here the doors are rarely marked with anything so homespun as the Finnish *Naisille* (women) or *Miehille* (men). Instead, a language of greater social standing is used. In hotels built during the Russian period, at the time when upper-class St Petersburg spoke French, the doors carry the words *Dames* and *Messieurs*; those of later date are marked with the Swedish *Damer* and *Herrar*; and in the newest hotels the current admiration for things Anglo-Saxon is reflected in the simple announcements *Ladies* and *Gentlemen* in English alone.

These snobisms belong to the towns. They mean nothing in the country, where society and the family are so closely knit. The conception of the family as the basis of social organization is as strong in Finland as anywhere else in Europe; but to it must be added the notion of the family as a working unit, which derives from a predominantly agricultural system where most farms are run by the family, with little or no outside help. Large families have always been common in Finland, and in the country the traces of the ancient patriarchal system still remain. In later mediæval times the people of eastern Finland lived, like the Russians, in 'great families' under one roof. As many as fifty people – parents, all their sons and their wives and children – might crowd into one large house, and when the parents died all the sons continued to live together. Today it is not unusual to find three generations living together on one farm in eastern Finland, but there, too, families are breaking up more quickly. The young people either tire of battling against the conservatism of their elders or see little hope of adequate gain from the shared farm profits, and leave in search of work elsewhere. In the towns, there are few flats large enough to house more than one generation and its young children, and the exile of the aged to institutions, benevolent as they may be, is becoming as normal in Finland as in the other non-Latin countries of Europe.

Many of the traditions of the farm family have been carried over to the urban family, and their influence is seen both in the role of the woman and in the upbringing of children. Finland was the first country in Europe and the second in the world to give women the vote (1906). For centuries women had carried an equal burden of work on the farms and often run them alone in the long years when their menfolk were away fighting Sweden's wars. For a considerable time men and women have been equal in law, and all professions except the Church and the armed forces have been open to women. At least half the married women in Finland do a job in addition to running the home, and the proportion of those of working age, i.e. under sixty-seven, is significantly higher than a half. In a number of occupations the proportion of women is exceptionally high. They account for more than eighty per cent of dentists; a third of the employees in the sawing industry, where heavy work is the rule; more than eighty per cent of bank employees; and, to the surprise and often pleasure of male visitors to Finland, for nearly one hundred per cent of 'barbers'.

Equality of opportunity between the sexes, then, appears complete. This is far from the case. Men will themselves quote an old proverb from this land of waters: 'The man steers, the woman rows.' Today, the woman's contribution in sheer hard work is expected and welcomed; but the direction and the steering must be left to the men, who sometimes exercise it only nominally. It is not unusual to find a woman to all intents and purposes running an office, although her salary and status are those of a junior employee. The problem is complicated by the extraordinary dynamism of the Finnish woman. The more dynamic she is, the more likely to marry a dreamy or ineffectual male. She is often sufficiently clever and charming to avoid giving any impression of 'wearing the trousers', and to merit instead the verdict, 'She's made a man of her husband'. But the man, unless qualifying for sainthood, has to compensate himself somehow, and the easiest way is by taking it out of his female colleagues, or at least preventing their advance. Bitterness being no part of the Finnish character, the women generally accept the situation without resort to militancy, and the men with commendably good grace. More than that, they treat women with a courtesy rare in Europe, and rarer still elsewhere in the North, where equality is held to make superfluous any further concessions to the female sex. The little bow and word of thanks which husband and sons offer to the housewife as they get up from the table may be a formality, but it is a pleasant one; so is the gift of flowers to the hostess, especially in winter when they are scarce and exorbitant in price.

Divorce is easy in Finland, and requires little more than the serious decision of both parties and the lapse of a year between application and the decree. The divorce rate is slowly mounting as more people leave the countryside, where broken marriages are rare. It is a little higher than in Britain, but considerably lower than in the United States or Sweden. The principal cause, according to official statistics, is 'broken relations', a term which must cover a large number of cases of incompatibility, for which Finnish obstinacy allows no mitigation. It probably also covers a large amount of drunkenness, as the number of divorces specifically so ascribed scarcely accords with observation. Adultery is listed as the cause of less than a quarter of all divorces. Almost invariably the wife is given custody of the children. Whether or not the comparative ease of obtaining a divorce leads to a greater number of broken marriages is debatable; but the number of successful and durable second marriages seems to be very high.

Certainly parents of the large families which are common in Finland make strenuous efforts to avoid a break. For the Finns hold their children in great affection, and regard boarding-schools as the ultimate in misfortunes. But, along with this often permissive affection, there is the unquestioned assumption that their offspring will put away childish things at an early age and become responsible members of the family, able, if in the country, to take a share of the farm work. Discipline in most families seems directed to one end – to make the child self-reliant, tough and responsible as quickly as possible. So far Finland has escaped most of the teenage troubles that have beset other countries, but whether they will increase as industrialization is intensified is yet to be seen. For the present, at least, society has neither the intention nor the inclination to treat hooligans lightly.

In a country which has so recently left behind an agricultural way of life, one could expect the Church to play a dominant role in society, as, indeed, it did until the middle of the last century. From the Reformation onwards, the Lutheran parsonage, austere in its condemnation of cards, dancing and alcohol, was the centre of rural life. Local government and education were largely in the hands of the clergy, who were so zealous in the pursuit of these secular ends that those who failed to learn to read often found themselves in the stocks. When, in the nineteenth century, these tasks passed to the laity, the Church withdrew into a deep conservatism. Its attitude was reinforced by the various pietist and revivalist movements which still have their adherents, particularly in the north of Finland, and whose precepts remain disconcertingly narrow and austere.

From this conservatism, the Church has only recently begun to emerge. But at a national and social level, its impact is not strong, and institutions such as 'Prayer Saturdays' and sermons preached at the opening of parliamentary sessions do not go far beyond tradition and formality. The clergy, with a very few notable exceptions, seem to find little in common with the laity, and the ordinary Finn has acquired such a built-in resistance to the cloth that he automatically retreats into doleful silence when a man in clerical garb comes in sight. One suspects that the root of this particular trouble is the lay conviction that alcohol and the clergy are mutually exclusive; for the parsons who are able to make real contact with the people are enormously popular.

So the Finns find themselves in an ambivalent situation where they neither wish to attend the Church nor to cut themselves off from it. Ninety-four per cent of the population are registered as Lutherans and pay their church taxes as such, but only about five per cent are churchgoers. It is a simple matter to have one's name transferred to a civil register without tax obligations, yet the percentage of registered Lutherans has remained more or less constant since the element of compulsion was removed forty years ago. The Finn is not anti-religious; his daily conversation moves easily and often on to a religious or metaphysical plane. But his roaming, sometimes undisciplined spirit refuses the trammels of formal religious observance. That his temper is devout is evidenced by the deep spiritual quality – and the response it evokes – of many of the new churches, often so revolutionary in design.

These striking buildings have played their part in the modernization of the Church which is now slowly taking place. Their priests have realized that there is no place in these new vessels for the old wine of outdated forms and clichés, and met with correspondingly greater appreciation among their flocks. The northern *aggiornamento* has received its principal impetus from the report, early in the 'sixties, of a committee which enquired searchingly into the work of the Church and recommended many non-traditional ways of renewing and strengthening the ties between Church and people.

The failure of the Church to provide in Finland the cement that it has given to society in many other countries points to one of the great enigmas of Finnish social life. There is no apparent unifying factor; no community feeling, engendered over generations, by the parish-pump politics of the villages; an interest in local government which is developing only slowly as urbanization increases. The Finns themselves can point to no distinct cementing element other than the practice of resistance to absorption by Sweden or Russia. The underlying unity of the Finnish people, whether Finnish or Swedish-speaking, is more than anything an affair of the emotions, among which love of the land itself is uppermost. The sense of community derives more from intuitive feeling than from the practice of co-operation. When, before the Winter War broke out in 1939, Paasikivi went to

Moscow for a crucial round of negotiations, his departure was unannounced, and known only to a few people. Yet an enormous crowd gathered at the railway station in Helsinki to wish him godspeed, and there spontaneously began to sing Luther's hymn 'A Mighty Fortress is Our God'. In this, as in other respects, Finland still has some of the characteristics of a large family rather than a small nation.

CHAPTER SIX

The Arts and Entertainment

Both the Finns and the Icelanders claim to be the biggest book-buyers in the world, and the Finns can offer ample visible evidence in support of their claim. Helsinki has an enormous bookshop which is said to be the largest in Europe; but even more impressive is the number of small bookshops to be found in the most remote places. A village may have four shops – if so, it is rather well served – and one of them, often the largest, will be a bookshop. On its shelves translations of the great European classics, Greek and Latin included, may jostle with well-known foreign and Finnish contemporary works as well as a quota of the ephemeral and the trashy. In an industrial worker's home it is not unusual to find a couple of hundred books. In the more sophisticated circles of Helsinki there is some speculation as to whether these books are bought to be read or to furnish, but one may safely assume that the proportion intended for the second purpose is small. Reading is a habit born out of isolation from other spare-time occupations; and television, its only real rival in remote areas, collaborates with publishers with the aim of stimulating, rather than preventing, further reading.

This lively interest in literature is typical of the Finnish approach, at every level of society, to all the arts. In Finland there is no cultural dichotomy, no need for conscious efforts to take the arts within the reach of more ordinary people. The idea that literature, music, art or theatre belong only to a privileged or highly educated class does not occur to the Finn. Whatever the level of his own tastes, he regards the arts as an important – if not the most important – expression of Finnish nationhood and national character.

Since the early nineteenth century there has been a constant interaction between nationalism and the arts. The first impulses of the nationalist movement were primarily literary; later, when nationalism was denied its normal political expression, it voiced itself inside and outside Finland through the arts. Finnish literary history begins with the nationalist movement which took shape after Finland became a Grandy Duchy of Russia in 1809. At that time the country's small published literature was in Swedish, the language of the schools and the printing presses. But, as scholars had already been aware for many years, there existed in Finnish a vast unwritten store of folklore and legends, which had for centuries been handed down orally by the rune-singers of the eastern part of the country. After the separation from Sweden nationalist aspirations fastened on this folk poetry as a living witness of native Finnish, as opposed to Swedish-inspired, culture. In 1831, the Finnish Literature Society was founded, with the dual aims of collecting the existing oral literature and assisting the development of writing in the Finnish language.

The publication of the *Kalevala*, a long collection of folk ballads, in 1835, was the Society's first, and possibly greatest achievement. It was the work of a doctor, Elias Lönnrot, whose passionate interest in folklore led him to practise in remote areas where he could hear the ancient runes and set them down on paper in his spare time. In addition, he made several long trips in Finnish and Russian Karelia as far north as Petsamo and as far east as Archangel. Eventually he welded into a connected whole the thousands of legends and fragments which he had collected. The final version of 23,000 lines tells the story of the struggle between Kalevala, a mythical land which is part of Finland, and Pohjola, or the Northland, for the possession of the *sampo*. This *sampo* is a magic mill which grinds not only corn and salt but also money, and so assures the everlasting prosperity of those who possess it. Between the runes which recount the forging of the *sampo* and the struggle waged to obtain it, there are interspersed a multitude of other episodes, some retailing magical feats, some the events of everyday life as it had been lived during the thousand years in which the legends had been passed down by the rune-singers.

The impact made by the publication of the *Kalevala* was enormous. The Finns were assured by it that they possessed a literary heritage of their own, and that they were capable of creating a literature in the future. The *Kalevala* had come out of the mouths of unlettered people from their own farms and villages, proof that the making and enjoyment of literature was not to be limited to a small group of intellectuals. But in some respects the circumstances of its publication gave the *Kalevala* an exaggerated or distorted reputation. It acquired the standard description 'the Finnish national epic', and evoked unjustified comparisons with the *Iliad* or the *Nibelungenlied*. To say that the *Kalevala* has few epic characteristics is not to detract from its poetry, its charm and its interest. Indeed, all these derive chiefly from the fact that its themes are homely, naïve or fanciful, often rooted in the daily life of farmers and fishermen, and far removed from the heroic deeds of the aristocratic warriors of epic poetry.

The nationalist movement was further stimulated by the works of J. L. Runeberg (1804–77) and Z. Topelius (1818–98). Both made use of patriotic Finnish themes, although they wrote in Swedish. Runeberg, still regarded as one of the giants of Finnish poetry, is best known for his collection of poems dealing with the war of 1808–9, *The Tales of Ensign Stål*, although his purely lyric qualities are more appreciated today. The many-sided Topelius has been described as 'one of the main popularizers of the national movement'; as a newspaper editor, poet, novelist, children's writer, historian and university professor, he was the man from whom Finns of all ages and classes learnt about their country.

The first great prose writer and dramatist to use the Finnish language was Aleksis Kivi (1834–72), best known abroad for his novel *Seven Brothers*. Kivi brought to the novel and the stage a strong sense of realism which had rarely been present in Swedish-language writing, and was able to depict the harshness and poverty of the rural life which he himself shared. Of the many novelists who have followed Kivi, those who have become best known outside Finland, through translation, are the Nobel prize-winner F. E. Sillanpää (b. 1888), one of whose chief works is *Fallen Asleep While Young*; Mika Waltari (b. 1908), whose prolific output includes *Sinuhe the Egyptian* and a number of other novels which have been best-sellers in several languages; and Väinö Linna (b. 1920), author of the war novel *The Unknown Soldier*.

As the use of the Finnish language grew, the people who had for hundreds of years been accustomed to the rhythms of spoken poetry naturally developed an appetite for the written line. Poetry has remained one of the most flourishing of literary forms, and until recently a Finnish poet could expect a volume of poems to run through several editions, even in his small country. There remains also in Finland a desire for participation in literature which must spring in part from the habit of participation in rune-singing. Finnish publishers are constantly deluged with manuscripts, chiefly novels, written by amateurs in every walk of life. The vast majority are naïvely unsuitable for publication, but one cannot help being touched by the enthusiasm with which the factory worker or farm labourer pursues his literary ambitions.

If his ambitions lead him to the stage, rather than to literature, he will find them easier to satisfy. The theatre, amateur and professional, is the consuming passion of the Finnish people, their most native and natural talent, whether as actors or spectators. This passion enables eighty-five theatres to give regular performances, and about five thousand amateur groups to play all the year round. The Finns readily acknowledge their need for the catharsis of drama. Their intense, emotional temperament is largely concealed by their everyday containment and calm; but in the theatre, whether on the stage or in response to the stage, their emotions burst out. This makes them highly satisfying as an audience, though often a little exaggerated as performers.

The theatre in Finland also owes part of its vitality to the impetus originally given to it by workers' amateur movements in the days when the higher positions in the country were all held by Swedish-speaking Finns. Then amateur movements developed among Finnish-speaking workers as a means of expression of their own Finnish culture. The continuing result is that the worker is as staunch a patron of the theatre as the intellectual, and a more catholic patron than might be expected. The theatre has been created by the people for their own enjoyment; not, as in the past, for the enjoyment of the court, nor, as in the present elsewhere for the profit of the management. There is no commercial theatre as such in Finland; and hence, in any season, a far wider range of plays can be seen than in countries where box-office considerations are paramount. Thirty-five theatres receive a state grant, and are considered as educational institutions; some are also subsidized by the municipality. All are organized on a repertory basis. The remaining fifty theatres are half professional, half amateur, and manage to maintain their premises and their two or three professional actors from their receipts. Such is the enthusiasm – and the supply – of amateur actors that it is never difficult to make up a cast headed by only one or two professionals.

At the centre of the vigorous theatre life of Finland is the Finnish National Theatre in Helsinki, the oldest and largest theatre in the country. It was founded in 1872 by Dr Kaarlo Bergbom, who had then for close on a decade been working, ahead of many of his contemporaries elsewhere, to create a theatre of the people, rather than a theatre of fashion. Today, ably headed by Arvi Kivimaa, it can give an impressive account of itself in facts and figures: three stages, playing to audiences of 1,100, 300 and 100; 600 performances a year, over nine and a half months, with between sixteen and twenty plays in the yearly repertoire; one performance every week for schoolchildren only; an annual attendance of 200,000, high when compared with figures for cities of a size comparable to Helsinki; and a repertoire ranging from Shakespeare and Molière (to whom even the amateurs of the backwoods are devoted) to the most recent Finnish, British, American and French plays. This is achieved in competition not only with the nine other theatres in Helsinki, but also those in Tampere, so noted for their productions that they can draw people living two hours away by rail.

Tampere, besides its orthodox theatres, has a unique open-air summer theatre, whose beautiful site is a promontory jutting out into a lake, and providing varying backdrops of hillside, forest, meadow, and water. To utilize them all, a revolving auditorium, seating 800, is set in the middle of what might be termed the stage; a change of scene is marked by a half or quarter revolution of the entire auditorium, while the audience remains seated. The number of plays which can be adapted to this form of theatre is few, but summer is short, and the open-air theatre has had sufficient outstanding successes since it was opened in 1959 to guarantee its permanence. It has also inspired an amateur group in southern Finland to build its own version of the outdoor revolving auditorium.

The Finnish theatre has been undeservedly isolated from the rest of the world, for a variety of reasons. The foremost is that Finland has produced no great universal playwright. The Finns say, in explanation, that they are too emotional a people, that the writing of drama is primarily an exercise of the intellect for which they are less well endowed. Language difficulties have, in any case, stood in the way of the translation of plays into more accessible tongues such as English and French, though they need not have prevented the export of actors. But those who have played abroad prefer to act at home, reflecting that, in spite of mediocre pay and the hard work of repertory, which may keep them acting in five plays concurrently, 'Finland is the actor's paradise'. Nevertheless, since the war the National Theatre has become more closely integrated than formerly in the European theatre. Its outstanding directors have been responsible for productions in other countries, and the theatre has given guest performances in several European capitals.

The vitality of the professional theatre, great as it is, is dwarfed by the exuberance of the amateur theatre. With at least five thousand groups scattered over the country, it can be estimated that a minimum of a hundred thousand Finns are acting and rehearsing all the year round. A village which consists of only a dozen houses and eighty to a hundred inhabitants may have its own amateur dramatic group; larger villages may have as many as six groups, particularly in Ostrobothnia, where the amateur movement is strongest. Industrial firms have their own groups; so do hospitals, where patients well enough to get on their feet can forget about their own ailments and perhaps act someone else's. So do prisons, where warders form one group and prisoners another. A prisoner has even been known to ask for his release to be delayed until after the performance of the play for which he was rehearsing.

Most of these groups are affiliated to two central organizations, which send directors and coaches round the country to advise them and to run courses for amateur producers. These organizations also hold annual drama competitions which are often enormously complicated by the number of group-entrants. The development of television in Finland has barely dented the enthusiasm for amateur drama, although, during the first two years or so, there was a slight falling-off in membership and attendance. But then, apparently, the Finns could no longer contain themselves in front of the box watching other people act; they had to get up and out and act themselves. Now the situation has been reversed: the best of the amateurs frequently give television performances, and the hope of like achievement stimulates the rest.

The interaction of art and nationalism is as powerfully reflected in music as in literature, and has served to strengthen the reverence and respect in which Sibelius, 'the uncrowned king of Finland', was held during most of his lifetime. For his countrymen, Sibelius was not only a great composer but a great Finn who made the name of Finland resound round the world; not only the composer who stirred their patriotism when the nationalist movement was reaching a peak, but the man who, in later and less turbulent days, could echo their vast landscape in sound as no painter has succeeded in doing on canvas.

Finland had its slender musical traditions long before the sudden upsurge of the late nineteenth century. Tsarist persecution and the threat of absorption into the Russian Empire provoked artistic self-assertion in many forms. In the musical world, it took the form of the foundation, in 1882, of the first Finnish symphony orchestra and of the Institute of Music, now the Sibelius Academy. The founder of the orchestra was Robert Kajanus, a conductor and composer of courage and energy, and a pioneer who first made Sibelius known outside Finland. Then, in 1899, Sibelius composed *Finlandia*, which was so stirringly nationalist that it rapidly became an unofficial national anthem, expressing in music what the Russian censorship of the press prevented the Finns from saying in words. The following year enough money was raised by public subscription for Kajanus to take his orchestra on a tour of Europe which culminated in Paris, then the scene of a World's Fair. The orchestra introduced to Europe *Finlandia* and other of Sibelius' works, and at the same time aroused fresh sympathy for the small and distant country which was battling to preserve its identity.

In these circumstances Sibelius acquired, outside Finland, a reputation as a national romantic composer which he never completely lost. No one would deny the patriotic and programmatic content of many of his earlier compositions. But his later and greater works, from the Second Symphony to *Tapiola*, are Finnish only in the sense that they echo the mood of landscape and seascape with their spaciousness, their primeval harshness and mystery. Without either programme or the inspiration of folk music, these later works cannot be classified as national or romantic, only as Finnish. Few of Finland's artists seem to succeed when they attempt to deny or suppress their Finnishness, but only the greatest can be both as Finnish and as universal as Sibelius.

Many of the multitude of composers who have followed Sibelius have lacked the combination of the Finnish and the universal, or have sacrificed one to attain the other. Many contemporary composers, in particular, have struggled to free themselves from the Sibelian tradition, and suffered from the unwillingness of the outside world to interest itself in any Finnish music except that of Sibelius. Apart from Selim Palmgren (1878–1951) and Yrjö Kilpinen (1892–1959), Finnish composers are less known outside Finland than they merit. This may be in part because both their number and their output are of a size to confuse the outsider. In the early 'sixties, for instance, a score of living composers had between them produced more than sixty symphonies, in addition to numerous other works by themselves and an equal number of non-symphonic composers. The Finnish public has a zest for new composition which gives a hearing to the good and to the indifferent; but in music and the other arts its admiration of creative activity for its own sake may sometimes impair its real judgment. Thus modern Finnish composers, in particular, have to await the workings of the sieve of time before a more lasting assessment of their worth can be made.

This zest for composition is part of a wider zest for musical activity at many levels. In Helsinki, where a concert is held almost every day in the season, there are two large symphony orchestras, and a third attached to the Finnish National Opera. The larger provincial cities have their own professional orchestras, and in many other towns professionals and amateurs combine to form a municipal orchestra. Purely amateur orchestras and operatic societies flourish in many out-of-the-way places and small organizations.

But it is as singers that the Finns are most distinguished internationally, and as singers that they are the most active as amateurs. Few instrumentalists have won real acclaim abroad, but the list of singers – and women especially – who have appeared in the great opera houses of the world goes back to 1830. Similarly Finnish choirs, and particularly male voice choirs, have won praise all over the world. These choirs are merely the best of hundreds which exist all over Finland, in villages, factories and offices, and which include almost as many enthusiasts as the amateur theatre movement.

The scale of amateur musical activity derives largely from the belief, apparently accepted by parents at every level of society, that their children shall either sing or learn an instrument, even if the latter is only the accordion so popular in the North. Thus music-making in the home, and the quartet formed within the family, are not unusual. Nor are the musical evenings, which can often entail suffering as well as enjoyment on the part of the audience. Television may now be displacing these *soirées*, with their nineteenth-century flavour, but if and when it does, the loss will far outweigh the gain.

Of all the arts, painting is the least successful and the most admired in Finland, the field in which enthusiasm far outstrips performance. Finns have rarely excelled in any of the graphic arts; they have a strong sense of form which is seemingly frustrated when they have to work in two dimensions. The pioneers of architecture and industrial design often lag behind the rest of the world in pure art.

If one accepts that art grows in the first place out of the landscape, one can immediately grasp the difficulties faced by Finnish painters. Their landscape rarely offers a composition complete in itself but rolls on endlessly on a scale too vast for canvas. In summer it is too monotonously green to tempt the palette; in winter so monotonously grey-white that all but a few shapes and outlines disappear. When colour enters into the landscape in spring or, more strikingly, in autumn, it is of a brilliance that becomes unreal on canvas, as does also the dazzlingly clear light of Finland.

The development of painting in Finland coincided with the rise of the nationalist movement in the late nineteenth century. The painters of the time strove to create a 'Finnish school', and so rejected the more universal influences of European painting of the day. At the same time the public suffered, and continues to suffer to a lesser degree, from a lack of yardsticks. A country with a long history of poverty could afford to buy for its national museum only two or three paintings by the great European masters, and had no other means of seeing the paintings of the past.

Finnish painters, until modern times, have tended to concentrate on the pictorial and the symbolic, using a brush both sombre and heavy. Their work displays the gloom and melancholy which the outside world often associates with the northern temperament, but which finds little expression in Finland's other arts. More recently, they have abandoned their quest for an exclusively Finnish style, and shown increasing readiness to experiment and invent, without, however, producing any name of note in the European context.

Yet in few countries has the patronage of the visual arts developed on so considerable a scale. The individual Maecenas has never existed in Finland, but the individual minor patrons are legion. The walls of their homes are overcrowded with originals of varying worth, while reproductions of the works of great European masters are rarely to be seen. State grants, administered by the Finnish Artists' Association, provide a number of travelling scholarships and bursaries; and 1 per cent of all public money spent on buildings must be devoted to murals, sculpture and decorative art. And all the while amateurs paint feverishly, in the unquenchable hope that next year they will be able to exhibit and eventually break into the ranks of the semi-professional artists.

It is to sculpture rather than to painting that one must look for a reflection of Finnish creative energy in pure art. In the last thirty years or so there has arisen a flourishing school of sculptors working on an international and universal plane. For them, unfortunately, problems of transport often stand in the way of the international recognition they deserve; and much of their major work is so dispersed all over the country that even the visitor to Finland cannot easily appreciate its range and variety.

The pioneer of Finnish sculpture of this century was Väinö Aaltonen (1894–1966), an artist so versatile that he could turn from imposing civic statuary to jewellery and silverware. He earned particular distinction from his use of the native granite in all its subtle colourings, and showed an extraordinary ability to soften and lighten it without sacrificing anything of its primitive strength. His work includes the well-known bust of Sibelius, the mobile figure of the Olympic champion runner, Paavo Nurmi, and a vast number of classical marble reliefs, modern busts, and abstract and almost surrealist themes. He was an eager experimenter, and could point to abstract models created long before abstraction became a recognized trend. But always he returned to the classic forms which he believed must lie at the base of all sculpture. In some pieces of civic statuary, this led him into an untypical orthodoxy – shared, however, by a number of Finland's civic sculptors.

This is more than redeemed by the gaiety and humour of much

of their smaller works, notably the small heads and statues of Hannes Autere, Mikko Hovi and Ben Renvall. The same humour is also evident in the work of one of the younger and most outstanding of Finnish sculptors, Eila Hiltunen. Using welding techniques and materials such as iron, copper and sheet metal, she has produced animal and human figures remarkable for their fluidity and movement. On a far different, and immense, scale is her great abstract composition which won the competition for a memorial to Sibelius. Made entirely of welded steel pipes, it is designed in relation to its setting in a wooded park in Helsinki. It so defies the rigidity of its material that it seems to form an organic whole with the trees around it, and combines the hard severity of pine and spruce with the flowing grace of the birch.

Finnish sculptors owe much of their success to the fact that the best of their work is widely sought after. Public statuary is a feature of all the larger towns; the purely decorative is frequently far more interesting and original than the commemorative, and some statues of public men have little to commend them. Commercial firms, as well as public authorities, habitually commission sculpture from the hands of the foremost artists, and the stark outlines of a factory entrance are frequently softened by a graceful statue. The post-war demand for war memorials, which gave such an impetus to the Finnish sculptor, is now over; but sculpture has become, for the Finns, so essential a part of everyday life that it is likely to flourish for some time to come.

Part Two

HISTORY AND POLITICS

CHAPTER SEVEN

Under Swedish Rule

The history of Finland is largely the history of her neighbours, Sweden and Russia, of their rivalries and their attitudes to the land that lay between them. The unaggressive Finns had chosen to make their home in the path of two ambitious, expansionist powers, who both sought the advantages that control over their neighbour would bring. For Sweden, the east exercised a magnetic pull from the ninth to the eighteenth century; Russia's desire for a commanding position in the Baltic began abortively with Ivan the Terrible, and became, from the time of Peter the Great, a decisive factor in policy.

It was the Swedish drive to the east that made Finland part of the kingdom of Sweden. The Swedes were a restless people, whose commercial instincts were already highly developed in Viking times. While the Norsemen and Danes sailed westward in search of adventure and conquest, the Swedish Vikings, or Varangians, turned to the east. Their end was not conquest but trade with the Byzantine Empire and the Orient. Their route led through the Åland Islands, which they had settled in the seventh century, and along the southern coast of Finland. The Finns were drawn into the movement of trade, and the furs they trapped were taken by the Varangians to be exchanged for the silks and spices of the East. The Swedes gained control of many Russian towns on their route, and most significantly of Novgorod, later to develop into a powerful and independent trading centre which regarded as enemies both the Swedes and the Tavasts of central Finland.

By the middle of the twelfth century Swedes and Novgorodians alike had begun to cast a predatory look on the disorganized, disunited Finland between them. They were competing for control of raw materials and trade, and they shared the pious if subordinate intent to christianize the semi-pagan Finns. At this time, Sweden was by far the stronger power, and her intervention has been exaggerated in history by the name 'northern crusade'. According to a legend which persisted into recent times, the Swedish King Erik himself led the attack on the Finns, who were easily overcome by his well-armed soldiers. He left in Finland an Englishman, Henry, the Bishop of Uppsala, to carry on the work of converting the pagans. Henry met with little immediate success. The pagans rallied unwillingly to Christianity, and Henry was killed by a peasant on the frozen surface of a lake – but he eventually became the patron saint of Finland.

Recent research has not been able to authenticate this picturesque legend; it has merely underlined the fact that Finland's conversion to Christianity took place gradually and sporadically from the eleventh century onwards, and that the absorption into the kingdom of Sweden was an equally gradual process. There was neither a dramatic crusade nor a single conquest by force of arms, although there were raids and minor attacks in plenty, which little by little consolidated Sweden's hold on Finland. The Swedes certainly played a part in the conversion of the reluctant Finns; but it was an Englishman, Bishop Thomas, formerly a canon of Uppsala, who placed the Church in Finland on a firm foundation during the thirteenth century. In 1216 the Pope made Finland part of the ecclesiastical province of Uppsala, and the seat of the Finnish diocese was eventually transferred to Turku. Most of Bishop Thomas's mediæval successors in Turku were native Finns, educated at the University of Paris or, later, at the Charles University of Prague.

The relationship between Sweden and Finland in the Middle Ages was for much of the time indefinite and undefined. Sweden had not yet become a unified state, although she had advanced further than Finland towards a form of political organization. Finland was no more and no less than an outlying part of Sweden, inhabited by men who had the same rights in law as the Swedes and who were regarded as equals by the Swedes. From Sweden came men to colonize the coastal areas of south-west and north-west Finland, and there they probably felt no farther removed from Stockholm than their compatriots in the north and west of Sweden. It was only as the power of the Swedish Crown developed, and as Sweden became a more unified state, that the Finns began to be subject to the central authority in Stockholm. (They did, however, send their own delegation to the election of the king.) From the fourteenth century onwards,

Finland was divided into 'castle counties', administered by Swedish bailiffs representing the king and living in their castle-fortresses. They collected the taxes due to the Crown, and those near the eastern border were held responsible for the protection of the people against the Russians. For there was little peace in the Middle Ages between Sweden and Novgorod. The Swedes, still dreaming of their Varangian conquests, had as their objective the control of the mouth of the River Neva, where Leningrad stands today; the Novgorodians constantly repulsed them and counter-attacked, and when Muscovy absorbed Novgorod in the fifteenth century it absorbed, too, Novgorod's antagonism to Sweden-Finland.

In 1523 Gustavus Vasa became king of a Sweden that was emerging as a centralized and independent state. Now the Finns were to become more aware of their subservience to Crown and government in Stockholm, but it was a subservience hardly touched with resentment, and Finns as well as Swedes profited from the energy of this first hereditary monarch of Sweden. Gustavus Vasa found his kingdom in severe financial difficulties; the Roman Catholic Church of Sweden-Finland possessed wealth and property which would solve his problems. Accordingly he made the Lutheran Reformation the pretext for the divorce of the northern churches from Rome and for the confiscation of their property. He made himself head of the new church, responsible for the appointment of the clergy and the payment of their meagre salaries, but showed no concern for questions of doctrine. Lutheran belief and practice displaced the Roman forms only gradually, and it was not until the end of the century that the Lutheran faith became officially and generally accepted throughout the kingdom.

In Finland the adoption of the Protestant faith had a major influence on the development of the Finnish language. Luther's insistance on the use of the vernacular instead of Latin in church services prompted the Bishop of Turku, Michael Agricola, to translate into Finnish the Prayer Book and the New Testament (1548). These, and a Finnish-language primer he had written a few years earlier, were the first books to be published in Finnish, and made Agricola celebrated as 'the father of Finnish literature'.

Meanwhile the power and influence of the Swedish Estates were slowly developing, complemented by the provincial assemblies which dealt principally with taxation. To the Four Estates of nobles, clergy, burghers and yeomen, the Finns sent representatives; the provincial assemblies included both nobles and yeomen. Thus the ordinary Finns had their share, from early modern times, in the developing political organization of Sweden; and if this was not democratic in the modern sense of the term, it nevertheless gave the common yeoman and the ordinary peasant opportunities, rare in many other European countries at that time, of voicing their complaints and of speaking as free men.

From Sweden there also came the stimulus for other modern developments. Gustavus Vasa's efforts to increase economic activity and to free Swedish trade from the grip of the Hansa cities had their repercussions in Finland. He founded Helsinki in an unsuccessful attempt to divert Russian trade from Tallinn, and encouraged Dutch merchants at the expense of the Germans. Thus by the end of the sixteenth century the Dutch were well on their way to the domination of the Baltic trade, and were firmly entrenched in Finland's coastal towns, many of which had been founded by the Swedes. Later, the most famous of Swedish governors-general of Finland, Count Per Brahe, in his two mid-seventeenth-century missions, founded, with the University of Turku, the intellectual life of the country. He equally laid the foundations of the modern economic state by beginning the exploitation of mines and forests, and developing towns, roads and postal services. The Swedes who settled in Finland became the intellectual and commercial leaders of the country, bringing with them their legal system, their culture and their language, which was gradually to become, for administrative and literary purposes, far more important than Finnish.

But if the Swedes brought to Finland many and incalculable benefits, they also imposed on the Finns the duty of fighting with them in their recurrent wars, of standing always in the front line between Sweden and Russia. From the time of Gustavus Vasa until 1809, when Finland was ceded to Russia, she was the battleground of wars which never spread to Swedish soil. The Finns not only had to provide men and money; they had to suffer the devastation of their land and their crops, the pillaging of their farms and the destruction brought about by the total warfare of the time. There were other enemies besides the Russians; the Finns had to take part in the

Thirty Years' War (in which they provided one-third of Gustavus Adolphus' army) and in the wars between Sweden and Poland and Sweden and Denmark, which drained Finland's population although they did not devastate her land. During the three centuries before Finland was ceded to Russia in 1809 she was involved in war for a total of more than eighty years, and at times further weakened by famine or plague. During eleven of those years – from 1710 to 1721 – the country was partly or completely occupied by Russian armies, whose vandalism and destruction brought normal life to a standstill, ruined whole towns, and reduced the Finnish population by a quarter.

These recurrent wars laid a heavy strain on Finnish *sisu* and Finnish loyalty to the Swedish Crown. That loyalty survived along with *sisu* is a measure of the overall good relations that existed between the Finns and the Swedes. There were the inevitable points of tension and sources of friction; but on the whole, Swedo-Finnish relations up to the end of the seventeenth century were remarkable for their placidity. However, this equable state could not be maintained in the face of the development of centralized and autocratic rule in Sweden and of a new sense of nationality in Finland. When the eighteenth century dawned, both countries were approaching positions which were bound eventually to divide them.

The absolute monarch of Sweden, Charles XI (1660–97), was the first to proclaim as an objective the total absorption of Finland in the Swedish realm. His intentions were summed up in the words: 'One religion, one language, one law, identical customs.' Already Swedes and Finns shared a common faith, a common legal system, and many common customs. Language was the stumbling-block to complete unity, and the Swedes immediately set about removing it through efforts to convert the Finns to the Swedish tongue. Swedish was made the language of the army, and even churches attended mainly by Finnish-speaking worshippers were ordered to hold services in Swedish every three weeks for the Swedish-speaking upper class. In the schools Swedish replaced Latin, which had previously been the language of instruction. As time went on it became increasingly clear that there was no future for men of the upper and middle classes unless they spoke Swedish, and preferably also took a Swedish name. Thus by the latter half of the eighteenth century most of the 'gentry' and the burghers spoke Swedish. The movement accelerated by Charles XI had already gathered considerable strength; it was later to create for Finland social problems which still have their echoes, however faint, at the present day.

But the men who were obliged to adopt the Swedish language soon demonstrated the weakness of the theory that language and nationality went hand in hand. The increase in the number of Swedish speakers was matched by an increase in Finnish national feeling. For a long time this was neither violent nor assertive. It took the form of a generalized conviction that Finland constituted a natural national entity, distinct from Sweden; but this conviction was coupled with a growing fear that separation from Sweden might mean annexation by Russia. These two strands of thought met in a minor movement among Finnish army officers, led by G. M. Sprengtporten, which aimed at making Finland a semi-independent state under Russian protection. Such a formula, they somewhat naïvely thought, would rid them simultaneously of Swedish domination and the spectre of total Russian domination. The movement was as unsuccessful as it deserved, and found, in any case, little support throughout the country. The mass of Finns, indeed, remained undisturbed by the absolutist tendencies of the Swedish Crown, and those who lived in the remoter areas were probably hardly aware of the political developments of the time.

The cession of Finland to Russia in 1809 was part of the redrawing of the map of Europe which took place during the Napoleonic Wars. The details of the ensuing relationship between Finland and Russia will be discussed in the following chapter. What must be emphasized here is that it was, paradoxically, during the century in which Finland was a Grand Duchy of Russia that the inheritance of the Swedish period was consolidated and strengthened. Though separated from Sweden, the Finns had no wish to disown the institutions which had been developed under the aegis of their western neighbour. Some of their political institutions were not truly democratic: the power of the Estates, in particular, had been drastically reduced by the autocratic Gustavus III. But these institutions provided a basis on which Finland was able to build, even while subject to Russia, one of the most democratic countries in Europe.

An outstandingly important element in democratic stability was the Swedish Law of 1734. This monumental work of more than two hundred chapters dealt with both criminal and civil law; it covered all the contentious matters of everyday life – marriage, inheritance, ownership of land and property, building rights, trade, and so on – in simple terms which were generally understood by the ordinary people. From the outset it applied equally to Sweden and to Finland, and became available in a Finnish translation in 1759. In the settlement with the Tsar Alexander I after 1809, the Swedish Law of 1734 was accepted as the continuing basis of Finnish law. This it has remained ever since, and today it still gives to Sweden and Finland a wide area of commonly-held legal practice.

In Sweden's 'Age of Freedom' (1718–73), liberal ideas were abroad, and took root also in Finland. In 1766, the censorship was abolished, partly as a result of the efforts in the Estates of a Finnish Lutheran clergyman and liberal economist, Anders Chydenius. Sweden-Finland thus became one of the first countries in the world to allow the freedom of the press. Finland was not able to maintain this freedom throughout the period of Russian rule, but it was revived at the first opportunity. Chydenius was a champion of religious freedom, and it was largely due to him that Roman and Greek Catholics and Jews gained the right to hold their own services undisturbed in Sweden-Finland. Throughout the nineteenth century and beyond, Finland maintained both the Lutheran faith which she shared with Sweden and the right of other sects to freedom of worship.

All these things – political institutions, the law, the idea of freedom of speech and worship – represented an enormous and positive inheritance from the Swedish period, particularly when contrasted with the dissimilar ideas and institutions which held sway across the Russian border. They were in part conferred by Sweden on Finland, in part evolved and shared by the two countries. Whatever their source, they conformed so well with Finnish inclinations that they had come to be a natural element of their life. They had made Finland part of Western European civilization, and neither tsarist oppression nor the vicissitudes of independence could eliminate or weaken them.

But from the Swedish neighbour Finland also inherited the 'language problem', the rivalry of the Swedish and Finnish tongues, which has continued to recur, in different forms and varying degrees of severity, right up to the present day. The language problem was closely related to the independence movement, and as such it had its positive aspects; but, by and large, over a long period it absorbed time, energy and emotions which could have been put to better use in other branches of public life.

After the annexation of Finland by Russia, Swedish remained the language of administration and instruction, and therefore of the educated classes, as it had been for more than a century. There was a fear, in some quarters, that if Swedish were rejected, the new overlords would insist on Russian taking its place. But in the event the Russians showed no wish to make such a move, and so the time seemed ripe for the advancement of Finnish. Besides, the time had come for the crystallization into a more systematic form of the vaguer feelings of nationalism and independence which had been growing over several decades. A group of Swedish-speaking Finns took up the unlikely task of advancing the Finnish language at the expense of their own. Foremost among them was J. V. Snellman (1806–81), teacher, editor and administrator, who devoted himself to a crusade to persuade his compatriots that unity and independence could never be achieved until the whole country spoke and used the Finnish language, and only the Finnish language. A country, he affirmed, in which the bureaucracy and the cultivated class spoke Swedish and the rest Finnish, was a country divided against itself, and one which laid itself open to the imposition by the Russians of their own language. It was therefore the duty of the Swedish-speaking Finns to learn and adopt the Finnish language, and so identify themselves with the nation as a whole. (The many-sided Snellman also drew up plans for the administrative and economic reform of Finland – plans which he was later able to put into operation himself as head of the equivalent of the modern Finance Ministry.)

Eventually Snellman succeeded in persuading Tsar Alexander II to order the wider use of Finnish. The Language Decree of 1863 put Finnish on an equal footing with Swedish in all matters concerning the Finnish-speaking population, allowing twenty years for it to become generally used in government, administration and public life in general. In the event, the adoption of Finnish on fully equal terms with Swedish was not completed until 1902, and by that time the language problem had divided the country more deeply and bitterly than ever before.

Snellman and his supporters (known as the Fennomanians), though originally Swedish-speaking themselves, had sought a solution of the problem in what they believed to be the interests of the majority and of the whole of the Finnish people. It was nevertheless a drastic one, since it involved the suppression of Swedish. Against them there arose a counter-movement whose adherents were known as the Svecomanians, and which worked in the interests only of the Swedish language. The leader of the movement was Axel Olof Freudenthal (1836–1911), a Swedo-Finnish university professor. He asserted that nationality derived from language, and the more extreme of his followers held that the 'Swedish race' in Finland was vastly superior to the 'Finnish race'. They disregarded the patent facts of intermarriage and adoption of the Swedish language by pure Finns, and asserted that any form of unity between the two language groups could never be achieved.

The Svecomanians' arguments could not fail to widen the gulf between the two groups. The pure Finns were bound to resent sharply the insults that were heaped on them. Unfortunately, they often tend today to remember these insults and to forget that it was due to the Swedish-speaking Snellman and his followers that the Finnish language eventually attained its pre-eminence. But underlying the mixture of bitterness and stupidity in the Svecomanions' arguments was a practical factor which still operates today: Finnish, the language of the majority, is rather difficult to master, while Swedish is relatively easy. Thus the Swedish-speaking *élite* was put at an immediate disadvantage *vis-à-vis* the pure Finns. Their lack of command of Finnish would inevitably be a handicap to them in the pursuit of advancement to the higher posts which they had previously monopolized. Even today, when many of the major differences have been smoothed out, a Swedo-Finn is under a handicap if his command of Finnish is less than perfect; on the other hand, a pure Finn can reach the highest position – that of Prime Minister, for instance – with no more than a sketchy knowledge of Swedish. Linguistic equality can never be complete in practice as well as theory where one language is spoken by a majority like the ninety-three per cent of Finnish-speakers in Finland. The Swedo-Finns of the nineteenth century must have realized, if only dimly, that the official use of the Finnish language would ultimately weaken their own political, social and educational position.

In 1902 another decree regarding the language of the law courts and administration gave Finnish and Swedish this complete theoretical equality. A further series of decrees, made since Finland became independent, have clarified the language position on a local basis, and communes are now officially designated as unilingual or bilingual, according to the ten-yearly census. The Swedish-speaking population is relatively compact, living in the western and southern coastal areas and in the south-western archipelago. In some communes in these areas Swedo-Finns constitute over ninety per cent of the population, in which case the commune is designated as unilingual Swedish and its affairs are dealt with in Swedish by the central government. Conversely, communes where the Swedish-speaking population does not exceed ten per cent are treated as unilingual Finnish. A bilingual community should have, as a rule, a minority of at least ten per cent, or 5,000 people. Several towns in the south – Helsinki-Helsingfors among them – are regarded as bilingual communities. These will probably grow in number as the two linguistic groups tend to mingle more in industrialized and urban centres. (In the country, on the other hand, the demarcation is often very clear, and one village may be almost completely Swedish-speaking while the next village, a few miles away, is completely Finnish-speaking.) In all secondary schools pupils must learn either Swedish or Finnish as their second language; but outside the bilingual areas Finnish speakers, in particular, seem to forget much that they have learned, and often speak English more readily than Swedish.

In spite of guarantees and safeguards in law and in spite of the scrupulous fairness with which the law is observed, the position and future of the Swedish language in Finland are by no means assured. A large number of pure Finns recognize the great value to Finland of a native Indo-European language which gives them a bridge to the West, and, perhaps more important still, a common means of communication with the other Scandinavian countries. But there are others who attach less importance to the Swedish language and fail to see any need to maintain and encourage its use. However, there are many signs that in the coming years Finland will be drawn more closely into the Nordic group, and the use of Swedish, which is easily understood by the Norwegians and the Danes, will therefore be stimulated.

But in more general terms the great improvement in relations between the two linguistic groups which has been evident since the Second World War represents a positive and important gain to Finland. The part played by the Swedo-Finns in the Finno-Russian wars demonstrated beyond doubt their devotion to Finland; and the passage of time has now removed the old class differences between Swedo-Finns and pure Finns. In many respects the tensions between the two groups (apart from the occasional personal animosities and prejudices) are less marked than, for instance, those between the English and the Scots. It is to the great credit of the Swedo-Finns that they have accepted both their changed social position and the unavoidable disadvantages of their minority position with such equanimity.

On the other side of the Gulf of Bothnia, in Sweden, there is now a modern corollary to the long-standing language problem in Finland. Emigration from Finland to Sweden – from the poorer country to the richer – goes back almost as far as the records. In the years since the war, in which Sweden has been rapidly industrialized and become unable to supply all her own manpower needs, more and more Finns have left their own country, with its hitherto endemic unemployment, for Sweden. There are now more than 200,000 Finns in Sweden. Many of them are Swedish-speaking; but for those whose mother tongue is Finnish the Swedish authorities have made special efforts, in the provision of Finnish-speaking schools or courses, to enable them to maintain their own language and traditions. Self-interest plays its part in these efforts, but they nevertheless reflect the easier and more generous relationship between Sweden and Finland which has developed since the Second World War.

CHAPTER EIGHT

From Russian Tsar to Finnish President

For Finland, the sea to the west has always been a kindlier border than the land boundary to the east, and the Swedish neighbour more predictable than the Russian. Relations between Finland and Sweden contain no real surprises nor enigmas; a clearly discernible thread runs through them, linking one event to another with the cool logic which characterizes Sweden today.

Finno-Russian relations, on the other hand, have always been erratic, subject to violent, though sometimes repetitive, change. Russia's attitude to Finland has depended at different times on different sets of circumstances. In times of general European upheaval, it has been governed by her other aims and commitments and the degree of security she has needed in the Baltic; at other times it has depended on her own strength, and Finland has often been able to snatch more freedom when Russia has been weak. It has also depended on the degree of liberalism in Russia, for which Finland has been a fairly reliable barometer. The one constant factor in Finno-Russian relations has been the Russian need to control the Gulf of Finland, and even this has not always been paramount. It was not responsible for that most freakish event, the annexation of Finland by Russia in 1809. The ambitions of the Tsar Alexander I all lay to the south-west; he had little interest in his neighbour to the north-west. He attacked Sweden-Finland reluctantly, to implement the agreement made with Napoleon at Tilsit; and having annexed Finland, allowed her to retain, by yet another freak of circumstance, a constitution which was to become far more democratic than any enjoyed by the Russians in the days of the tsars.

The annexation of Finland was the culmination of centuries of warfare between Russia and Sweden, in which Sweden had sometimes been the aggressor, and had controlled territory inside the modern Soviet Union for long periods. To undermine the power of Sweden in the Baltic and to secure an outlet to the northern waters thus became an important objective in Russian policy. Ivan the Terrible was the first to attempt to break through to the Baltic. He was successful in his attack on Livonia in 1558, but when he tried to wrest Estonia from the Swedes in 1575 he was beaten back, and lost all he had gained in the Baltic. By the time his dreams were revived by Peter the Great, Sweden had become a power far more formidable than she had been in Ivan's time. The triumphs of Gustavus Adolphus and Charles X had made the Baltic a Swedish lake, and by the end of the seventeenth century Sweden controlled, as well as Finland, Ingermanland, where Leningrad now stands, Estonia, Livonia and Pomerania. Peter's ambitions of making Russia a European power and an economically viable state both demanded an outlet to the Baltic. He accordingly set about systematically and vigorously, in a war which was to last twenty-one years, to clear the Swedes from as many of these territories as possible. His first success was the most decisive and far-reaching in its effects on Finland. In 1703, he captured a Swedish fort at the mouth of the Neva River; here he laid the foundations of a new town and named it St Petersburg. It was to be his capital, and he therefore immediately built a fortress to defend it, which he called Kronstadt, on an island lying in front of the embryo city. Since that time, the security of St Petersburg, Petrograd or Leningrad, has never ceased to trouble the Russians and to colour their attitude to Finland. 'The belief [in 1938] that Finland represented a dangerous gap in Russia's defences was one of the hardiest clichés of Russian strategic thinking,' a Finnish commentator, Max Jakobson, has pointed out. '"The ladies of St Petersburg could not sleep peacefully as long as the Finnish frontier ran so close to our country," wrote Peter the Great in explanation of his conquest of Viipuri and Karelia.' (These areas were returned to Finland in 1812; but more than two hundred years after Peter, they represented the Soviet Union's most crushing territorial demand when Finland was defeated in the Winter War of 1939–40.)

Not content with Viipuri and Karelia, Peter advanced through Finland, capturing Helsinki and Turku and conquering the whole country. The Russian occupation of Finland, known as the Great Wrath, lasted eight years. At the Peace of Uusikaupunki (Nystad), Sweden surrendered to him south-eastern Finland, Livonia, Estonia and Ingermanland. He could presumably have demanded the whole of Finland, but was satisfied with only Viipuri and Karelia. He had occupied the entire country, he said, so that he could bargain from strength when the peace treaty was made. In any case he needed his army of occupation to fight a new war against Persia and extend his territory in the south-west. Thus Finland escaped the complete absorption into the Russian Empire that came to Estonia and Livonia. But Russia had obtained a firm foothold on the shores of the Baltic and turned her face for ever to the west. A sequence of events had begun which was to influence Finland's destiny right up to the present day.

As the eighteenth century wore on, Sweden's power waned while the Russian Empire grew in strength. Inside Finland there were many besides Sprengtporten (see page 90) and his supporters who suspected that Finland would eventually be forced to exchange the Swedish king for the Russian tsar. Henrik Gabriel Porthan (1729–1809), the 'father of Finnish history', observed: 'We must pray to God that Russia will succeed in situating its capital in Constantinople . . . But now that its capital city is located so near, I am afraid that Finland will sooner or later fall under the power of Russia.' Porthan was no mere prophet of doom: he took active steps to encourage the people of Finland to think of themselves first and foremost as Finns. Through his research into Finnish history, language and folklore, and his work as a professor at the University of Turku, he awakened a generation of Finland's intellectual leaders to a real understanding of their country, its needs and its future. This was the generation which, after Finland was annexed by Russia, was to uphold the western democratic traditions which had for so long been shared with Sweden.

Annexation by Russia, at the outset, defied the prophets of doom. Finland's position under Russia seemed possibly less unfavourable than had been feared. The war against Sweden which Napoleon had forced on Alexander I was not a planned part of Russian policy, and was unpopular among Russian leaders. The Tsar found himself, after the armistice of 1808, in possession of Finland but without precise plans for her future. Moreover, he had some vague and rather flabby liberal notions, and seemed open to proposals from the Finnish side. A group of leading Finns suggested that the Estates should be convened. Alexander agreed. Elections took place, and the first all-Finnish Diet met at Porvoo in 1809. It was formally opened by 'the Emperor and Autocrat of all the Russias and the Grand Duke of Finland' as Alexander now styled himself. He promised, in return for the allegiance of the Finns, to maintain the existing religion, laws and constitution of Finland, now an autonomous Grand Duchy of Russia. He had, in addition, previously agreed that, Finland being in personal union with him, the Finns should deal directly with him, and not through the Russian government. This personal union was to form the basis of the relationship between Finland and Russia for the next ninety years.

The Finns then set about organizing their own government and administration. They became responsible for the conduct of all their affairs, except defence and foreign affairs. They could not, it is true, introduce new legislation without the consent of the Tsar, but administratively they were completely autonomous. They had their own legal system, they controlled their own churches and schools, their finances were separate from those of Russia, and they continued to enjoy the same rights and liberties as they had done under Sweden. They were officially designated as 'Finnish citizens and Russian subjects', whereas they had previously been Swedish citizens and Swedish subjects. Their situation *vis-à-vis* Russia was as enigmatic as it has ever been since. The Tsar was, in his own country, an autocratic and imperial ruler; in Finland he was the ancestor of the modern constitutional monarch. The Finns possessed a degree of democratic freedom unknown in Russia. In spite of certain limitations, they had, it appeared, drawn some advantages from the change of overlord, and lost at the same time the constant menace of attack from the east. For few defeated countries has war had so fortunate an issue. And Alexander got, as far as his strange mind can be read, what he wanted: a country on whose loyalty he could count while he dealt with his commitments to Napoleon and with the war with Turkey which he already had on his hands.

When Nicholas I succeeded Alexander in 1825, mutual trust between Finns and Russians seemed firmly established. As well as conducting their own affairs in Finland, the Finns could, if they wished, spread their wings and serve in the armed forces or the civil administration in Russia. Such service attracted men who felt the lack of opportunity in their own small country, and also those Finns for whom the wider world has always had a fascination for its own sake.

Over the rest of the century Finland provided the Russian armed forces with, it is said, four hundred generals and admirals, together with a steady stream of other officers. (One of the last of these was Mannerheim, who entered the Imperial Guards in 1890 and, after commanding the Finnish armies against the Soviet Union from 1940 to 1944, became President of Finland.) The upper classes of Finland and Russia visited each other's capital cities, and some Finnish and Russian families were joined by marriage.

However, there were already men in Finland who feared that this harmony was the prelude to absorption, and who set to work to convince their countrymen of its dangers. The celebrated slogan of the times became: 'We are no longer Swedes, we will not become Russians, so let us be Finns.' The earliest proponent of the national movement was a lecturer at the University of Turku, Adolf Arwidsson; but he fell foul of the Russian authorities and was dismissed from his post, after which he left for Sweden. Snellman took over Arwidsson's task; but, as has already been seen, the language dispute absorbed the major portion of nationalist energies, and set Finn against Finn rather than Finn against Russian. The year of revolutions, 1848, found the Finns barely touched by the liberal political currents which were surging through Europe. Over the nineteenth century, their nationalist aspirations appeared in many different forms, but they never developed into a fully-grown political movement.

But towards the 'sixties Finnish liberals began to press for changes in their constitution, which had, as it were, lain dormant for half a century. The Diet had not been convened since 1809, and in the end, Alexander II (1855–81) was persuaded to summon the Estates in 1863. The liberals were unable to secure the many reforms they had hoped for – among them the adoption of a parliamentary régime and the abolition of the censorship. But the Tsar did agree to convene the Diet every five years and to grant it the right to initiate limited legislation. These concessions, coupled with the Language Decree giving Finnish parity with Swedish, marked a considerable step forward in the country's development; a later move which allowed the Finns to have their own army increased both their self-esteem and sense of security. The Russian motives for granting these concessions are far from clear, particularly given Alexander's repressive treatment of the Poles. Possibly the Tsar thought that in view of the current international situation, the price he paid for peace on the borders of his capital was not too high. The Finns had again demonstrated their capacity for loyalty to the Tsar during the Crimean War, which had reached the defences of Helsinki, and a Russia weakened by the conflict had reason to be grateful to them. (The Finns' experience, it must be admitted, was not particularly unnerving. The British Admiralty sent an expedition to the Baltic with the aim of deflecting Russian naval forces. British warships went into the attack with flags flying and the band playing, and the action was more appropriate to a Gilbert and Sullivan opera than to the annals of naval history.) The statue of Alexander II which the Finns spontaneously set up in Senate Square in Helsinki, and which remains there today, was a monument to a ruler who was idealized, perhaps mistakenly, and viewed as a benefactor.

For the reign of Alexander II was a good time for Finland in other respects. The country began to develop as an economic entity, independent of Russia or Sweden. The first steps towards a Finnish monetary system were taken when the Bank of Finland began to issue quarter-rouble notes called *markkas*, and eventually Finnish and Russian currencies ceased to bear any relation to each other. Roads, railways and canals were built. A telegraph line from Helsinki to St Petersburg was constructed in 1855 by the Russians, who later further extended the telegraph system. It was the only Russian institution – though manned by Finns – in the Grand Duchy of Finland. The woodworking industries began to take on a more modern form, and the foundations of many other industries were laid.

But in Russia itself reaction against liberalism was already developing and oppressive measures were multiplying. The terrorism of the revolutionaries, which was responsible for the assassination of Alexander II in 1881, was countered by reaction and repression which gathered strength in the reign of Alexander III. Government control of the universities, the law courts and the press was intensified. The periphery of the Russian Empire began to suffer from the pan-Slav policy. Poland was mercilessly russified; the Russian language was enforced in Estonia and Lithuania; Jews everywhere were persecuted. Only Finland remained largely undisturbed by this growing extremism. Her degree of freedom and self-government, and the 'special status' of personal union with the tsar, thus became highly distasteful to the reactionary Russian government. The frontier of contagious liberty ran far too near to St Petersburg for the reactionaries to sleep in peace. Nevertheless the only measure which Alexander III took against his Grand Duchy, to which he was personally very attached, was the abolition of the independent Finnish postal service, and this was without any noticeable effect.

Finland's turn for oppression came when Nicholas II succeeded Alexander in 1894 and inaugurated for the Finns a period of russification and repression which was to last, with some intermissions, until 1917. On his accession, Nicholas swore to uphold Finland's constitution, and the loyal Finns took him at his word. But by 1898, when a new governor-general, Nicholas Bobrikov, was appointed, it had become clear that he and his fellow Russian nationalists would be content with nothing less than total russification. Bobrikov viewed as a heresy the idea of a personal union between Finland and the tsar, and aimed at making the Grand Duchy an integral part of the Russian Empire. Russians were to be allowed to hold administrative positions in Finland, and Russian was to be made the administrative language of the country and be taught as the principal subject in all secondary schools. The Finnish army was to be absorbed in the Imperial forces. The Finnish Diet was about to reject this last proposal when Nicholas issued an Imperial manifesto transferring all Finnish legislation to the Russian government. At a single stroke Finland's autonomy was destroyed.

The Finns made immediate and heroic efforts to regain their rights. The Diet declared the manifesto invalid; half the adult population signed a protest to the Tsar, and sent a deputation of five hundred to deliver it to him personally. He refused to receive either this, or the international deputation carrying a similar protest and appeal for the restitution of Finnish rights, which was signed by more than a thousand of the great names of Europe.

So the process of russification continued and the censorship became more and more severe. In 1901, largely at the instigation of Bobrikov, a new conscription law was forced on Finland. The Finnish army was to be disbanded and conscripts were in future to serve under Russian colours. This was the signal for passive resistance. More than half the conscripts failed to report at the appointed place and time. The Russians made two further attempts to round up the Finns, but with little more success than at their first. They then abandoned the whole plan and demanded a levy of money instead of men. The Finns had won their first engagement and freed themselves from the obligation of fighting for the masters they were learning to hate. Resistance spread to judges, civil servants and local government officials. The nation became bitterly divided between the Constitutionalists, who defied Russia in their struggle to maintain Finland's constitutional rights, and the Compliants, supported, among others, by Lutheran bishops and some higher government officials who deemed it wiser to avoid a head-on collision. Constitutionalists in high positions were dismissed, imprisoned, or even exiled, and their places were taken by Compliants or Russians. By 1904 the time for desperate measures had come. The governor-general, Bobrikov, was assassinated in the government building by a young civil servant, who then killed himself.

Meanwhile the Russians' war with Japan had brought them defeat after defeat. At home the Tsar was under pressure both from liberal elements and workers' organizations. In October 1905, after the end of the Japanese war, Russian workers mounted a general strike, which spread to Finland. There it was purely a demonstration against the autocratic rule of the Tsar and his government; it was joined by civil servants and supported by employers, who showed their sympathy by continuing to pay their workers' wages throughout the strike. The Tsar was forced to make concessions both in Russia and in Finland. He repealed the illegal acts of the last few years, and the Grand Duchy recovered her autonomy.

There followed, in 1906, one of the most extraordinary developments of the whole Russian period. With the consent of the Tsar, the Finns disbanded the outmoded Estates, in which the growing number of industrial workers had no representation, and replaced them with the most modern and democratic parliament of the Europe of the day. It was the only unicameral parliament of its time, and the only one whose members were elected by women as well as men. (Outside Europe, one other country, New Zealand, had just previously given women the vote.) Universal franchise was established, and the electoral roll was thereby increased tenfold. In the subsequent general election, the Social-Democratic Party, founded in 1899, gained 80 of the two hundred seats in the new parliament. All this was achieved with remarkable speed and absence of friction. The country had found a new unity in resistance to Russia, and it knew that a strong and representative parliament would be a powerful weapon in any struggle with the Tsar.

Elsewhere in the Tsar's domains democracy could not be achieved as simply and effortlessly. Poland's demand for autonomy was answered by martial law. Inside Russia the Tsar paid only lip-service to democratic government, and three times limited the powers of the Duma. It was hardly surprising that the Russians' resentment once more rose against the small Duchy on their doorstep, which seemed in so many ways more advanced than the great Russian Empire itself. And the fact that Finland was becoming the refuge for revolutionaries (Lenin and Stalin are said to have met there for the first time) helped to turn resentment into mistrust.

So the reign of liberal democracy in Finland was only an interlude. In 1908 the Tsar suddenly brought to an end the personal union between the Grand Duchy and the Russian sovereign which had existed for exactly a century. Finland became part and parcel of the Russian Empire, subject to the legislation of the Russian government. Russians were appointed to the Finnish administration, which was forced to use Russian as its official language. Finns who resisted were imprisoned or sent to Siberia. By 1914 normal government, as the Finns had known it, had come to an end, and the outbreak of war gave the Russians the pretext for further extension and intensification of repressive measures and rule by force.

For some years already activist groups had been working to overthrow Russian rule and establish Finnish independence. The Finns were able to remain neutral in the First World War; they had no army of their own, and the Russians did not consider them sufficiently trustworthy to be enlisted in their armies. The activists took advantage of their neutrality to try to develop their military strength. They looked first to Sweden for training for their forces; but the Swedes were already deeply confirmed in their policy of neutrality and unwilling to risk training their neighbour's rebels. The Finns then turned to Germany, out of expediency, not affection. Germany was at war with Russia; Russia's enemies were Finland's friends. (The overriding determination to be rid of Russian rule led to this, and another dangerously simple equation supported by other groups in Finland: the Bolsheviks were the Tsar's enemies, and therefore Finland's friends. Both these equations were eventually to have disastrous consequences.) So, in 1915 and 1916, about two thousand young Finns were sent in secret for training in Germany, where they were formed into the Jaeger Battalion. In the event it was the Russian revolution, not the efforts of the activists, that precipitated the achievement of Finnish independence. The activists later helped to consolidate it.

When, after the revolution of March 1917, the Provisional Government took over in Russia, the constitutional position of Finland was obscure. Had the Provisional Government inherited from the Tsar the 'personal union' with Finland? Would it restore Finland's former autonomy? The Socialists were in a majority in Parliament, and they led the government which was formed after the revolution. They were not without sympathy for the revolutionaries, and Kerensky himself visited Finland in an attempt to secure Finnish loyalty to the Provisional Government.

Nevertheless in July Parliament passed the 'Power Law', which transferred to itself all the powers formerly vested in the Tsar, except those relating to foreign affairs and defence. The Provisional Government refused to ratify this law and dissolved Parliament – an action which made the Finnish Socialists look more favourably on the Bolsheviks to the left of Kerensky, who were intensifying their campaign inside Russia. The new elections held in October gave the Finnish Parliament a 'bourgeois' majority. But a week after it assembled on 1 November, the Bolshevik revolution changed the whole situation in Russia and Finland alike. The Finns realized that they had no alternative but to take matters into their own hands. On 15 November Parliament passed a resolution which empowered it to exercise all the powers formerly belonging to the Tsar and Grand Duke. The Bolshevik government raised no objection, and on 6 December Finland formally declared her independence. On the last day of 1917 Lenin's government recognized the new state, and Finland stood alone before the storms that were brewing at home and raging abroad.

The country had long since found its identity and become an entity. The struggle against Russia had taken the form, in part, of artistic self-assertion, and great cultural strides had been made in the previous three decades. Economically Finland had developed into a unit separate from Sweden or Russia, and the foundations of the modern industrial state had been laid. Technically the transfer of power was painless, because the Finns not only had their own democratic constitution and machinery of government but were experienced in using them. The Russians' great gift to Finland was the autonomy which made the transition to independence little more than a theoretical exercise. But political development had been delayed by Russian reaction, and the Finns lacked experience in foreign affairs, and in both internal and external politics enormous problems already faced them.

Throughout 1917 the rumblings of a class conflict had been growing louder. The years without normal government had created serious social problems and many reforms were long overdue. The war had provided in Finland, no less than in other countries, opportunities for profit which benefited the middle and upper classes; the working classes, on the other hand, were impoverished and their condition was aggravated by the unemployment and near-famine which the country experienced towards the end of the war. Neither side seemed disposed to come to terms with the other. During the summer of 1917 there were strikes and disturbances, partly engineered by Russian soldiers in Helsinki, which culminated in a brief general strike in November. All these took place in a virtual vacuum, as Finland had no army and few police, the Russian gendarmerie having been disbanded. In this vacuum, two private, unofficial armies began to take shape. The Red Guard represented the extreme wing of the Social Democrats and the workers' organizations, and was supported by Russian soldiers turned revolutionary. Linked with the Red Guard was the Central Revolutionary Council, composed of those Finns who, in the hope of ridding Finland of the tsarist overlords, had made common cause with the Bolshevik revolutionaries. Against the Red Guard there arose a counter-organization known as the White Guard, drawn from the 'bourgeois' parties and reinforced by Finnish officers from the disbanded Russian Imperial Army and, later, by the Jaeger Battalion from Germany.

The aim of the Central Revolutionary Council was to seize power and set up a Socialist Workers' Republic; it had been urged to do this at its conference in November, attended also by a young Russian revolutionary visitor, by name Josef Stalin. The majority of the Social Democrats were opposed to violent methods, but the extremists at the conference won the day. A wave of terror swept over the country, and in January 1918 the Civil War broke out. The White Guard was organized as the government army by General Mannerheim, who had recently returned from Russia.

The issues were primarily domestic, but, given the world situation, other issues and other powers became involved. At the time of the Russian revolution there were at least 40,000 Russian troops in Finland, and the new Soviet government made no attempt to withdraw them. Many of these troops joined forces with the Red Guard, and the liberation of Finland from the Russian garrisons thus became one of Mannerheim's most important objectives. His White Army was based in Ostrobothnia, while the Reds controlled Helsinki and southern Finland. The White advance was not rapid. Against Mannerheim's wish, and without his knowledge, the government asked Germany for help. German forces and equipment were landed in Finland in April, and by the middle of May the Reds were forced to surrender.

The Civil War was over, but the attitudes which had fanned its flames remained. Finland had avoided the setting up of a Marxist state and the possibility of only nominal independence within the framework of the U.S.S.R. But she emerged from the war with a government which was overwhelmingly pro-German, in a technical state of conflict with the U.S.S.R., with unsolved constitutional problems, and with political divisions which took a score of years to heal.

The body which met to deal with the new constitution was a rump parliament, from which ninety-one Social-Democrat members had been excluded on the grounds that they had taken part in the rebellion. Their absence left the parliament dominated by the pro-German element, which felt the need for the protection of a stronger power. It favoured the organization of the army on German lines and with some German direction; this policy precipitated Mannerheim's resignation from his position as commander-in-chief of the armed forces. The pro-Germans pressed for the establishment of a monarchy instead of the republic which had originally been envisaged with the support of the bulk of the nation; they proposed that the crown be offered to a German prince, and as late as October 1918, when the imminent collapse of Germany was obvious to most of Europe, Parliament elected, as King of Finland, Prince Friedrich Karl of Hesse, the Kaiser's brother-in-law. The armistice in November brought this plan to a fortunate end, and Finland was squarely faced with the independence which she had so long desired, yet begun to fear once it was within her grasp. To deal with its problems Mannerheim was summoned from abroad and appointed regent.

Gradually the political climate moderated. The Social-Democratic Party was reorganized on a moderate parliamentary basis by Väinö Tanner, and its extreme left wing split off to form the Communist Party. When a general election was held in 1919, the Social Democrats returned to their traditional position with eighty seats. Eventually a republican form of government was agreed, and in July the first President of Finland, Professor K. J. Ståhlberg, took office. In other respects constitutional changes were small. The Parliament Act of 1906, then far in advance of its time, needed no alteration, and the new Form of Government Act repeated and elaborated many of the essential principles by which Finland had been governed under both Sweden and Russia.

In 1920 the technical state of conflict between Finland and the Soviet Union was brought to an end by the Treaty of Tartu (Dorpat). The Soviet Union recognized Finland as an independent republic and ceded to her the Arctic port of Petsamo. Various small adjustments to the frontier were made, and Finland agreed to neutralize some islands in the Gulf of Finland commanding the approaches to Leningrad, of which the most important was Suursaari (Hogland). The Karelian question, however, remained as a source of friction between the two countries. Eastern Karelia had always been part of Russia, and the population, though linguistically related to the Finnish Karelians, had developed on Russian lines. But the Finns felt that this relationship gave them a certain vested interest in Eastern Karelia, and they secured from the Soviets a promise that it should be granted autonomy and national self-determination. Later the Soviet Union was to view the Finnish interest in Eastern Karelia as unwarranted interference in its own internal affairs.

The Treaty of Tartu brought down the curtain on the period of Russian rule. Finland's situation appeared to be stabilized, but the Russian neighbour remained to play a dominant role in her independent life. The very nature of the later Russian period, together with the growing pains of nationalism, had fostered in Finland a deep political bitterness. For the absence of personal bitterness in the Finnish character is counterbalanced by an intensity of public and collective feeling which can corrode national life over a generation and more. The Finnish view of the U.S.S.R. combined the mistrust engendered in the last twenty years of tsarist rule with an almost fanatical loathing of Communism. The Soviets, for their part, could not forgive Finland for throwing out the revolution and adopting a thoroughly bourgeois solution. Inside Finland, the civil war and the relationship of the Finnish Left to the Russian revolutionaries created a deep rift in political and social life and gave rise to prejudices which have still not been totally dissipated. The young republic was already caught between Communist Russia and neutral Sweden, and Nazi Germany was to arise to the south of the Baltic. Independent Finland was born, not with a silver spoon, but with a dagger, in her mouth.

CHAPTER NINE

The Stormy Years

To the Finns, the years between the two world wars seemed a time of peaceful and hopeful development. They had affirmed their neutrality shortly after they became independent. Two decades later, they believed, like the other Scandinavian countries with which they were associated in the 'Oslo group', that this neutrality could be maintained without common defence measures while preparations for war were piling up around them. But for the Finns the choice between neutrality and belligerence had been eliminated, though without their knowledge, before the outbreak of the Second World War. Stalin made the situation brutally clear in the autumn of 1939 when he said to a Finnish delegation: 'I well understand that you wish to remain neutral, but I can assure you that it is not possible. The great powers simply will not allow it.' This was no bluff, but the plain truth. The great powers – by which Stalin meant the Soviet Union and Germany – had between them already decided Finland's fate. The miracle, in retrospect, is that she so narrowly escaped the worst that had been plotted for her.

But long before the Soviet-German treaty of the summer of 1939 the Soviet Union had been casting a strategic eye on Finland. Soviet-Finnish relations had not improved in the inter-war years; they had rather deteriorated as a result of suspicions, both well-grounded and groundless, on both sides. Finland had overthrown the revolution which the Russian Bolsheviks hoped would succeed, and for a time had intrigued with the White Russians; her Communist Party had been driven underground, and hostility to the Soviet system was openly expressed. The Karelian question was raised from time to time, and the Finns appeared to the U.S.S.R. to be interfering in internal Soviet affairs when they made representations to the League of Nations concerning the Eastern Karelians. While there was in Finland a general orientation towards Germany, no agreements existed between the two countries. But the Soviet government was convinced, rightly, that Hitler would eventually launch an attack on Russia and would use Finland as a northern base; in more extreme moments, it was convinced, wrongly, of joint Finno-German designs to serve that end.

In April 1938 the Soviet Union began a series of somewhat oblique approaches to the Finnish government with the aim of including Finland, through various general measures, in the Soviet defensive system. The Finns rejected these approaches outright and reaffirmed their policy of neutrality. By the following spring, Soviet policy had taken a more definite shape and was directed to certain strategic areas. The Finnish government was asked to lease to the U.S.S.R. for a period of thirty years certain islands in the Gulf of Finland which commanded the passage to Leningrad. All these islands, of which Suursaari was the largest, had been neutralized by the Treaty of Tartu in 1920. In return the Soviet Union offered Finland a strip of Russian territory north of Lake Ladoga. General Mannerheim, then Chief of the Council of Defence, had been an officer in the Russian Imperial Army, and he well understood the strategic ideas which the Soviets had inherited from a long line of tsars. He urgently recommended that these islands, of no value to Finland, should be handed to the Soviet Union, and also suggested that the Finnish frontier should be withdrawn five or six miles farther west of Leningrad. Neither President nor government would listen to his views, and the Soviet request was refused.

In August 1939 the world was startled by the Soviet-German Treaty of Non-Aggression. Hitler had bought, at least temporarily, peace in the east and the certainty that he would not have to fight simultaneously on two fronts. The secret clauses of the treaty carved up Europe into spheres of influence, and the Baltic States and Finland were assigned to the U.S.S.R. After war broke out between Britain and Germany in September the Soviet Union lost no time in securing its north-western defences. Estonia, Latvia and Lithuania all yielded to its demands for military bases. The Finns did not doubt that their turn was to come, but they resolutely affirmed that they would 'never submit to a Baltic solution'.

The Soviet demands to Finland were made in October. They included the lease of the Hanko peninsula, which commands the mouth of the Gulf of Finland, for thirty years, the cession of the islands previously discussed, and of a part of the Karelian Isthmus. The Finns made limited counter-proposals to which the Soviet Union refused to agree. Mannerheim again counselled compromise and concession, but was not heeded. For more than a month a Finnish delegation shuttled between Helsinki and Moscow. In the end it became clear that further negotiation was useless, and on 30 November, Soviet aircraft bombed Helsinki. Even at this twelfth hour, attempts were made by Finland to reach an armistice through the mediation of Sweden. This was refused by the Soviet Union, which had already set up a puppet Finnish Government near the Soviet-Finnish border. It was headed by Otto Kuusinen, a Marxist Finn who had fled to Russia during the civil war and risen to be secretary-general of the Comintern. The Kuusinen government made no converts in Finland, and after a few weeks it faded into nothingness. But its establishment convinced the Finns that they had no alternative but to fight if they wished to continue to exist as an independent democratic state.

The Winter War, as it came to be called, lasted one hundred days, and was heroically fought by a small Finnish army which received only a minimum of supplies from abroad. Praise and admiration for the struggle of this David against the eastern Goliath poured in from all parts of the world; they may possibly have raised the army's already high morale, but they could not compensate for the hopeless lack of equipment of the nine Finnish divisions which found themselves facing twenty-seven larger Soviet divisions, with at least a hundred tanks. Yet Mannerheim's forces met only with success in the first six weeks of the campaign, and the Finnish ski troops were more than a match for the Soviet machines, unsuited as they were to terrain and climate. But by mid-January Soviet forces were reorganized to take the offensive. They were aided by the winter, the most severe for many years. Fifty degrees C. of frost froze the sea so hard that the Russians could bring their tanks across the Gulf of Finland and attack the Finnish lines from the rear. In February they broke through the Finnish defences, and in March the government was compelled to sign a peace treaty.

By its terms Finland was obliged to cede the Karelian Isthmus, and with it Viipuri, one of her largest and most important towns; also territory in the Kuusamo-Salla area in the north and the small islands in the Gulf of Finland. She also leased to the Soviet Union the port of Hanko and a part of the surrounding land. Throughout the peace talks, the Soviet representatives insisted that they did not fear Finland but a German attack through Finland; the cessions made by Finland made possible the defence in depth of Leningrad and protected the Murmansk railway. Molotov held that the terms of the treaty were generous. Perhaps they were, but only when compared with what was exacted from other defeated countries later in the war. Moscow had not pressed the war further when the Soviet armies held the advantage, and no political limitations were placed on Finland. She was defeated, but neither conquered nor occupied. By occupation Stalin would have risked a total break with Britain and France; and being convinced that Hitler would eventually attack the Soviet Union, he hoped to maintain some sort of connection with the West. But, while Finland's democratic form of government was intact, her wounds were severe. More than 25,000 men were killed; as a result of the territorial cessions ten per cent of her land and industrial production were lost, and every eighth Finnish citizen was deprived of his home and his livelihood.

For the next fifteen months the Finns lived in a state of half-peace that was far more perilous than war. They were endangered by every circumstance, and by the extremes to which war had pushed their own temperament. The Winter War had been epic and glorious in spite of its final disaster. It had intensified the fervour of Finnish patriotism and the power of Finnish obstinacy. Undisguised hatred of the Soviet Union got the better of reason and judgment and was matched by an almost pathological Russian suspicion of Finland. A high degree of secrecy surrounded all government moves, and censorship prevented the Finns from following the course of the war beyond their borders.

What they did learn of it prompted them, in the summer of 1940, to write Britain off as defeated and to look upon Germany as the power which would dominate the Europe of the future. Many other factors contributed to the development of pro-German sentiment: Finland's general pre-war German orientation, the German training of a number of senior officers who had belonged to the Jaegers twenty years earlier, the idea that German troops had saved the country from the 'Red menace' in 1918 and might do so again. Except among a few extremists there was little sympathy for Nazism as such; some blinded themselves to its evils and many were unaware of their extent; the majority succumbed to the smug belief, which recurs from time to time in all the northern countries, from Scotland to Finland, that all great powers are bad and all equally to be despised. Germany was only too ready to exploit this mood. The Russians broke their trade treaty with Finland and refused to send further supplies of grain. She was cut off from all other sources of supply, and Germany willingly stepped into Russia's place as provider. From September 1940 German troops began to travel to and from Norway through Finnish territory, and an increasing number of German 'cultural' and 'business' missions visited Finland. All this was done with the agreement of the Finnish government, which had observed similar German operations in Sweden, and had also given transit facilities to the Soviet Union. The government, however, did not know until the secret talks between Molotov and Hitler were reconstructed after the war, the extent to which Finland's destiny was being decided by Germany.

When Hitler and Molotov met in November 1940, Hitler was apparently already planning to attack and dispose of the Soviet Union before turning his attention to the invasion of Britain. Finland had therefore become essential to Germany as a northern base for attack. Molotov, for his part, was equally anxious to consolidate the Soviet Union's hold on Finland as a defensive outpost, and his remarks suggested the intention of occupying and annexing the whole country. Hitler made it clear that he would not allow the Soviet Union to use force in Finland, and Molotov was no doubt aware that, given the Finnish mood, nothing could be achieved without force. The question was closed without further significant negotiations between the two countries. Hitler had effectively prevented any chance of a Soviet occupation of Finland; he had other plans for her.

Early in 1941 German military leaders began to drop hints to Finnish staff officers about Operation Barbarossa, the plan to attack the U.S.S.R. In May a delegation of Finnish military experts was invited to Salzburg and there told of the possibility of war with Russia by General Keitel and General Jodl. They did not disguise the fact that they hoped for Finnish support, particularly in the drive on Leningrad.

To the Finns there appeared no way out. No declaration of neutrality would have been respected; indeed the Germans, like the Russians, were already present on Finnish soil and their numbers were steadily increasing. To enter into an alliance with the Soviet Union, were it even remotely possible, would have been to invite a German attack. The government confined itself to affirmations that Finland would not depart from neutrality unless attacked, when she would be forced to defend herself. German preparations for war continued, and on 22 June the attack on the Soviet Union was launched by German forces. Inevitably hostilities recurred between Finnish and Soviet forces, and three days later President Ryti announced that Finland was again at war with the Soviet Union.

Finland's only aim now was to recover her lost territories, and it was an understandable and reasonable aim. Her belief that the Soviet armies would be defeated in a matter of weeks was shared in responsible quarters in other countries; but the logic of the argument that Finland's war was entirely separate from that being waged by the British and their allies was not appreciated by the British government which, after several warnings, declared war on Finland in December 1941. British and Finnish forces, however, never met in any form of engagement.

At the same time there was, in the outside world, some misunderstanding of the Finnish position. There was no formal alliance between Germany and Finland; the Finnish and German armies fought under separate commands and there was little or no co-operation between the respective Chiefs of Staff. Political decisions relevant to the conduct of operations by the Finnish forces were taken by the Finns, not by the Germans. Although Finland was regarded by many as a German satellite, like Hungary, Rumania and Bulgaria, she never, in fact, sacrificed her independence or her institutions to Nazi Germany.

The German and Finnish forces both had considerable success at the outset of the Second War and within three months the old frontier on the Karelian Isthmus had been reached and part of Eastern Karelia occupied. Those dispossessed by the 1940 peace treaty hastened back to their old homes and farms and began to repair and rebuild them in the lee of the advancing Finnish army. But, as 1942 wore on, it became increasingly clear that the Soviet forces along the whole European front were not to be driven back and defeated by the Germans as easily as the world had hoped or feared. Inside Finland opposition to the war grew – chiefly among moderate members of the Left who, though without sympathy for the Soviet Union, realized that their country's entry into the Second War could end only in disaster. The strict censorship of the press imposed by the nearness of military operations, and the fact that Parliament was rarely consulted on more important issues, prevented such views from being openly voiced and discussed.

By the middle of 1943 the demand for peace began to be made more openly. The United States' offer of mediation made in the spring had been rejected, although at that time the Finnish armies had come to a standstill. A number of prominent citizens addressed an appeal to the President to begin peace negotiations. This, too, was disregarded, while right-wing newspapers continued to predict success for German arms, and left-wing papers to urge the government to reconsider its position. In the background there lurked always the problem of food supplies. If Finland were to leave Germany's side, who would defend her against starvation? And what course of action might the Germans take?

In February 1944, after America had issued her severest warning to Finland, negotiations were opened between the Finnish and Soviet governments. The Finns declared that the Soviet peace terms, which included a return to the 1940 frontiers and the payment of a heavy indemnity, were unacceptable. In the summer Soviet forces launched a fresh and successful offensive against the Finnish lines in the Karelian Isthmus, and at the same time German setbacks increased in other theatres of war.

By August, when Marshal Mannerheim became President of the Republic and a new government was formed, the Finnish people had become fully aware of their situation. By this time, too, Sweden had agreed to supply Finland with grain and other vital foodstuffs for a period of six months. Peace negotiations were opened once more, and on 4 September 1944 the war with the Soviet Union came to an end.

Two weeks later, the armistice terms were announced. Finland was to return to the 1940 frontiers, thus losing the Karelian Isthmus definitively. She was also to cede the Petsamo area which she had gained by the Treaty of Tartu in 1920, and an area near Kuusamo in

Finnish Lapland. Porkkala, a headland west of Helsinki and immediately opposite Tallinn, was to be leased to the Soviet Union for fifty years as a military and naval base. (In demanding Porkkala, the U.S.S.R. looked back forty years to the strategy of Imperial Russia. After the war with Japan, the Russians considered fortifying Porkkala and the offshore islands as part of their outer defences, but the project was abandoned.) Finland was to be immediately responsible for the evacuation of all German troops and was to pay the Soviet Union war reparations in kind to the value of 300 million American dollars over a period of six years. In keeping with the unreasoning mood of the times, the Soviet Union required Finland to bring to trial those deemed responsible for her entry into the Second War.

The clause which obliged the Finnish forces to rid their country of German troops provoked what is called the Continuation War. The Finns had believed that the 200,000 Germans stationed in Finland would accept the situation and evacuate themselves. Instead, they retaliated for the negotiation of a separate peace by a policy of scorched earth and devastation. It was not until the end of April 1945 that the Germans were finally expelled after many fierce battles.

Thus was brought to an end this most ill-starred of adventures. Up to the present day criticism has continued to be heaped on those who embarked upon the Second War. But in retrospect it seems unlikely that the Finns could have changed their destiny after October 1939. Once they had decided on the course that led to the Winter War there was little real possibility of avoiding the disaster of the war of 1941–44. Had they allowed the Germans, as they would have been forced to do, to use the country as a base for attack on the Soviet Union, Finland would have become a ravaged battlefield or a German satellite. Had they agreed to the Soviet demands in 1939 and so avoided the Winter War, they would have risked – to put it no higher – the absorption into the U.S.S.R. that was the lot of the Baltic States; and Hitler would have had no scruples about attacking the Soviet Union through Finland. The chances of Finnish neutrality being respected were, from the outset, minimal or non-existent.

Yet, looking back, it seems as though fortune, however, heavily disguised, was with the Finns after all. Neither Peter the Great nor Alexander I had been able to spare the troops from their other adventures to occupy Finland; Stalin had good reason for not doing so after the Winter War; Hitler prevented the Soviet Union from annexing Finland at a later stage. When the Finno-Russian war ended in 1944 Berlin was the overriding objective of the Soviet armies; whether or not Stalin wanted to occupy Finland, he could not detach the necessary forces. So Finland emerged from the Second World War as the only belligerent country on the European mainland that had never been occupied either by Germany or the Soviet Union; the only country, other than Britain, that had managed to maintain her democratic parliamentary system intact from the outbreak of war to its end. For so small a country the survival of democracy was, in 1945, a triumph of heroism and determination, as well as a stroke of fortune.

But in 1944 and 1945 the Finns had little time to reflect on what might have been. The task that now lay before them was almost more daunting than war itself. Political policies, internal and external, had to be reshaped in the new context in which they found themselves; the colossal burden of war reparations to the Soviet Union had to be shouldered immediately; close on half a million refugees from the ceded territories had to be resettled and rehoused. All this had to be done in total isolation; Finland was without allies or partners, and there was no place that she could safely occupy in the realignments of the post-war years.

The great and dominant figure of those years was Juho Kusti Paasikivi, who became Prime Minister in 1944, and President of the Republic in 1946 when Mannerheim resigned for reasons of health. It is not too much to say that Finland owes in large measure everything she possesses today – freedom, independence and prosperity – to Paasikivi's wisdom and statesmanship. Mannerheim, the more dramatic figure, has become today the object of something like a cult; but historians of the future may well judge Paasikivi as the greater man of the two. When war broke out in 1939 Paasikivi was Finnish Minister in Stockholm; he was sixty-nine, and apparently at the end of a succcessful, though not outstandingly distinguished, career. But few Finns knew Russia and the Russians as he did, and when it became necessary to send an envoy to Moscow to negotiate in October 1939 he was an obvious choice. He had studied in St Petersburg and spoke Russian well; he had negotiated the Treaty of Tartu in 1920; above all, he had retained an objective attitude towards the Soviet Union, unclouded either by sympathy for or hatred of Communism.

His reasonableness was combined with a firmness and determination to preserve Finland's independence of which he soon made the Soviet leaders well aware. They, for their part, from 1939 until his retirement in 1956, accorded him more respect than they gave to any other Finnish politician or diplomat. In 1944 he was the only man of real stature who commanded respect both in Finland and Russia, and so was again an obvious choice for the first post-war Prime Minister, and subsequently for the President of the Republic.

Paasikivi put on record in 1939: 'Russian interests in regard to Finland have always been strategic, whereas other (economic or ideological) considerations have never played much part.' This conviction remained unchanged for the rest of his life, and has been borne out by events up to the present day. It led, in the immediate post-war years, straight to the heart and basis of his policy: to secure and maintain the confidence of the Soviet Union, and to convince its leaders that Finnish territory would in no circumstances be used as a base for attack on Russia. The formula appeared simple enough; but it was the first time it had been enunciated and adopted in the long centuries of endemic conflict between the two countries. It was also the first time that the Finns had been asked to perform a psychological somersault and to make their heads instead of their hearts govern their collective attitude towards their eastern neighbour.

They responded with that tacit, intuitive grasp of the situation and its needs which they had shown at other, though not all, times of crisis. They had to succeed in the apparently impossible task of securing the confidence of the U.S.S.R. while containing communism inside Finland. In all their dealings with the Soviet Union the Finns behaved with the greatest correctness; a considerable contribution to the improvement of relations was made by the press, which reported all the facts with sobriety, but eliminated the sensational attacks on and abuse of the Soviets so common at the time in the press of other Western countries. Even the most private citizens considered it their duty to refrain from making any derogatory remarks about the Soviet Union, although the Communists of Finland and of the satellite countries never shared this immunity. The Finns were too honest to make any false claims of sympathy for the Soviet system. In the parliamentary debate on the peace treaty of 1947, the opposition spokesman did not hesitate to express the view that the treaty did not conform to the principles of justice. But he added: 'It is our firm resolve, nevertheless, loyally to carry out the terms of the treaty and to strive to establish good relations between our country and the Soviet Union.'

As early as 1948 it looked as if the good-neighbour policy was beginning to succeed. The U.S.S.R. had concluded with the satellite countries – Rumania, Hungary and Czechoslovakia – treaties of mutual assistance, and Finland was asked to discuss a similar treaty as a guarantee against possible German aggression. The result was the Agreement on Friendship, Co-operation and Mutual Assistance, signed in April 1948 and valid for ten years. This agreement, which was renewed in 1955 for a further twenty years, has become the cornerstone of Finno-Soviet relations. Its preamble noted 'Finland's aspiration to stand aside from the conflicts of interests of the Great Powers'; it consists of eight Articles, of which the most important are the following:

> In the event of Finland, or the Soviet Union across the territory of Finland, becoming the object of military aggression on the part of Germany or any State allied with the latter, Finland, loyal to her obligations as an independent State, will fight to repel the attack. Finland will in such cases use all her available forces to defend her territorial integrity by land, sea and air, and will do so within the frontiers of Finland in accordance with the obligations prescribed in the present agreement, and, if necessary, with the assistance of, or jointly with, the U.S.S.R. (Article 1)
>
> The parties shall confer with each other if it is established that the threat of an armed attack as described in Article 1 is present. (Article 2)
>
> The parties confirm their pledge, given under Article 3 of the Peace Treaty signed in Paris in February 1947, not to conclude any alliance or join any coalition directed against the other party. (Article 4)
>
> The parties pledge themselves to observe the principle of mutual respect of sovereignty and integrity and that of non-interference in the internal affairs of the other State. (Article 6)

The particular interest of this Agreement lies in its points of difference from the treaties made by the Soviet Union with Rumania, Hungary and Czechoslovakia. Finland was obliged, according to Article 1, to fight only within her own frontiers in the event of attack; the Eastern European satellites were obliged to assist the Soviet Union over an undefined area with all military and other resources. Article 2 called for a conference between Finland and the Soviet Union if the threat of an armed attack from Germany were established; the Eastern European countries agreed to discuss with the Soviet Union 'all important international problems', and this meant in practice the subordination of their foreign policies to that of the U.S.S.R.

From the Finnish point of view the Agreement formalized an existing reality; Finland's determination to remain neutral and to pursue a good-neighbour policy towards the Soviet Union which still governs the conduct of her external affairs. The clause relating to an attack on Finland or the Soviet Union by Germany looked backwards rather than forwards, and the passage of time has steadily decreased its relevance to modern warfare. But the passage of time has not diminished the Soviet Union's suspicion of Germany, which was so much sharpened by the sufferings of the 'Great Patriotic War', as the Russians call the part of the Second World War fought on their own soil. The Finnish recognition of this basic element in Soviet political psychology has made a considerable contribution to the development of better relations between the two countries.

In domestic politics, the first few years after the war were also critical, and freedom and independence were only narrowly secured. The sole change in the parliamentary system after 1944 was the resuscitation of the Communist Party, which had been driven underground between the wars. In the first post-war election in the spring of 1945 the Communists and their allies gained 49 of the 200 seats in Parliament, and joined the Social Democrats and the Agrarians in a coalition government. The Communist leader Yrjö Leino was made Minister of the Interior; when Paasikivi became President of the Republic in the following year, he was succeeded as Prime Minister by Mauno Pekkala, also a Communist. It soon became clear that normal democratic processes were being tampered with, and that Communist activities extended beyond a justifiable point. The Communist coup in Czechoslovakia in 1948 was followed, in Finland, by rumours and fears of a similar event.

A timely investigation into the state police revealed that it was largely composed of unqualified Communists, some of them former convicts. Other irregularities were uncovered and probed. There was a sharp general reaction against this extension of political influence, and a vote of no-confidence in the Minister of the Interior, Leino, was passed in Parliament. In 1948 he was forced to resign, in accordance with a constitutional clause which lays down that Ministers must enjoy the confidence of Parliament. By the time of the then triennial election in July of the same year anti-Communist opinion had hardened to the extent that the People's Democratic Union (as the Finnish Communist Party and its fellow-travelling group are named) lost eleven of its seats in Parliament, and with them its place in the government. Both the bourgeois parties and the Social Democrats were united in their refusal to consider a government in which the Communists were represented, and remained so until 1966.

The political demands of the Soviet Union brought about in Finland a general, but not drastic, reorientation of internal and external policies. The economic demands, in the form of reparations, provoked an upheaval and an effort which would have crippled many nations, but which have been miraculously turned to good account by the Finns. The war reparations were to be in kind, and consisted of a long and immensely varied list which included items such as complete industrial plants, fully equipped with machinery, ships, locomotives and machinery of all kinds. Two-thirds of all the reparations had to be produced by the metal and engineering industries, which were so relatively small that their pre-war exports had amounted to only four per cent of Finland's total; machines and appliances, in fact, had made up one fifth of all imports. There were in Finland in 1944 neither the workshops nor the trained workers nor the raw materials to meet the Soviet demands. But these were immediate, and allowed the Finns no time to reorganize themselves and seek supplies of raw materials. Deliveries had to be made according to a monthly programme, and failure to complete this programme each month involved a fine of five per cent of the total value of the delivery. All this was exacted from a country worn out by war, as near starving as it had been at any time in this century, and lacking housing, clothes and the normal commodities of everyday life.

The reparations demanded in the form of ships provide one indication of the problem and of the way it was tackled. The Soviet

Union was willing to take one-fifth of the total tonnage specified in old ships. (This meant that, through war and reparations, Finland lost more than half her merchant fleet.) But the Finns were allowed only a fortnight to deliver them. Many were on the high seas and had to be summoned back to Finnish ports in haste; some could not be traced until the last moment; some were in Norwegian ports and Norway was still occupied by Germany. It scarcely seemed possible that they could be delivered on the appointed day, but they were, and the Finns had to start immediately on the task of building 578 new ships for the Soviet Union. These included tugs, lighters, trawlers and ocean-going schooners. The last two had never been made before in Finland, and there was not a single trawler or schooner expert in the country. There was nothing to do but to start making drawings and keep on making drawings until a satisfactory ship was produced. But it was a desperately expensive project. The Soviet Union paid $15,000 for each of the schooners; it cost Finland twelve times as much to produce them.

All over the country new factories, new workshops, new wharves had to be built and old ones enlarged. Workers had to be trained and houses built for them near the factories. The world had to be scoured for raw materials which were then in short supply, and the Finns had to pay high prices to supplement their own small mineral resources. Little by little the obstacles were overcome, and production gradually swung into a normal rhythm. The harshness of the situation was somewhat mitigated when the Soviet Union extended the period of delivery from six years to eight and made some reductions in the total demands. But when all deliveries were finally completed according to schedule in September 1952, the cost to Finland was infinitely greater than had been envisaged in 1944. At the armistice the value of reparations demanded was fixed at $300 million, and prices of individual items were calculated on the basis of world prices in 1938 plus ten to fifteen per cent. The steep rise in prices after the war made this figure unrealistic by 1952; and the deliveries of reparation goods involved so many other major expenditures that their total cost to Finland has been estimated at more than $700 million or, over the period of eight years, an average of eleven per cent of the state budget. One of Finland's leading economists took the view in 1952 that the country could never recover from this enormous drain. Happily he was proved more than wrong. The Soviets may have hoped to weaken Finland by their colossal demands; to meet them, the development of an almost new industry was enormously accelerated and the most up-to-date techniques were adopted. In the event they helped to turn her into a highly prosperous country.

CHAPTER TEN

New Bearings

The completion of the reparations deliveries in September 1952 marked the end of the era of anxiety in Finland. Problems were far from disappearing overnight, but they gradually grew less dangerous, more manageable. Already in 1952 Soviet suspicions of their small neighbour were diminishing, and the death of Stalin in the spring of 1953 and the subsequent thaw in Soviet policies were further to improve Finno-Russian relations. At home, communism had been contained, though the margin of safety was still small. The half-million displaced Karelians had been resettled, though for many of them life remained hard and meagre. A creditable number of new houses had been built and, even more surprising, all ration cards had been thrown away while the British were still queueing up for their weekly allocation of meat to the value of one-and-sixpence.

Now the slate had been wiped clean. Finland could make the fresh start which was denied her at the moment of independence. There were still some serious limitations, it is true, but now it was possible to move and breathe within them. Finland had been since 1944 in a situation where any step could be a false step. After 1952 she began to build up a new and more positive national personality. The shape of her relations with the Soviet Union, with the other Scandinavian countries, with Europe and the world, acquired firmer and clearer outlines. She became a prosperous and significant industrial country, and consolidated and increased her world reputation for architecture and design. This achievement, by a country of under five millions which, at the end of the war, was far less advanced industrially than most Western European countries, has been far less publicized than the German *Wirtschaftswunder*. But in retrospect it seems equally, if not more remarkable.

The course of relations with the U.S.S.R. over the next decade was to confound the pessimists, particularly those outside Finland who held obstinately to their view of a small country almost entirely at the mercy of its powerful neighbour. Tensions relaxed to the extent that Finland, who in 1947 found it prudent not to participate in the Marshall Plan, was able to become in 1955 a member both of the United Nations and of the Nordic Council, and in 1961 an associate member of E.F.T.A. The first hurdle was politico-economic and concerned the metal and engineering industries which had been built expressly to manufacture reparations goods for the Soviet Union. Economists had for some time been anxious about the post-reparations future of these industries. The home market, with its pent-up demand, could absorb their output for a certain time, but not indefinitely. Being young and small compared with the industries of Western Europe, they could not hope to compete in overseas markets; nor could the industries be wound up and workers dismissed without serious unemployment and some economic and possibly political dislocation. The Soviet Union and Eastern Europe were at that time the only outlet of any size for their products. The U.S.S.R. immediately showed itself willing to take, in the form of free exports, approximately the same items as it had demanded in the form of reparations. This, however, was not sufficient to dispel anxieties, and some feared that the Soviet Union could use Finland's economic dependence on it for political ends. But with only one exception the trade treaties made between the two countries at regular intervals in the following years were without political significance, and as much in the Soviet interest as in Finland's. More than that, the certainty of the Soviet market was for the Finnish metal and engineering industries a springboard which enabled them to expand and grow more competitive, and so export to the West as well as to the East.

A far more significant change in Finno-Soviet relations took place in 1955, when the U.S.S.R. dismantled the 900 square-mile military base at Porkkala and returned the territory to Finland. At the same time the Agreement on Mutual Friendship, due to expire in 1958, was extended to 1975. It was not believed in Finland that this gesture was motivated wholly by the regard of one neighbour for the other; but it was thought that the Russians would not have made it unless they had acquired a certain respect for the Finns and confidence in their good faith and good intentions. The Soviet Union, however, had a clear interest in proclaiming to the rest of the world that it had abandoned a foreign base while the Americans were increasing theirs.

And, in the event of nuclear war, Porkkala could have little or no value. The extension of the Agreement on Friendship for a further twenty years had, on the other hand, considerable value to the Soviet Union.

For the Finns, the return of Porkkala had the important effect of stabilizing their neutrality. The Soviet Union acknowledged Finland as a neutral nation, along with Sweden and Austria, for the first time in 1956, and subsequently Russian political commentators referred to the Agreement on Friendship as a pact to guarantee neutrality rather than a treaty for mutual assistance. The Russians in Finland had been as correct in their behaviour as had the Finns and had given no cause for offence; but as long as they occupied an extensive military base within a few miles of the capital, the Finns never felt, psychologically, either neutral or free. Paasikivi said in a broadcast after the Soviet Union had offered to relinquish the base: 'For us, the return of Porkkala is an extremely important matter. The provisions as to Porkkala were one of the heaviest stipulations of the 1944 armistice treaty. The rights which were secured by the Soviet Union, not only as regards the base area of Porkkala, but also in connection with free passage along all means of communication and with all means of transport from this base area to the Soviet Union, coloured Finland's neutrality and the whole of Finland's international status.'

A further territorial concession was made in 1962, when the U.S.S.R. agreed to lease for the use of Finland the sector of the Saimaa Canal which had passed into Soviet territory at the end of the war. This canal connects the vast waterway system of eastern Finland with the Gulf of Finland, and had a considerable economic value before the war, particularly for the transport of export goods to the coast. It was built in the middle of the last century, and so by 1962 had become quite unsuitable for use by modern vessels. The Finns have gone to great expense to widen, deepen and modernize it, but there is some doubt whether their efforts will prove economically worth while. In Finland many political moves are judged primarily by psychological criteria, and it may be that the psychological advantages of the virtual return of the canal will be greater than the economic benefits.

The Soviet Union could afford to make these territorial concessions. It could eventually accept, without demur, Finnish membership of the United Nations, the Nordic Council, and E.F.T.A. But if, over the wider fields of policy, mutual confidence grew, there were still some blind spots and lingering suspicions which concerned individuals rather than policies. A clause in the Agreement on Friendship pledges the two parties to 'the principle of non-interference in the internal affairs of the other state'; but the U.S.S.R. has, at times, appeared to wish to influence indirectly the course of domestic policies in Finland by voicing its dislike of certain prominent politicians.

Finno-Russian attitudes have been coloured throughout the centuries, not only by calculated strategic considerations, but by personal and psychological factors amounting to a love-hate relationship of the kind that develops between members of a family or individuals who have lived next door to each other for too long. The Finns and the Russians admit at times that there is between them some personal affinity which puts them, as it were, on the same wavelength. The direct approach of one person to another, the absence of 'presence' and pretence, the dominance of heart over head are characteristics shared by Finns and Russians as individuals. They tend to reinforce the theory that a strain of common blood has survived in both nations from the time, deep in history, when they lived in much the same areas of Russia. (That the Finns will openly discuss this is an index of the evolution and relaxation of their feelings since the war. In 1948 the very subject was taboo. Now they will say lightheartedly: 'Of course we and the Russians have some common blood; but that doesn't mean that it's Communist blood, does it?') Research suggests that Muscovy itself took shape on lands occupied by Finno-Ugrian tribes, in particular the Merya, as late as the twelfth century. One authority, Henryk Paszkiewicz, believes that the people of Great Russia are actually descended from the Merya who, unlike other Finno-Ugrian tribes still in Russia (Veps, Cheremissians, Mordvinians, etc.), lost their own language and entity and adopted the Slavonic tongue.

Whether or not this thesis is accepted in its entirety, there is no denying the importance of individual relations between Finns and Russians which have influenced national affairs for good and ill. Relationships in which personal feelings play a great part are likely to be either better or worse than those confined to formal diplomatic exchanges. Stalin and Paasikivi got on very well personally; Kekkonen, who succeeded Paasikivi as President of the Republic in 1956, after having been Prime Minister (Agrarian) several times, was on excellent terms with Khrushchev. Personal goodwill contributed to or was elevated to national approval. On the other hand, Väinö Tanner, a Social Democrat to whom Finland stands in great debt, incurred the hostility of the Soviet Union after the First World War and remained more or less *persona non grata* until his death in 1966. The Russian attitude may have derived in the first place from Tanner's observation to Stalin in 1917 that he supported the Mensheviks; it led to his imprisonment as a 'war criminal' in 1946, although he had consistently pressed for an early end to the Second War with the Soviet Union. When he came out of prison and was elected chairman of the Social-Democratic Party, Soviet hostility extended also to the Party and to governments in which it participated. The bourgeois parties, naturally, were only too ready to make capital out of the Soviet attitude; thus it was never quite clear to what extent the exclusion of the Social Democrats from a number of governments was due to the opposition of the Soviets and to what extent to the opposition of other Finnish political parties. But certainly the Social-Democratic Party's fortunes began to improve after Tanner's retirement in 1963.

A more sharply-pointed exchange between Finland and the Soviet Union took place in the autumn of 1961. A presidential election was to be held in the spring of 1962; Kekkonen had again been nominated by the Agrarians; the Social Democrats had put up, with the support of the Conservatives and the Liberals, Olavi Honka, the Chancellor of Justice, who was considered a very strong candidate. Suddenly the Soviet Union invoked the 1948 Agreement on Friendship and Mutual Assistance, and requested consultations on joint defence measures 'in view of the threat from Western Germany' (in particular, Western German participation in N.A.T.O.). Eventually Kekkonen went to Russia for a meeting with Khrushchev; after it, communiqué recorded Khrushchev's 'high regard for the political experience of the Finnish President and his goodwill and ability to maintain and strengthen Finland's policy of neutrality', and announced that the Soviet Union could therefore put off the military consultations it had requested.

The next event was Honka's resignation of his candidature 'for the sake of the fatherland'. Kekkonen was then left without serious contenders. He was re-elected by a comfortable majority, whereas in the previous election he had received 151 votes to the 149 obtained by his Social-Democrat opponent, K. A. Fagerholm. Before the presidential election which took place in 1940 the Soviet Union made known its opposition to four out of five potential candidates, presumably with the aim of securing the election of Risto Ryti, the man whom it favoured. Ryti was in any case the strongest candidate, and became President. It is not easy to tell whether the complicated manœuvre of 1961 was intended to serve a similar end, but it achieved a similar result. The Finns are well aware of the part played by individual personalities in their relations with the U.S.S.R., and are united in regretting its less fortunate consequences. They are less united in their choice of a course of action in these circumstances: Honka resigned immediately; but Tanner remained chairman of the Social Democrats until 1963.

The Soviet attitude sometimes influences, one way or another, the Finns' own attitude to some of their politicians; but it has never seriously disturbed their democratic institutions. No one claims today that Finno-Soviet relations are perfect; the Finns know that they must always walk carefully and realistically. But few people in 1944 could have dared to hope that the atmosphere would improve so dramatically within a score of years, and that the enmities of five centuries would be so much diminished in so short a time.

Finland was not able to become a full member of the United Nations until 1955. Her application to join in 1947 was vetoed by the Soviet Union as part of the display of shadow-boxing which included the Western refusal to admit several Communist states (Albania, Bulgaria, Hungary and others). She was, however, able to take part before 1955 in the non-political and constructive work of several of the specialized agencies, and this she has continued to do to a greater extent than any country in Eastern Europe, the Soviet Union included. Participation has been beneficial to herself and others. She has received a number of loans from the International Bank and medical advice and supplies from the World Health Organization; in return, as a member of the Food and Agricultural Organization, she has been able to give valuable assistance to other countries in forestry matters, in which so many Finns have distinguished themselves.

This practical work is more in keeping with Finnish inclinations and the limitations of Finnish neutrality than are the diatribes of the General Assembly. Since her admission to the United Nations, Finland has studiously and quietly avoided joining in condemnatory resolutions, and concentrated, within her narrow means, on the encouragement of conciliation and negotiation. President Kekkonen summed up his country's attitude in his address to the General Assembly in 1961: 'We see ourselves here as physicians rather than as judges; it is not for us to pass judgment nor to condemn, it is rather to diagnose and try to cure.' This unspectacular role, combined with a determination to remain outside the conflicts and differences of opinion of the great powers, often prevents Finland from voting with either East or West – although no pressure is put on her by the U.S.S.R. On the other hand, she is often able to share the common Scandinavian approach to U.N. problems, which is formulated at the almost daily meetings of the delegations of the five Northern countries. Finland's neutral but constructive policy has enabled her to play a practical role more important than her size and resources would suggest. She has provided troops for the U.N. forces in the Middle East and in Cyprus, and observers in the Lebanon and Kashmir. One of her most distinguished men, Sakari Tuomioja, was twice personal representative in Laos of the Secretary-General of the United Nations, and was U.N. mediator in Cyprus at the time of his death in 1964.

For Finland, by far the most far-reaching and significant development of the years since 1952 has been the rapid and successful growth of co-operation between the five Scandinavian countries (Denmark, Finland, Iceland, Norway and Sweden). The Scandinavian method of reaching this objective is so unspectacular that an achievement of considerable importance has gone unnoticed while the quarrels of the Common Market have occupied the headlines. The basic notion of inter-Scandinavian co-operation is a very old one (the first meeting of jurists of the Northern countries was held in 1872); but in practice the will to common planning and common decisions tended, up to the Second World War, to be weakened by divergent attitudes to international politics and defence. As Max Jakobson has said: 'A defensive alliance presupposes a common enemy. [In the late 1930s] the Scandinavians could not agree who the enemy was. Finland feared Russia; Denmark feared Germany; Sweden could not make up her mind which to fear more; Norway felt secure enough to fear neither. . . . "A Nordic defence alliance belongs to Utopia," the Prime Minister of Denmark said in 1937.' Attempts to remedy the situation during and after the war were no more successful. The Soviet Union vetoed the defence plans drawn up by Finland and other Scandinavian countries, in particular Sweden, after the Winter War. In the immediate post-war period, Denmark, Norway and Sweden considered the formation of a neutral bloc. The Soviet Union, then bent on dividing the North, expressed disapproval of what it suspected to be an anti-Soviet military plot. The Swedes were, at that time, particularly susceptible to Soviet arguments. They feared that any departure, apparent or real, from their strict policy of non-alignment might result in a tightening of Soviet control over Finland, and wished to avoid this for their own and the Finns' sakes. Thus, when Norway and Denmark joined N.A.T.O. and Sweden and Finland become more deeply committed to neutrality, the Scandinavian countries seemed more hopelessly divided than ever.

Yet the will to co-operate over a wide field of activities had now become too strong to be affected by defence policies. The five Scandinavian countries took the commonsense course of working together as far as was practicable in all spheres other than military. In 1953 an instrument of co-operation was created in the Nordic Council, and its aims and functions were formally codified in the Helsinki Convention of 1962. It gave official shape to the practice of collaboration which had already grown naturally out of the habit which private and voluntary groups have long had of consulting their counterparts and opposite numbers in the other countries. Thus, while foreign ministers and finance ministers are discussing weighty problems, shoe designers from all five countries may be jointly planning next season's styles, dentists may be holding an inter-Scandinavian congress, and amateur drama groups may be taking part in an inter-Scandinavian competition. Co-operation on this scale becomes part of the life of the ordinary citizen, rather than a remote governmental policy, and it is undoubtedly to this groundwork of solidarity that Northern co-operation in general owes it success and momentum.

The Nordic Council meets annually and is composed of 69 representatives. The parliaments of Denmark, Finland, Norway and

Sweden each appoint sixteen, in proportion to the strength of the political parties, and the Icelandic parliament five. In addition, the governments appoint their own representatives, who have no vote. The Council has no legislative authority; it makes recommendations to governments, who are obliged to inform the Council at its next session of what action has been taken. In the ten years following its inception in 1953, the Council made more than two hundred recommendations, covering a very wide range of questions, and of these a high proportion became operative. In 1962 the Helsinki Convention codified the areas of existing agreement and of proposed co-operation between the five countries. Broadly speaking, its forty Articles deal with uniformity of civil and criminal law, equivalence of examinations, cultural exchanges, inter-availability of social benefits, a common labour market, economic co-operation, the establishment of a single passport zone, and co-operation in the development of communications.

All these forms of co-operation, other than economic, were well advanced in 1962, so the Convention represented reality rather than pious hopes. The value of common and uniform practices in a group of five countries with a total population of no more than 20 million is obvious. More stimulating and fruitful is the growth of co-operation in common projects, and of projects undertaken by one country to serve all five. In the first category can be mentioned the joint efforts to provide for the Lapps, and to develop the 'Calotte', or northern areas of Norway, Sweden and Finland. (The Soviet Union is also involved in this area, and a power station has been jointly built on the Russian border by Finland and the U.S.S.R.) Also in this category come the development of roads and ferries linking one country and another, and the increasing number of radio and TV programmes intended for all the Northern countries. The second category of institutions set up by one country to serve all five includes the Institute for Theoretical Nuclear Physics at Copenhagen, the Institute of Maritime Law at Oslo, and the Institute of Arctic Medicine which the Finns are establishing as part of the University of Oulu.

Economic co-operation has offered more difficult problems, most of which still await solution. A Scandinavian customs union has been discussed at intervals since 1945. The idea was abandoned, in part because of doubts of its viability, but mainly because it was thought wiser to concentrate first on making E.F.T.A. succeed. Denmark, Norway and Sweden became members of E.F.T.A. when it was formed in 1960. The following year arrangements were made for Finland to become an associate member, on terms which would not affect her trading arrangements with the U.S.S.R. Through common membership of E.F.T.A., internal Scandinavian barriers were removed, and tariff reductions have greatly stimulated inter-Nordic trade. However, the possibility of a customs union has not been entirely ruled out, in spite of the many technical problems it would present. Many economists feel that either a customs union or some form of closer economic co-operation will eventually impose itself, whatever other developments take place in Europe as a whole. The Scandinavian countries are too small to provide for their own needs or to offer an economic market in today's terms for their own manufactures. A common economic policy could mean, ultimately, that each country concentrated on what it could do best.

For Finland, these great strides in Northern co-operation have had and will continue to have enormous importance. They have already consolidated the pattern of activity characteristic of the Northern democracies, and made this pattern irreversible and inescapable. Thus Finland's democratic institutions have been given additional protection and security. As a member of the Scandinavian family she is automatically part of Western Europe, though without commitment to any bloc or power grouping. This is the fortunate outcome of the years of isolation between 1946 and 1952, when the sense of world loneliness sometimes invaded ordinary, individual Finns, and made them falter in their optimism and determination. The remarkable development in co-operation has made the Finns feel psychologically, as well as politically, more secure, and more satisfied that they are able to play a part in European affairs.

A negative neutrality sits ill on the Finns, and they have welcomed the opportunities they have had since 1952 of breaking out of the confinement of the eight preceding years. They have been able both to soften the rigidities of post-war neutrality by association with other countries, and to give it a more positive character. Neutrality, nonetheless, is no new concept for the Finns. When a Grand Duchy of Russia, Finland was not involved in Russia's wars and was able to remain neutral in the First World War. On independence she proclaimed her neutrality, and would have maintained it in the Second World War had she not been attacked by the Soviet Union. But Finnish neutrality has changed in character over the years, and has had to be rethought and reshaped in the light of changed circumstances.

Post-war neutrality is properly described in the Finno-Soviet Agreement on Friendship and Mutual Aid as an 'aspiration to stand aside from the conflicts of interests of the Great Powers', and Finland has faithfully followed a course which accords with this very generalized 'aspiration'. But the overriding aim of Finnish neutrality is to prevent the conflicts with Russia caused by Swedish or Russian aggression from which Finland has suffered since the thirteenth century. In 1943, when Finland and the Soviet Union were at war, President Kekkonen, then an ordinary M.P., addressed a group of Swedish parliamentarians in Stockholm. He then stated unequivocally: 'We must choose either a policy directed against Russia, or a policy of neutrality ... It cannot be in our interest to adopt a policy directed against a Russia which remains a great power. In an era of mechanized warfare a small state cannot stand forever armed to the teeth.' His views coincided with those of Paasikivi, and have since become embodied in what is called 'the Paasikivi-Kekkonen line', which has been accepted in Finland since 1944. Seen in this light the provisions of the 1948 Agreement on Friendship, provided they are respected by both sides, are useful to the Soviet Union, but far more so to Finland.

The cliché-criticism 'neutral in peace, but not in war' has at times been applied by outsiders to Finnish policy, particularly in relation to the Soviet Union, but it in no way corresponds to the facts. Finland is committed to fight only if her own territory is invaded or attacked by Germany or a power allied with Germany. This was reaffirmed by President Kekkonen in 1965, when he said: 'Finland has engaged herself to defend the inviolability of her territory within her own boundaries, which she would do in any case, treaty or no treaty. But this self-evident point was included in order to clarify the nature of the Agreement. In the event of an attack on the U.S.S.R. by another route than over Finnish territory we shall not, under the Agreement, be involved in the war. On the contrary, we shall then take every conceivable step to remain neutral. ... From a Finnish point of view, it is especially important that the Agreement is not hinged to any automatically released mechanism, as is the case in N.A.T.O. and the Warsaw Pact.'

A former Finnish foreign minister has said: 'No nation can rely on being able to take refuge in neutrality unless it has created the basis for such a policy in good time before the outbreak of a conflict.' Both as Prime Minister in the early 'fifties, and as President since 1956, Kekkonen has felt the need to strengthen and consolidate Finnish neutrality by encouraging a zone of limited non-commitment round Finland. The post-war realignments of Europe and the great powers have left her, and to a lesser extent Sweden, in a potentially vulnerable position between the N.A.T.O. and the Warsaw Pact countries (to neither of which either belongs). These two military organizations meet on the Norwegian-Soviet border which leaves the Arctic west of Petsamo and joins the Finnish border near Lake Inari. Kekkonen has on various occasions put forward proposals for the formal creation of a Nordic nuclear-free zone. The other countries concerned have made no positive response, although all four together constitute, in practice, such a zone, Denmark and Norway having refused to allow American nuclear bases on their territory. More recently President Kekkonen has shown a particular concern for the area in the region of the N.A.T.O.–Warsaw Pact border, which, in his view, could threaten Finland's security in a conflict between the great powers. He has suggested that a treaty between Norway and Finland to safeguard the 'Calotte' area would protect the Norwegian-Finnish frontier.

It is, inevitably, in the area of defence that Finland feels most keenly the divergent policies of the Nordic countries, with whom she otherwise collaborates so easily and profitably. The policies of Denmark, Norway and Sweden both influence and are influenced by Soviet policy towards Finland. When the Russians gave up Porkkala they removed a source of tension in the rest of Scandinavia. Equally, the refusal of Denmark and Norway to permit American bases on their territory contributed to the Soviets' abandonment of their policy of dividing the North, and made it possible for Finland to be much more closely associated with the other Scandinavian countries.

The achievement of a degree of security in the Baltic has also concerned the President, and has led him to speak out against the formation of a Multilateral Nuclear Force connected with N.A.T.O. The

German question is constantly in the Finns' minds. They are perhaps more aware than people farther west of the extent to which it colours all Soviet thinking, and they know that their own relations with the Soviet Union are liable to deteriorate or improve as tension between the West and the Soviet Union increases or relaxes. After the war they realized that their neutrality must be punctiliously observed in all their dealings with Germany. They have never recognized either the Federal Republic or the German Democratic Republic; they do not maintain diplomatic relations with either state, but keep only commercial and consular representatives in East and West Germany. This, in practice, has been the only major limiting factor of neutrality since 1952. But shadows are cast here and there; for instance, an extension of the European Common Market to include the present E.F.T.A. countries would pose considerable political and economic problems for Finland, and could, in some circumstances, conflict with her policy of not joining in an alliance which the Soviet Union might regard as being directed against her.

But it is Finland's constant hope that the divisions between East and West, particularly in Europe, will be gradually, if slowly, broken down. Despite the intractability of the German problem these divisions appear more artificial to the Finns, placed as they are geographically, racially and temperamentally, than they do to people farther west. The Finns know and understand the Russians, and their imprisonment in history, better than do most Europeans; they have long-standing ties of sympathy with the Poles; they have a kinship, if remote, with the Hungarians; and they are part of the Scandinavian family. They could perhaps use their neutrality and their position, on the modest scale that their numbers and resources allow, to help to bridge the divisions in Europe. In the meantime, they are content to accept their situation and to use their particular talent of making a virtue of necessity. Like so many people of great creative ability, they do their best work, individually and collectively, within the discipline of a prescribed framework. Neutrality has provided that discipline.

CHAPTER ELEVEN

Political Life

Although many of Finland's institutions are similar to, even identical with, those in the other Scandinavian countries, her political life and institutions present many divergencies. The Finnish political system has developed in different circumstances, at a different time, and it reflects the differences between the Finnish character and the true Scandinavian character. There is nothing in Finland of the sober monotony and righteousness of politics in Denmark, Norway and Sweden. No one could complain that Finnish political life is uneventful, whatever its other shortcomings may be. Temperamentally, the Finns are less politically inclined than the Danes, the Norwegians and the Swedes. They are more emotional, less rational, and less given to abstract theory and ideology. They have far greater difficulty in adjusting their immediate plans to the hypotheses of a more distant future. It is only recently that they have taken to longer-term planning, and what they have done has been largely non-political.

Historically, both necessity and choice have made most of the Finns unpolitical animals. When Finland was part of Sweden, Finns sat in the Swedish Estates, but they represented, not Finland, but their own social class. The Finnish Estates, convened when Finland became an autonomous Grand Duchy of Russia, did not begin to meet regularly until 1863, and it was only in 1906 that modern parliamentary politics began to take shape. However ardent the Finns' desire for independence, it did not – and at times could not – find any political expression. It asserted itself through the arts, through the Finnish language, event through sport, but never in a great organized national movement. The sharp cleavage between the Swedish-speaking upper class and the large Finnish-speaking majority served to reduce the latters' interest in politics. The Swedo-Finnish minority held all the administrative posts, and as a result of their experience had a greater understanding of matters of government. The pure Finns, excluded from such positions, compensated themselves by other forms of self-assertion. Today it still cannot be said that the Finns, as a whole, are really interested in political theory and ideology, as opposed to practical politics – although, as is natural in a small country, gossip about political personalities is eagerly passed on, and political manœuvres are closely followed.

One of the most surprising features of political life is the conservative, almost patriarchal character which has remained one of the most powerful reflections of the old agricultural society. This conservatism has resulted in the two contradictory elements of stability and instability which now seem firmly rooted in the political structure. Stability is expressed in the Finns' unchanging voting habits, which rarely produce more than marginal variations in parliamentary representation when the quadrennial elections are held. Political parties are based on class interests rather than on doctrine, and the rigid class domination of political life contrasts strongly with the relative absence of class distinction in social life. The Finn votes as his father and his grandfather voted before him; he is considered a traitor if he votes against the party which supports the interests of his own class. Even among the supporters of the Communist Party, where ideology is so much more important than in the other parties, there are many who vote Communist merely because their fathers voted so before them. However, there are signs today that this hereditary approach is being gradually weakened. The more independent of the young people in the towns insist on making their own political choices. It may take time for this attitude to spread all over the country, but there is little doubt that it eventually will, and it may then change a pattern of voting which has varied little since Finland became independent.

A change in voting patterns might help to reduce the chronic governmental instability from which Finland has always suffered. Finland had fifty governments in fifty years; their length of life ranged from one month to three and a half years; only fourteen lasted more than a year, and eighteen lasted only six months or less. This kaleidoscopic situation is only slightly accentuated by the custom which obliges a government to resign when a new President is elected. Its major cause is the failure of coalition governments to agree among themselves. The multi-party system based on proportional representation has meant that the largest single party in Parliament has rarely gained more than about 80 of the 200 seats, and since 1944 no party has had more than 56 seats. The alternatives, then, are coalitions, which have been the rule, or minority governments, which have been the surprisingly successful exception. The coalitions are often finely-balanced constructions which depend for their continued existence on a willingness to compromise and to give and take which does not come easily from the obstinate Finns. Minority governments, in spite of their obvious disadvantages, are spared the constant need for accommodation within the cabinet, and can assert themselves more strongly in Parliament.

A further impression of instability is given by the fairly lengthy periods during which Finland is without effective or normal government. After a government has fallen or resigned, it may take several weeks of bargaining or manœuvring before a new Prime Minister succeeds in forming a new cabinet. The outgoing government remains, technically, in office until a new one is formed, but its role in this interim period is necessarily indecisive. Finland also has a recurring institution, unknown in most European countries, called a 'professional' government. This body is drawn from among experts, civil servants and other high officials to run the country when the politicians have reached such a point of disagreement among themselves that it is impossible to form a normal government. During the lifetime of the Republic, there have been six such 'professional' governments, which have held office for a total of thirty-three months. They have a tendency to deal out harsher medicine and work faster than the politicians would dare; sometimes the first act of a 'political' government, after taking over from the 'professionals', has been to reverse some of their decisions.

The results of this governmental instability are manifold. There is no stimulus to fundamental political thinking and programme-building; a party has little incentive to bring out a strong and clearly-defined programme when it knows how small its chances would be in a coalition of putting it into practice. Ministers, with a few exceptions, command little respect among the already irreverent Finns; there is a certain lack of dignity about the way they are obliged to pop in and out of office, and often men of real ability cannot stay long enough in a government to make their mark. Parliament usually dominates the government, but, since no single party dominates Parliament, its lead is not always clearly defined. It may even be confused by the opposition of each party to all others. The most important result is that the President frequently has to make full use of his wide powers, and on him falls the responsibility of assuring a large measure of continuity and stability. Many of his functions are exercised by the Prime Minister in present-day monarchies, and since the war foreign policy in particular has been largely in the hands of the President. His powers can be considered too great, but they compensate in large measure for recurrent governmental instability, and make it possible for the life of the country to continue relatively undisturbed by the absence of a government.

Finnish political parties developed, at the end of the last century and the beginning of this, in response to certain practical situations rather than to the evolution of political ideas. They have now become slightly more theoretical, but their chief appeal is still to sectional interests. The Conservative Party, farthest to the right, draws its voting strength mainly from big business and from among landed proprietors, and also from officials, executives, teachers, etc. It secures, on an average, fifteen per cent of the seats in Parliament. The Centre Party is the name recently adopted by the powerful Agrarian Party in recognition of its changed character and sources of support. It was originally formed to press for the advancement of the small farmer, whom it still seeks to defend against powerful financial interests. Eventually it grew into a large party, drawing support from a high proportion of the rural population, and also from middle-class voters in the towns ('asphalt Agrarians', as the jibe went when this trend began). In the whole life of independent Finland, it has been absent from only six political governments. Since the war, it has generally won about a quarter of the seats in Parliament. It still gives priority to agricultural interests; in other matters, its attitude is such as to justify its new name, and it accepts a fair degree of social reform.

The Finnish Liberal Party also stands in the centre, opposing both Conservatives and Social Democrats, and aiming at representing the intellectual and professional middle classes. The Swedish Party, liberal to moderate conservative, exists to support the interests of the Swedish-speaking minority but does not claim all its votes. Swedish-speaking industrial workers, for instance, may often vote for one of the left-wing parties. Since the war, Finnish Liberal representation in Parliament has varied between five and thirteen seats, and the Swedish Party's between eleven and fifteen.

The Social-Democratic Party, formed in 1897, both represents the growing industrial population and competes with the Agrarians for the votes of the smallholders. It follows a moderate Socialist doctrine, and can be distinguished from all other parties except the Communist by its insistence on the political education of its members. Since the war it has had a series of vicissitudes. The revival of the Communist Party drew off many of its votes in 1945, and in the 'fifties a small left-wing group split off and further weakened it. However, in the 'sixties it began to show signs of returning to its former strength, and in 1966 it secured more seats than at any election since the war. From the first parliamentary election in 1907 right up to 1945, the Social-Democratic Party was always the largest single party in Parliament. This suggests that fundamentally Finland has the same bias to moderate socialism as have the other Scandinavian countries, although the established and stable framework in which it could develop has been lacking at times.

The character and strength of the Communist Party provide one of the great enigmas of Finnish political life. It regularly secures between twenty and twenty-five per cent of the seats, and is, proportionately, the third largest Communist Party in Europe, following behind those of France and Italy. After its post-war excesses, the Party settled down into a milder state of mind, and many of its leaders and members are sufficiently moderate to be left-wing socialists. It is often the mildness rather than the violence of the Communists that provokes comment. They have officially renounced the intention of seizing power by a *coup*, and those of the hard core who still talk of 'revolution' and 'class warfare' are viewed as out of date by their fellows. This moderate policy may be associated with expediency rather than conviction, but there is no doubt that a substantial number of Party members and voters are without real extremism of feeling, and that if obliged to choose between Finland and world communism they would put their country first. One hears of Communist M.P.s who give considerable help and support to large industrial enterprises in their constituencies (while, of course, decrying private enterprise in general); one hears of Communist employees who are described by their employers as excellent and agreeable workers, and sometimes also shareholders in the company. A good number of Communist voters must, indeed, also be members of the Lutheran Church, since ninety-four per cent of the population is registered as such.

This relative mildness may account for some of the support which the Communist Party receives; but there are other, more important reasons, many of them historical. In the early years of this century the industrial workers, who were already becoming numerous, had no place in society or in the political system. They were not represented in the outdated Estates, and were untouched by social reform. They were thus receptive to the Marxist ideas which came across the border from Russia and represented opposition to the tsarist régime which had become so oppressive in Finland. The Russian revolution in 1917 made further converts to communism, and those Finns who already had leftish inclinations made common cause with the Bolsheviks in order to overthrow the hated tsars. These inclinations were reinforced during the Civil War, and the Finnish Communist Party proper was founded in 1918. Thus many of the older members of the Party today are men who thought in 1917 that the way to independence ran via communism; and they now have sons who perpetuate their fathers' voting habits.

The Communist Party was made illegal in 1931, and not allowed to come out into the open again until after the Second World War, when the Soviet Union demanded its reinstatement. It emerged in a strong position as the one party which had been neither in Parliament nor the government during the war, and therefore could not be blamed for the defeats and disasters of that time. The Communists and their allies immediately gained forty-nine seats, drawing especially strong support from the isolated smallholders and lumbermen of north Finland, where life is poorer and harder than elsewhere. However, Finnish communism appears to thrive almost as well on prosperity as on poverty and isolation; Communists represent some of the industrial areas where conditions would be the envy of any worker, industrial or professional, anywhere in Europe. This kind of Communist success is sometimes attributed to the failure of the Social Democrats during the 'fifties to provide a sufficiently radical and vital programme to attract the younger voters, who have turned to communism instead. Finally, the Finns are habitually guided by self-interest in their choice of political party; and no party makes a greater appeal to self-interest than the Communist.

The Communists have been highly active in the trade unions, and a long-drawn-out struggle between the Social Democrats on the one hand and the Opposition Social Democrats and the Communists on the other led to a split in the central trades union organization in 1957. Eventually three separate groupings emerged: the largest, consisting of unions affiliated to the Communist-dominated central organization; a smaller group, affiliated to the Social-Democratic organization; and eighteen unions which refused to affiliate with either body. The trade union movement has never been particularly strong in Finland, and its membership is, proportionately, much lower than in the other Scandinavian countries. This is due mainly to the large number of workers in agriculture and forestry, and of women workers, both of whom are difficult to organize. The split inevitably weakened the trade union movement as a whole, and over the years repeated efforts have been made to restore unity.

The conservatism of Finnish voting habits can be gauged from this table, which shows how relatively little change in representation there has been since the war:

	1945	1948	1951	1954	1958	1962	1966
Centre (Agrarian)	49	56	51	53	48	53	49
Communist	49	38	43	43	50	47	41
Conservative	28	33	28	24	29	32	26
Liberal	9	5	10	13	8	13	9
Social Democrat	50	54	53	54	48	38	55
Opposition Social Democrat	—	—	—	—	3	2	7
Swedish	14	14	15	13	14	14	12
Others	1	—	—	—	—	1	1

From this it can be seen that the problems of government since the war have centred firstly on the creation of a fairly stable coalition cabinet, and secondly on the containment of communism. After the near-disaster of the Agrarian/Social Democrat/Communist coalition of 1946–48, no party was willing to work with Communists, who remained in opposition until 1966.

As long as there was general agreement to exclude the Communists from office the obvious basis for government appeared to be an Agrarian/Social-Democratic coalition. Together these two parties represent roughly half the electorate. They are both near enough to the centre to find certain areas of agreement; both are opposed to powerful financial interests, though for different reasons; both are in favour of social reforms, though in different spheres. And many members of both parties are convinced that the only real hope of stable government lies in a coalition between them. In practice, however, difficulties have constantly arisen. Personal frictions have often been present, though they have not been allowed to bulk too large. The universal problems of wages and prices have been more intractable; the Agrarians have been bound, in the interests of their smallholder supporters, to seek higher prices for farm products; the Social Democrats have been bound to oppose them because they would increase the cost of living to their supporters. More important still was the Soviet prejudice against certain prominent Social Democrats, which helped to keep the party out of office from 1959 to 1966. As a result, for more than three of these seven years the inclusion of the Conservatives shifted the government farther to the right than at any time since the war, but without Soviet criticism.

The 1966 general election led to a reversal of the trend of politics over the previous eighteen years, and over the previous seven in particular. The Social Democrats, with 55 seats, came back to a stronger position than they had enjoyed at any time since the war, and the leftward movement of voters also increased Opposition Social-Democratic representation from three to seven members. This movement did not, however, benefit the extreme left, and Communist representation fell from 47 to 41. The Centre Party's loss of four seats was relatively small, and it was left with 49 seats.

After lengthy negotiations the Social-Democratic leader Rafael Paasio formed a government whose fifteen members included Social Democrats, Centrists and three Communists. It commanded 152 of the 200 votes in Parliament, and so had the numerical strength necessary if some unpopular economic measures were to be carried through. The Conservatives, the Swedish Party and the Finnish Liberals maintained their opposition to collaboration with the Communists. But elsewhere it was felt that the time had come to experiment with a government representing the entire left. The general thaw in the international climate had spread to Finnish political parties. The Soviet Union and the Finnish Social-Democratic Party had abandoned their previous mutual distrust and Finnish Communist attitudes had moderated considerably. Thus it seemed that this experiment could be made without danger to democratic government or threat of change in Finland's established foreign policy. However, the introduction of the Communists into the government did not fail to arouse consternation in many quarters, although this subsequently moderated; and comfort was drawn from the fact that the key role in both domestic and foreign policy, and particularly the latter, would in any case continue to lie with the President of the Republic.

The powers of the President are such that he stands as a fixed and stable point in the political structure. His term of office lasts six years compared with the parliamentary term of four years, and he can thus assure continuity and stability of policy in all major issues, and in particular in foreign affairs; he also acts as a moderator, who must aim at reconciling the different views of the often heterogenous cabinet over which he presides. When the constitution of the independent republic was drawn up in 1919, Finland had had several years of experience of a multi-party system and a single-chamber parliament. The need had already made itself felt for a Head of State who would provide both the continuity necessary to counterpoise the changing and not always unanimous governments, and the checks and balances of the upper house in countries with a bicameral system. The Finns showed considerable practical wisdom when they recognized this need, but they laid a heavy burden on their Presidents. In 1919 Finland's role in Europe and her internal political life were far less complex than they are today; but even then, the duties and responsibilities assigned to the President were demanding. Today the Presidency requires almost super-human physical strength and great qualities of mind and character if the degree of individual responsibility it involves is to be exercised wisely and well.

The President is chosen by an electoral college of 300, elected by the whole voting population. There may be as many as six candidates, put forward either by the political parties, acting individually or in groups; or by smaller groups drawn from several parties to support one particular candidate. Although the election of a President is primarily a political affair, support for the candidates often cuts across party loyalties. The President is invested with supreme executive powers, can exercise a suspensive veto on legislation, and dissolve and summon Parliament. He has the right of initiating legislation and final control of foreign policy. He is the supreme commander of the armed forces and is responsible for a number of high official appointments.

In principle the President cannot take any major political action without the concurrence of the government, and important international agreements have to be ratified by Parliament. But, given the frequent changes of government, many Presidents are in a strong position to promote their own personal policies; cabinets, on the other hand, which owe their appointment in part to the President, are often in a weak position to oppose him. In general, both cabinets and Presidents try to avoid a collision; but if, exceptionally, there is a major clash on an important issue, the cabinet may have to resign.

The political inclinations of the President himself may often play an important part in determining the composition of a coalition. It has happened that a President has refused to allow the inclusion in the government of a party to which he was opposed. The relationship of the President to party politics is, in some respects, a contradictory element in the system. The President is generally expected to be above party politics, and at times the Finns have deliberately chosen a man with slender party affiliations, or none at all. But the number of suitable candidates to be found outside politics is few, and long experience of political life is, in itself, a major asset in a President. It is far from easy for any politician, on being elected President, to shed immediately the party bias of a lifetime. Some have been more successful than others in achieving a degree of impartiality; some have not wished to do so, and have rather followed the American model in their interpretation of the Presidency, combining the roles of Head of State and of a super-Premier. This presents few difficulties when the President shares the politics of the largest single party in power; but troubles may arise with a shift of leadership to a party of a different colour. Another disadvantage is the Finnish custom of regarding the President, like a monarch, as above criticism; if a President has marked political leanings this may confer some immunity on his party as a whole. However, in spite of its demands and its disadvantages, the office of President has served the Finns well during their period of independence; and today the trend it takes in Finland does no more than reflect the world's dangerous tendency to entrust its fate to a handful of super-personalities.

Part Three

INTO THE MODERN WORLD

CHAPTER TWELVE

The Vanishing Idyll

When the reparations deliveries to the Soviet Union were completed in 1952, economists were still unsure whether Finland was an agricultural or an industrial country. They were even less sure which way the country's economy would develop now it had met the Russian demands and was left to operate freely in the world market. A large number of ordinary Finns, on the other hand, had no such uncertainties: Finland had always been an agricultural country and would always remain so. The idea of it becoming an industrial country demanded a stretch of the imagination of which they were incapable. In almost all circles it was fashionable to deplore and decry 'the flight from the countryside'. Those who believed so deeply in the country's agricultural future were, as the Finns so often are, ruled by heart rather than head, and unable to accept the message of statistics which already showed how far agriculture was yielding to industry.

Yet their attitude was understandable. Many could look back to 1917, when independence was gained, when only one-seventh of all Finns lived in towns, and Finland could accurately be described as underdeveloped. Many more were dominated by their memories of the 'thirties, when the agricultural way of life was still so deeply-rooted, so widespread, even sometimes so primitive, that any real change seemed almost impossible. Finland had then only three cities, apart from the capital, with more than 60,000 inhabitants; at widely-separated points there were small country towns where leafy cobbled streets were lined by wooden houses, and where the sound of horses' hooves was heard more often than the rumble of motor traffic. By 1950 there were still only 60,000 motor vehicles in Finland; but there were seven times as many horses, and all but the few main roads were made for horses and carts or sleighs, not cars. More than half the population still lived in rural areas, although it did not necessarily work on the land; for the building of factories in remote areas had already begun to break down the traditional equation of industrialization and urbanization.

Ten years later Finland's way of life had been changed for all time. By 1960 industry had triumphed over agriculture, and townsmen had become for the first time more numerous than country-dwellers. Horses had been displaced by cars and tractors, new highways and railways had been built. Since the Finns first arrived in Finland they had been continuously engaged in the struggle to wrest food and a bare living from land and water in the face of a hostile nature. Now they had mastered and tamed nature itself, bought themselves prosperity through industry, and found a new standard of life and comfort in a new form of urban development. This had been, up to a point, a gradual process; but it gathered a dramatic momentum during the 'fifties. The transition, for the majority, from relative poverty and hardship to prosperity and ease was so swift that it had taken place before the people as a whole had time to grasp what had happened. The extent of this transition was startlingly demonstrated by the realization that their two apparently inexhaustible natural resources, wood and water power, were becoming insufficient. The world demand for the products of the woodworking industries had increased so fast that to meet it Finland had to start importing timber, rather than over-cut and jeopardize future supplies; the most thickly forested country in Europe began to buy timber from abroad in order to re-export it in processed form. At roughly the same time it became clear that even the vast hydro-electric schemes nearly completed would not be adequate to run the industries of the future, and plans were made to build a group of nuclear power stations in the 'seventies. What had happened was no less than a second industrial revolution. It had been at first retarded by Finland's conservatism and remoteness, then accelerated by war and the demands of reparations, and finally given greater momentum by the universal post-war expansion.

This industrial revolution manifested itself in many different ways. The growth of the woodworking industries was far greater than could have been expected before the war, and the newer metal and engineering industries found themselves exporting capital equipment to many parts of the world. Industry in general was modernized, mechanized, and sometimes automated. As a result of a big prospecting drive, several new sources of minerals were discovered. The mechanization of agriculture resulted in a big increase in production with a reduced labour force, and Finland even achieved a surplus in dairy products.

Statistically, the revolution expressed itself as follows: the proportion of the population engaged in agriculture and forestry dropped from 42 per cent in 1950 to 32 per cent in 1960, while the proportion in industry and the service trades rose correspondingly; industrial production rose between 1948 and 1956 by an average of 9 per cent a year; total production *per capita* in 1964 was 70 per cent greater than in 1948, and exports increased by 70 per cent between 1954 and 1964. By the early 'sixties Finland was among the first fifteen countries of the world as regards income *per capita.*

These statistics mean that life has been radically changed for the great mass of Finns. The impact of the industrial revolution has been felt by everyone, though perhaps least by those already living in large towns, because they have merely become more comfortable and more prosperous; some of the people in the remote parts of the country, however, have become poorer than before by comparison with the rest of the population; regional differences have been accentuated, and become too marked for the good of the country as a whole. Large numbers of people have left their lonely farms and settled in more modern homes in towns; many of them have bought cars and television sets, and spent holidays abroad. The industrial revolution has given the country an extraordinary mobility and nourished the Finnish passion for removing. It is estimated that in one decade close on a million people – more than one-fifth of the population – moved their homes, either from country to town, or from a small town to a larger one.

This movement to the towns has been almost all in one direction – to the mainland of the south-west. When the Finns first arrived in Finland they settled in the south and the south-west; over the centuries they pushed the frontiers of civilization northwards until they had established beyond the Arctic Circle farms which were viable, though barely so, compared with those of the gentler and more fruitful south. This trend lasted right into this century, when it began to be reversed by the growth of industry in the south. The Finns moved at first slowly, then rapidly, back to the areas where they had first settled and where roads and buildings were swallowing up some of the country's best agricultural land. The south-west has been the most heavily industrialized part of Finland since the woodworking industries began to set up their mills and factories near the mouths of the rivers which bring the timber from farther north, and also near the ports through which their products can be exported. Now the bulk of the country's activities is concentrated in an area bounded by a line which starts north of Pori, on the west coast, runs eastwards to take in Tampere and southwards to skirt Lahti, and ends east of Kotka on the Gulf of Finland. The centre and the north – and especially the north-east – have become in danger of depopulation, for here the great lakes and forests form a natural barrier to modern industrial and urban development. At the same time many islands in the south-western archipelago, the homes of small farmers and fishermen, have already lost their inhabitants to the mainland, for lack of means of transport, supplies and modern 'amenities'. The contrast between the mainland of the south-west, with its new towns, its modern buildings and industrial plants, and the wild, sparsely-peopled and under-developed centre and north has become more and more marked. The south-west is one of the most modern –and beautiful – industrial areas in Europe; much of the rest of the country, outside the towns, has preserved an archaic, traditional character which sites it in the nineteenth rather than the twentieth century.

This dichotomy has faced Finland with a problem which grows too fast for adequate solutions to be found. Present trends, if allowed to continue, could turn the country into two nations of haves and have-nots. In 1965, if one took the average income per head for the whole country as 100, the figure for the southern province of Uusimaa (which contains more than a quarter of all Finland's industry) was 157, while for Central Ostrobothnia and Northern Karelia it was 65. These inequalities are aggravated by great variations in the birth-rate. The population growth in Finland is one of the highest in Europe, but the increase has largely taken place in the least prosperous areas. The rate of growth is the highest in Lapland where, in the early 'sixties, half the population was either still at school, or too young to go to school. In all these more remote districts there is ample room for a bigger population, and agricultural production can probably keep pace with the increase; but there is not enough work locally for this sizable rising generation. The farmer who has acquired only a share of some farm machinery no longer needs all his children to help him on the farm. If there is no work in the neighbourhood, he sends them to Helsinki or one of the other big cities in search of employment – and in the long run no good will be served by allowing the south-west to develop into a giant reception area. The need, above all, is for industrial or semi-industrial work in the more distant agricultural areas.

The problem in its essentials was foreseen soon after the war; but then few people envisaged its eventual dimensions. Not until the 1960's did decentralization and the establishment of development areas begin to play a large part in national policy. Enough, however, had already been done to provide a basis for decentralization, though not to stem migration to the south. Lapland was the first 'development area', though it was not scheduled as such; necessity and enthusiasm, not policy, dictated its development. When the Second War with Russia ended in 1944, about 200,000 German troops were based on Finland, and most of them in Lapland. The Finns, as part of the armistice terms, had to see that they left the country. The Germans refused to evacuate themselves. Instead they sought out the remotest dwellings in the forests and burned them down or blew them up; they reduced the capital, Rovaniemi, to ashes; they demolished 925 of the 1,000 large and small bridges, and reduced Lapland to a state of almost complete devastation.

This was the first challenge to modernize. The Finns, still pioneers at heart, took it up eagerly. Lapland was rebuilt in an entirely modern style, with schools and hotels of which London might be proud, and a fresh searching look was taken at the economy of the land beyond the Arctic Circle. In many parts of Lapland the area of cultivated land has been at least doubled since 1945. But, with its fleeting, often frosty summers, Lapland could never feed its growing population without supplies from farther south, and the provision of non-agricultural work is more important than the development of farming. A great hydro-electric scheme has harnessed the broad rushing rivers of the Province, providing power for present and future development in the northern half of Finland. New wood-processing plants have been established in south and central Lapland, and if more of the enormous timber resources can be handled locally, instead of being sent to mills farther south, a good deal more employment will be created. A certain number of light industries have also been set up.

Lapland, however, is only one part of the problem. The whole of north Finland, including Lapland, most of the east, a little of the centre, and the south-western archipelago are now scheduled as development areas. In the mid-'fifties the first steps were taken to encourage decentralization and to try to reverse the southward migration. Already the most northerly university in the world has been opened at Oulu, on the Gulf of Bothnia; important institutions for higher education have been extended and developed in Tampere and Jyväskylä in central Finland; two other universities are planned in eastern Finland. The State has built wood-processing factories in under-employed areas; and the City of Helsinki has refused to allow any further large-scale industrial development within its boundaries. The removal of some government departments to Kuopio, a town 220 miles north-east of Helsinki, is under consideration, but this seems, at the time of writing, a controversial idea which has no appeal to the staffs concerned. Lapland represented frontier territory, a challenge to the pioneers; Kuopio would be exile without challenge.

The general climate of opinion will need to change if decentralization is to be as thorough and as successful as is necessary. The impetus to it has come largely from Agrarian governments; their opponents have tended to dismiss the whole idea as a political gimmick designed to benefit Agrarian supporters (which it would). Industrialists are very satisfied with their location in the south, and have little wish to move to areas that are economically less rewarding. They appreciate the nature of the problem, but want to solve it in their own way. This would probably mean the selection of a certain number of 'growth points' – or existing towns – in the development areas where industry and the service trades could expand side by side. The newer Finnish factories are so highly automated that they require very little manpower, and so cannot always provide the necessary employment in themselves. One of the corollaries of Finland's extensive modernization of industry and mechanization of agriculture and forestry must be an increasing dependence on the service trades for employment; and therefore a greater degree of urban development than has so far taken place.

This has perhaps been realized more clearly by people living in the development areas than by those in the south. Finnish town-dwellers have a lively civic pride and a desire to make their own town, whichever it may be, one of the most modern in Finland. Many small towns have organized architectural competitions for their redevelopment, and in doing so aroused interest all over the country. They have embarked on schemes whose cost would deter towns in wealthier countries, but have somehow managed to raise the money. Experience so far suggests that a new civic centre designed by a distinguished architect will do more to attract industrialists to the locality than all the exhortations of governments; although the inhabitants are spurred on, in the first place, by their passion for rebuilding for its own sake. This remaking of the faces of the towns is yet another aspect of the post-war transformation of Finland. Even the smaller places have rebuilt their main streets. The cobblestones have gone and cars ride swiftly along smooth, wide roads. The old wooden houses have been replaced by multi-storeyed buildings, including offices, shops, restaurants and flats in the modern manner. In many out-of-the-way places there are hotels, schools and hospitals as up to date as those in Helsinki.

More dramatic than this face-lifting is the radical replanning of towns, and sometimes of whole industrial areas, which has given so much of the country a new look. Under the inspiration of Alvar Aalto, architects and town-planners have since the war broken right away from the old notions of urban non-planning which had infected Finland from the West. The cramped narrow streets, the divorce of town and country, and the strange failure to use the space which is Finland's greatest asset now belong to the past. In the new towns and suburbs houses are set far back from the roads and surrounded by trees which are never cut down unless it is absolutely necessary. Stretches of woodland and grassland march right into town centres. When Aalto replanned the growing industrial town of Imatra in eastern Finland, he went further and insisted on thrusting wedges of agricultural land and forest right into the town. This was a human response to the Finn's need to see the countryside before his own eyes, and a protest against the classic opposition of town and country. No new town in Finland is now likely to fall far outside the 'garden city' classification. (Though this term, used by the Finns themselves, would often be better replaced by the description 'woodland town'.)

The development of communications has, of necessity, proceeded concurrently with industrialization, urbanization and decentralization. But for Finland all communications, and roads especially, represent an enormously disproportionate financial drain. It is not only that less than five million people are scattered over a country where more than 700 miles separate the northern border of Lapland from the Gulf of Finland in the south, and the mileage of roads needed is far greater than in a more compact country. Roads probably demand more maintenance in Finland than anywhere else in Europe. Throughout the winter they have to be constantly cleared of snow to keep the traffic moving; and with the spring comes the annual break-up of the surface, caused by frost which may penetrate three feet below ground. In recent years Finland has invested a higher percentage of the gross national product in road-building than any other European country, partly because she has made a relatively late start with a modern road network. Since 1959 at least 1,000 kilometers of new roads, some of them four-lane motor highways, have been built every year.

The construction of these roads has entailed few manpower problems. It has absorbed a number of seasonally unemployed workers, who have been reinforced by men convicted of driving after drinking alcohol, even in very small quantities. For these, road-making is now the standard penalty, and cabinet ministers and managing directors have wielded pickaxe and drill alongside more experienced workers for months at a time. But the road programme has proved so expensive in terms of money that in 1964 Finland asked the World Bank for a loan to assist further construction and maintenance, and also to finance a detailed study of the country's long-term transport needs. This was done by a Dutch consultant firm, which prepared a ten-year plan, co-ordinating all forms of transport, by road, rail, air and water.

In the meantime, Finland is one of the few European countries which are still extending their railway systems. This is necessary largely to allow the transport of freight, whether timber or manufactured goods. The railways meet fierce competition for passenger traffic from Finland's remarkable airlines. Finnair is the fifth oldest airline in the world, and claims to charge the lowest domestic fare in Europe, on the densest network per head of the population. Finnish airlines have profited in the past by the backward and limited rail and road communications, and now the Finns find a plane almost as ordinary and normal a means of transport as a bus. Thus Finnair, seventy-two per cent government-owned, needs no subsidy and can make an adequate profit.

This leap forward into the modern world has not been achieved painlessly, or without social problems. In less than a year you can build a highly modern factory; in less than two you can turn a Finn from a farm into a skilled worker, since he is by nature practical and adept with his hands. But it takes far, far longer to accustom him to factory life, with its resemblance to servitude by comparison with the life of a free man on the farm. It takes far, far longer to get him adjusted to town life, where he may have to live in a flat, and lack even the chance of working in a garden or on an allotment. Ideally, the sons of isolated farms ought to work in small industrial communities; but for many of them the streets of the big towns are still paved with gold, and the disillusionment and disappointment they find there are all the greater.

A certain *malaise* extends even to town-bred, industry-accustomed Finns faced with the rapid pace of industrialization. The tradition of town-dwelling is so short, of country-dwelling so long, that they feel that industrialization and urbanization are cutting them off from their roots. They fear anything that may diminish either the beauty of the countryside or its way of life. They suspect that work on the land is intrinsically better and more worthwhile than work in a factory, that the best qualities of the Finns are nurtured in the countryside and the worst in the towns. There is a nostalgia for the lost childhood in the country, where life may have been hard but was without worldly or urban complications. The old agricultural life has come to be viewed among the romantics as a vanishing idyll.

However, space and the modern town-planner may save the Finns from the type of industrial and urban life which Western Europe and the U.S.A. take for granted. In some of the newer communities, with their sophisticated town centres, yet semi-rural character, people undoubtedly live more happily and harmoniously than in the old industrial areas. The Finns may yet be able to get the best of both worlds.

Chapter Thirteen

Farm and Forest

The Finns are justly proud of their agricultural successes of the post-war years. They have made themselves largely self-sufficient against all odds, for few countries have been in the past less kindly to the farmer. Finland's conversion to an agricultural country whose cows have set world records for their milk yield is a triumph of determination. Some people, viewing all the unpromising conditions of northern soil and climate, might call it a triumph of sheer obtuseness. Certainly the cost of success in toil and hardship has been so great that it still helps to account for the Finns' deep emotional attachment to their agricultural background, as well as for their pride in achievement.

Finland is the most northerly agricultural country in the world. The whole of the country lies north of the great farming lands of southern Sweden, and in few other parts of the world does the climate present greater hazards. The growing season is brief enough already (a month shorter than in Denmark), without the frosts that can bite deep into summer or come as too early heralds of autumn. The grazing season rarely lasts more than five months in south-western Finland, and dwindles to three in Lapland. Throughout the long winters the animals have to keep their narrow quarters in byre and shippen. According to an old proverb from the province of Savo, by Michaelmas 'the animals must be in the byre and the women in the *tupa*'. For any time after Michaelmas the snows might start to fall, and the womenfolk were then expected to begin their traditional winter activities of spinning, weaving and baking in the *tupa*, or kitchen-living room, that was warmed by the great oven in the corner. The soil has done little to compensate for the hostile climate. The better agricultural land lies in the south-west, where the plains are often of sand and post-glacial clay. Here the soil has been steadily improved by the use of fertilizers, and by underdrainage, which is still rare, though increasing, in a country almost quilted by the open ditches that prevent the full rationalization and mechanization of agriculture. But in the north the soil becomes predominantly peaty, or in some parts stony and thin, and demands both extensive drainage and heavy artificial nourishment.

But nature mitigated the harshness and barrenness of the land with the great forests; and society from the early days saw that the farmer could not live without his portion of forest in addition to his arable and pasture land. The traditional rule of Finnish agricultural economy is that a farm must contain at least twice a much forest as field. However, it has recently been found that some of the larger and more highly mechanized farms of the south-west are able to prosper with little or no forest, but these are exceptions to the general rule. In the old days, the forest provided the materials for the farmer to build and heat his house and byre and shippen, and to make his implements, his sleigh, his boat, his furniture, his wife's spinning-wheel and loom, and all the smaller necessities of daily life. Today the forest yields a cash crop which he can sell to the great woodworking companies, and also provides work for himself, his men and his horse, if he still keeps one, in winter when the fields lie deep under the snow. The farmer may draw as much as three-quarters of his income from the forest; without it, he could not at times have reached subsistence level.

The small farmers who are so typical of Finland are still especially dependent on their forests. The sale of milk provides for their day-to-day needs; but the sale of timber pays for new machinery, new buildings and the like. Well over half the farms in Finland have only between five and twenty-five acres of arable land, and can hardly pay their way without forest land. They are owned by the farmers themselves and entirely run by the family, without help from outside. A tenant farmer is an extreme rarity, and there are ten farmers for every farm labourer. This self-sufficiency is particularly characteristic of the Finnish farm; it lies at the root of the traditions of independence and self-help which the Finns fear may be driven out by machinery and rationalization.

For these yeoman farmers, whether large or small, have sent agricultural production soaring up from the early 'fifties onwards. In 1950, taking all products together, Finland had reached 65 per cent self-sufficiency; by 1965, the figure was 105 per cent. The more dispassionate economists consider this too high, taking the view that

Finland would do better to aim at an eighty per cent sufficiency level. Agricultural subsidies – a built-in part of the system – would then be reduced, and surplus manpower could be used in the export industries, paying for imports of food from countries able to produce more cheaply than Finland. Moreover, this apparently high sufficiency figure hides the fact that Finland cannot supply all her own fertilizer needs, and that large sums have had to be invested in nitrogen and superphosphate factories in order to reduce imports or artificial fertilizers.

All this does not, however, detract from the remarkable achievement of such increased production of milk, bread-grains and fodder in this Arctic land. As a result of research, mechanization and land clearance, crop levels of wheat, rye, barley, oats and a variety of root vegetables have been greatly raised. Research has developed strains of bread-grains and fodder turnips suited to high-latitude farming, and able to thrive and grow quickly in the long summer daylight of the far north. The greatest contribution to animal husbandry has been made by the development of grass rotation in a country where both climate and soil make permanent grass impossible. This regular renewal of the grasslands is also essential to the production of the celebrated A.I.V., which is named after its Nobel prize-winning discoverer, Professor A. I. Virtanen. This is a green cattle fodder treated with chemicals so that it retains its original food value all through the winter, and so enormously increases milk production. Professor Virtanen is at present working on a new fodder based on wood pulp and nitrogen, and is optimistic that this will increase milk yield even further. (Milk is perhaps even more of an obsession in Finland than in the other Scandinavian countries; the Finns call it 'Agri-Cola', jokingly combining the names of their famous sixteenth-century bishop, Michael Agricola, and of the factory-bottled drinks which have reached them from the West. But they are nevertheless already exercised by the problem of their milk surplus and are looking a little anxiously for better export outlets for their dairy products.) Mechanization has taken place on a scale once thought impossible; now tractors, combine harvesters and other machines are to be seen almost everywhere; the small farmers who lack the money to invest in them are often able to share them with four or five others in the neighbourhood. Land clearance and swamp drainage have been pursued so energetically that the acreage under cultivation is now larger than before the war, and the ten per cent of cultivated land ceded to the Soviet Union in 1944 has thus been more than made good.

Animal husbandry has always been for the Finnish farmer a more profitable enterprise than cereal growing, being less at the mercy of the weather. Dairy production has now become so flourishing an enterprise that Finland exports considerable quantities of butter, eggs and cheese. Unfortunately, the excellence of Finnish dairy products is often masked abroad by the generalization 'Imported'. Finnish cheese is exported to more than forty countries, but is too often anonymously packaged, and the Finnish versions of the famous cheeses of other countries become indistinguishable from their originals. Until recently cattle have been bred chiefly for milk yield, and the Finns have concentrated on Ayrshires, which account for about a quarter of all cows, and their own Finnish breeds. The care of cattle has been almost entirely in the hands of the womenfolk, whether the wives and daughters of the farmers, or hired help. But when milking machines came into more general use – and now most herds of more than six cows are milked mechanically – men began to take a fresh interest in their animals, and to think of breeding for meat as well as for milk. They also take pig-breeding and poultry-keeping very seriously; but, on the other hand, the number of sheep has been allowed to dwindle to about one-fifth of the pre-war stock.

Between the isolated and sometimes primitive farms, the advanced research at the centre, and the wide export market, there often seems an enormous distance in outlook and methods as well as in space. The thousands of small, separate units sometimes seem as remote from each other as they are from the laboratories and their markets; yet they are all linked with an efficient modern organization at the centre. There are any number of specialist agricultural societies, many of which exist solely to give advice to farmers. They are concerned, to name only a few, with the breeding of pigs, horses, or fur-bearing animals, with reindeer-raising, or with swamp drainage and cultivation. All employ specialist consultants who travel from farm to farm to advise farmers on their individual problems and to keep them up to date with the results of recent research. Education, both vocational and professional, makes an equally important contribution to advance and improvement. It is relatively normal for the young people on the farms to attend vocational courses, lasting anything from six months to two to three years, at either general farming schools, or the more specialized schools teaching subjects such as animal husbandry, dairying, forestry or horticulture. They bring back to their elders on the farms knowledge of newer ideas and methods which are more often than not accepted and adopted. Of course the streak of conservatism asserts itself from time to time, and sometimes one hears more about the farmers averse to change than about the go-ahead. But the rapid increase in production during the post-war years proves that the work of both agricultural advisers and teachers has been largely fruitful.

At the other end of the process is the problem of marketing. This is met by the extensive co-operatives, without which the smallholders, in particular, could never have survived. Co-operation is both natural to the Finnish temperament and essential to the agricultural economy. The modern co-operative movement, which now extends to so many commodities, originated at the beginning of this century among the farming population, specifically to ensure the future of the smallholders. Today, when the milk from a small farm reaches the consumer, whether as milk, butter, cheese (or the ice-cream which is so startlingly popular in the Arctic midwinter as well as in summer), it has almost invariably been processed and marketed by a local dairy co-operative and by the national association, which also handles exports. Butter and cheese are rarely made on the farm; the co-operatives, with their modern equipment, can do the work far better. There are similar egg marketing co-operatives and slaughter-house co-operatives. Equally important for the small farmers are the co-operative purchasing organizations which buy items such as seed, fertilizers and equipment on behalf of their members. Although the co-operatives were originally launched to buy and sell in bulk, they have always been concerned with the improvement of quality and have played a great part in the raising of standards. As far back as 1916, Valio, the co-operative dairies' association, opened a laboratory for this purpose. It has since developed into the foremost biochemical research institute and teaching centre in Finland.

So, technically, the state of Finnish agriculture appears at best sound and healthy, and at worst in process of considerable improvement. But the farmer, whether poor or prosperous, stands at the centre of a skein of problems, political, economic, social and psychological, which is immensely difficult to unravel. The political problem of subsidies is common to many other countries; but in Finland it takes on a more acute form because it totally divides the two largest parties, the Centre (formerly Agrarian) supporting the farmer, and the Social-Democratic supporting the less well-paid consumer. More than one cabinet has broken down and resigned over questions as deceptively simple as the price of butter. When a third of the population still lives on the land, there is no real victory for either side in this politico-economic tug-of-war, which is likely to remain a feature of political life for some time to come.

Great social and economic problems are posed by a dual division of Finnish farms by size and situation. The proportion of smallholdings is far too great; so is the contrast between the larger modern and mechanized farms of the south-west and the smaller, sometimes backward holdings of the remoter north and east. During this century various circumstances have combined to increase the number of small farms with less than twenty-five acres of arable land. The really large farm, it is true, was never common, and divided inheritance split up many holdings. In 1918 reforms in land tenure made more than 100,000 crofters and cotters into independent small landowners. In 1922 further groups of landless people were enabled to acquire small farms.

Then, after 1944, the State was obliged to find land for the dispossessed farmers from the part of Karelia ceded to the Soviet Union at the end of the war. For them, and also for war veterans, war widows and the disabled, 45,000 farms had to be created elsewhere in Finland. Forty per cent of the land was provided by voluntary sale to the State; the rest was acquired compulsorily from state and communal land, mismanaged farms and the estates of 'hobby' farmers. It was realized then, and is realized more strongly today, that the farms so created were far too small. Yet what was economically wrong was then socially and psychologically right; the Karelians, given a fresh and eventually manageable stake in the country, settled down and soon began to make their lively contribution to their new surroundings. But it remains a hard fact that the possibilities of increasing production on these smallholdings are limited, so little suited are they to mechanization, rationalization or modern methods.

By now it has become far more difficult to increase the size of a holding than to reduce it. A government-appointed Agricultural Policy Committee made, in 1962, a number of far-reaching recommendations regarding the rationalization of agriculture and the economic improvement of conditions for the farm population. It observed that the minimum eventual amount of arable land per farm should be fifty to seventy acres – but saw no means of achieving this aim.

The problem of the small farm is aggravated when it is situated, as many are, in the wilder, more remote and beautiful north and east. The south-west is the Finland of today and tomorrow in agriculture, as in so many other respects; in the north and the east something of the hard, primitive pattern of life remains. Here are the family farms which have passed from father to son over several generations, but which no longer offer the young people the opportunities of financial reward and social life they seek today. Yet in much of this vast region there seems little possibility of providing sufficient employment outside the few towns, and no one wishes the countryside of the north and east to become a lifeless zone animated only by the summer cottages of the townsmen. Moreover, this is the part of Finland where traditions now on the way to idealization are the best preserved. Perhaps the farms are still made gay by the lively Finnish breeds of dog – the exuberant Spitz and the endearing and aptly-named Karelian bearhound – and by the wiry Finnish horse which has been replaced elsewhere by the tractor. Perhaps the great *tupa* is still the scene of mammoth 'bakations', for the bread and cakes of the farmers' wives today remain worthy of the eye and palate of a master-baker in Britain or the United States, and are often more nutritious than a good many of his products. And perhaps in winter the womenfolk still find time to weave beautiful table linen, rugs and hangings, which are sometimes not far removed from the work of textile artists of the capital. For the natural gifts of the Finnish countrywomen have been nourished and encouraged by the remarkable 'Martha' organization. This, the approximate equivalent of the Women's Institutes of several Anglo-Saxon countries, has given a sense of direction and modernity to women's activities in the home, and has been as successful in some of the towns as in the remote country districts. All in all, the way of life on these farms is one which few people wish to see disappear, yet few know how long it can be preserved in a modern economic context.

In spite of the extent of agriculture, it is the forest that asserts itself everywhere in Finland, dominating the farm, even hiding it from view. Few visitors could spend more than a day in Finland without being made aware of the role of the forests in the national economy; but they could stay for several weeks without catching a glimpse of the farms, often so distant from the roads. The farmers, large and small, own over sixty per cent of the 'green gold' of the forests; it is divided among so many of them that some of the great woodworking companies have to carry through about fifteen thousand transactions a year to purchase the wood they need. The State owns less than thirty per cent, and the remainder is divided among companies, communities and the Church.

The forests are overwhelmingly made up of the pine and spruce, which, in the slow-growing North, develop the long fibres which make good paper, newsprint especially. Less than a fifth is birch, much of it the tall, straight variety which grows so profusely and makes Finland the world's biggest exporter of birch plywood. In the paper and board industry, birch makes fluting (the middle layer of corrugated board) and milk cartons, and is being increasingly used, mixed with other pulps, for various types of papers. Now there is also a possibility that plastics can be made from birch wood; if it is realized, this wayward child of the forests, which grows and spreads so quickly, will acquire a new and considerable value overnight.

To the forest the farmer turns for work in the winter. If his own woodland is too small to take up much of his time in maintenance or felling, he can find work in the larger forests, owned by private companies or the State. He may go to one of the vast northern forests, so far from civilization that the lumbermen have to live in their own encampments. But the number of men needed for the winter work of felling, logging and bundling is decreasing, and the seasonal unemployment, or underemployment, of the farming population is thus aggravated. Now four men with power saws and forest tractors can do an amount of work that once needed fifty or sixty. Half of all transport in the forests is done by motor vehicles, but sometimes even the tank-like forest tractor cannot make its way through the deep snow of the roadless forest. Then the small, patient yet powerful Finnish horse still has to haul the heavy timber-laden sleighs over short but difficult distances.

The timber may then be transported along one of the many roads which have been built recently, but it is more likely to be left on a frozen lake or river. Here it is bundled into huge rafts on the ice, ready to float downstream when the spring thaw comes. Then it starts its journey towards the distant sawmill or pulp mill for which it is intended, and which may be two or three hundred miles away. The two great river systems of Lapland, dominated by the Kemi and the Oulu Rivers, drain down into the Gulf of Bothnia, where there are factories to process the wood and ports from which it can be exported. In south-east Finland the Kymi River combines with an enormous and intricate lake system to form a series of floatways which carry timber to mills and factories near the big ports on the Gulf of Finland.

Without these waterways the utilization and export of timber could never have reached its present scale, nor could Finland's whole economic development have been what it is. Their extraordinary fitness for purpose provokes as much wonder as does the sight of the enormous rafts of wood which float, apparently aimlessly, down some wide waterway, yet rarely lose their complicated way to their destination. Some routes are used by a number of mills, and floatway maps are here the counterpart of road maps. The mystery, to the onlooker, is how every raft finds its way through the labyrinthine lake system and the many river tributaries. The log sorter is the little genius who controls this form of traffic. It is his job to keep the rafts moving in the right direction; every log is marked with the owner's code after felling, and so is identifiable by the sorter. He operates at all points where routes converge or fork, a nimble figure balancing lightly on one raft, or sometimes on a single log, while he steers another raft with his long pike-pole. If he is unlucky he may be faced with a log-jam half a mile long, and more tangled than any city traffic jam; then it may take him several days to get it cleared. By comparison it is a far simpler matter for a steam tug to tow an assembly of logs several miles long across the calm waters of one of the great lakes.

The Finns have always had a knack for introducing an element of play into work, and the annual lumberjacks' games on the swift, wide rivers of north Finland are the playtime of the floaters and sorters. Here they demonstrate their skill by racing each other across floating logs, walking across narrow beams, standing perilously on a single log in midstream and treading it round at the same time. There are women as well as men sorters in Finland, and the star turns of these games have often been three agile and celebrated sorter sisters.

Floating and sorting require such skill and experience and carry so much responsibility that high wages can be demanded, and these may offset the cost of the alternative methods of transport by lorry or goods train. Now that new and splendid motor roads have been built all over Finland and the railways have been extended, an increasing amount of timber travels by road or rail. But where distances are great or communications less than adequate, as in Lapland, floating is likely to remain the most economic way of transferring the timber from the distant forest to the wood-processing plants near the coast.

The world demand for paper and wood products has grown so much recently that these plants have begun to need more wood to convert into processed goods for export than Finland can afford to cut. Timber has had to be imported, chiefly from Russia, to avoid over-cutting and running into a major shortage later in the century. Such a situation has never been envisaged in Finland, and even after the war no comprehensive afforestation programme was thought necessary. Legislation did no more than limit the amount of felling that could be done in any given year.

The import of timber made the Finns realize the need for a forest policy and a forest programme, and despite their aversion to planning they drew up the longest-term plan of their entire existence. A tree takes at least thirty years to mature in southern Finland; it may take as much as 150 years in the north. So allowing for an average growing-period of seventy to eighty years, the new forest improvement programme stretches well into the next century, and aims at so increasing the forest capital that twice as much wood as now can then be cut each year.

This programme was the work of M.E.R.A. (the Forestry Financing Committee). It aims in the short term to reach a position where about 50 million cubic metres of wood can be cut in a year without jeopardizing future supplies. In the long term, that is, in about seventy or eighty years, it aims at an annual cut of 80–100 million cubic metres. The Committee estimated that fifteen per cent of existing forests was insufficiently productive, and needed immediate reafforestation; and that there were in Finland between 10 and 12 million acres of swampland which should be urgently drained and seeded. Nurseries have been expanded and new seed stocks built up; there are programmes of forest fertilization, forest road construction, and training of forestry experts and workers. Both forest-owning companies and individual farmers have been exhorted and encouraged to increase and improve their forests, and special grants are made to farmers to push ahead with this work. The long-term intention is to alter the balance between forestry and agriculture so that the profitability of forestry is increased and overproduction in agriculture is decreased. Already in 1962 the Agricultural Policy Committee had recommended that no more reclaimed land should be devoted to arable farming; the M.E.R.A. recommendations went a step further in insisting on its use for the growing of timber.

Thus, in another generation, some of the farmer's economic problems may be eased by the extension of his forest land. There may also be solutions for some of the human and social problems of agriculture. But for the present the gap between incomes and living standards in industry and agriculture grows constantly wider. Electricity and television may have reached into many isolated farmsteads, but they do not help the small farmer to break out of the closed circle of his acreage. He cannot appreciably increase his income unless he can enlarge his farm; he cannot enlarge his farm without more money. The 'flight from the land', bewailed by the romantics and viewed as necessary by the harder-headed, is bound to continue as it has done now for a generation. It will probably result, in the long term, in the amalgamation of a certain number of smallholdings. But this will not be brought about easily, and it will not be brought about for some years. In their heart of hearts, the Finns fear the dominance of the large farmer for whom agriculture is a business and an industry. He neither belongs to their present way of life nor accords with the farming traditions of centuries.

Chapter Fourteen

Setting for a New Society

When a young man decides to leave the farm where his family has lived for generations and earn his living in industry, he is fortunate if he can get a job in Valkeakoski, or a place like it. This small town, with its population of 15,000, stands at the gateway to Finland's vast lakeland, and its own centre stretches into a narrow isthmus between two large and forest-fringed lakes. It is a lively modern town which draws its living almost completely from industry; yet there are few points in it where water or woodland disappear totally from sight. One of the biggest firms in Finland dominates Valkeakoski's life through its paper and cellulose mills, its paper-converting factory, its engineering works and its glass and chemical factory. These together employ a total of more than 3,000 people, while another 1,500 work in the rayon factory of another company.

Valkeakoski is one of the most attractive and successful of Finnish industrial communities; it is a town which has developed fairly recently and one in which man and machinery have come to terms particularly well. Industrialization might lose many of its anti-social terrors if it could always take place in settings like Valkeakoski. In Finland it often does, because here there is the space which so many industrialized countries lack. There are some places which, though without slums or tightly packed streets, seem drab and lifeless. However, many other Finnish manufacturing centres, larger or smaller, have much in common with Valkeakoski; but a number of factors, besides its beautiful natural environment, have combined to make this town outstanding. It is ideal in size, not big enough to become impersonal or to create distances too great to cover on foot, yet not too small to support a theatre and a wide range of social activities. The town's two big employers, Juuso Walden of United Paper Mills, and Baron Wrede who retired from Säteri Oy in 1966, have combined a high reputation among industrialists with a deep interest in social affairs and a determination to do their utmost for their employees and for the whole community. The town itself has a strong corporate civic sense, and for several years its council chamber was adorned by a large bronze wild boar – a trophy signifying that in the previous general election, Valkeakoski was the place where the highest percentage of the electorate went out to vote. Finally, it is the home of one of Finland's champion football teams, and that alone gives it a special civic status in the Finns' eyes.

When industry began to develop here, Valkeakoski was not much more than a straggling, unplanned collection of wooden houses. It took twenty years to demolish 400 of them, as they became vacant, and make way for the new, modern town centre. A few of the old wooden houses still remain here and there; with their particular grace and charm they stand as reminders of the past among the bolder granite and concrete buildings of today. The old traditional Lutheran wooden church also remains, but it has yielded some of its congregation to an impressive modern building which owes nothing to tradition. Its wide, clear windows look out on to the surrounding woodland; inside, green plants climb up its stark white walls, as evidence of the widespread Finnish wish to dissolve the division between the indoor and the outdoor, and keep, even when indoors, a sense of contact with the natural world. It would have been less surprising if the Finns had tried, instead, to shut out all evidence of their often harsh climate; but they seem to feel a need for wide vistas which leads them, even in the towns, to dispense with curtains that draw across the windows of their homes.

The small and charming Greek Orthodox church, its dark wooden structure tipped with white, is traditional and rustic in style. Both architecturally and symbolically, it offers a complete contrast to the modern Lutheran church. Here are no large widows or wide vistas. The world is shut out, and the church reserved for a tight group of believers for whom the gathering together is an essential part of the faith. This church was built for the Karelians who settled in Valkeakoski after their province was ceded to the Soviet Union in 1944. The Greek Orthodox Church was always strong in Eastern Finland, and since the cession of Karelia and the dispersal of the Karelians its influence has been felt in many other parts of the country. The monks from the famous monastery of Valamo on Lake Ladoga, the most north-westerly outpost of the Greek Church in Europe, were also dispossessed in the cession. They are now struggling to continue their traditions by another Finnish lake, but the number of Finns who are drawn to the monastic life is small.

The town centre of Valkeakoski is dominated by the group of buildings which comprises the town hall, the municipal library, with its first-class collection of Finnish and foreign books and music, and an evening school. Plans are in hand to build a 'Culture House', to include a theatre, a concert hall, and premises for other purposes, very near to the town hall. Valkeakoski is a prosperous 'property-owning democracy' if ever there was one, but it has strong leftish leanings. A Communist was its M.P. for several years, and its town council is composed of fifteen Social Democrats, ten Communists, and ten Conservatives. The mayor, as everywhere in Scandinavia, is a permanent salaried official, and the citizens are enthusiastic about the energetic way he is developing the town. Indeed, it is difficult to point to any major amenity that Valkeakoski lacks, or to any institution that is not thoroughly modern and up to date by international standards. The hospital has 110 beds, and no more than six in any one ward; one of its most pleasant provisions is a number of small lounges and indoor gardens where patients can sit and talk to their visitors, as here there are none of the regulations which oblige them to be unnecessarily in bed at visiting hours. Running costs are borne mainly by the commune, though a number of beds are maintained by the two big industrial concerns in the town, and all patients make a very small contribution to their upkeep while in hospital. There are an old people's home, a block of flats specially built for old people, two gay little day nurseries, and a splendidly equipped new secondary school where, as befits a manufacturing town, the emphasis is on practical training. Valkeakoski's chief drawback is its smell – the stench that pours out of the chimneys of the sulphate mill and the rayon factory and envelopes the town when the wind is in the wrong direction. The citizens accept it with resignation and the flat remark, 'It's our bread and butter', and the assurance that their health is in no way endangered. But experts are gripping the stench problem by the nose, as it were, and are optimistic that they can soon find ways of mitigating it.

Valkeakoski seems to reach the peak of its activity when the working day is over. The orthodox working day in the factories starts at

7 a.m. and ends at 4 p.m.; but some mills work twenty-four hours in three shifts. The Finns habitually have dinner about five or five-thirty, and by seven the citizens are all well launched into their evening occupations. The theatre and the cinemas are open, the library is crowded, and the evening classes are full, and a large number of the 150 clubs which this energetic town boasts are in full swing. The figure includes the numerous clubs and societies run by the factories, but it is high, even so. Sports clubs predominate, but there are also thirteen women's organizations, several youth clubs, a 'golden age' club for old people, and a flourishing English club. Between the end of May and September nearly all the clubs except those devoted to outdoor sports are closed, unable to compete with the outdoor attractions of summer. There are swimming and boating close at hand, and, almost in the centre of the town, two open-air platforms by the lake are ready for dancing through the white summer nights to the accompaniment of a jazz band – and the Valkeakoskians will be satisfied with nothing less than one of Finland's best known bands.

Impressive as are the activities of the town as a whole, the real dynamic is supplied by the United Paper Mills, one of the biggest industrial concerns in Finland, which has its headquarters and several factories in Valkeakoski. The majority of big employers in Finland have a long record of social welfare, and have shown so splendid a concern for their employees that they are occasionally accused of pampering the worker. United Paper Mills is, even by the high Finnish standards, one of the most energetic and imaginative of companies in this respect; and possibly its outstanding achievement is the provision of housing for its employees. It has always been fairly normal throughout Finland for industry to make available a certain number of homes for its workers; this has been essential when factories have been set up in lonely places, far from existing communities but near to the waterfalls which originally supplied their electric power. (*Koski*, Finn. = falls, rapids; Valkeakoski = the White Falls.) This tendency was accentuated at the end of the war, when employers had to share with the State the burden of rehousing both the dispossessed Karelians and the new workers they needed to produce reparation goods. Frequently houses or flats are owned by the company concerned and let to employees at rents which may be as low as seven or eight per cent of their wages.

Both United Paper Mills and Säteri Oy, however, are among those who have developed schemes to allow their employees to build and buy their own homes. These two firms own a few blocks of flats in which office and technical staff and some of the works foremen are accommodated. But the accent is put heavily on helping the workers to buy their own homes. Schemes to this end were started in a small way in the 'thirties and continued after the war on a much larger scale. Now more than 700 employees of United Paper Mills and 400 employees of Säteri Oy live in their own homes. In the first place, the company's architect draws up a plan for the building area and designs the houses; the town builds the roads and lays water, drainage and electricity. The prospective home-owner is able to buy his land at a very low figure. The company then gives a loan to the employee (who must have done a requisite number of years of service) which will cover about 25 per cent of building costs and is repayable over twenty years at $5\frac{1}{2}$ per cent interest. The rest of the costs can be covered by state and bank loans, but the company gives additional help by selling timber (the principal building material) at a reduced rate, and lending the employee building machinery.

This is especially valuable because the Finn finds it normal to build his own house, at least in part. In Valkeakoski it is estimated that the work of the owner and his friends can save between 15 and 20 per cent of the total cost. Often building is speeded by the traditional *talkoo*. This is an ancient institution in which neighbours co-operate to do a job which one of them cannot do alone, or at all. A poor widow may need a shed for her only cow; she can neither build it herself nor afford to pay for the labour. So her neighbours get together and put up the shed at the weekend. There are only two conditions attached to a *talkoo*: when the work is done the recipient of the help must provide coffee and something to eat, and the participants must have a party, which could be a dance in an empty barn in the village. When the *talkoo* comes to town and and is applied to larger enterprises such as house-building, help is given no less willingly but the price is likely to be higher, and the cost of bottles as well as building materials has to be included in the final reckoning. This is not low. Depending on the size of the house, it is the equivalent of four or five years' wages of a man earning the average hourly rate, and 15 to 20 per cent less with benefit of *talkoo*.

However, these are houses in which highly-paid professional people in Helsinki – or London – would be happy to live. The older ones, built immediately after the war, are rather dull and uniform, as in those days standardization and simplification helped to build more quickly and cheaply. But the new single-storey houses set among the pinewoods, and reminiscent of American ranch houses, look as though they had come out of the pages of an expensive home-making magazine. Many of the gardens, whether of old or new houses, share this more recent elegance. The Finns love flowers beyond the point of extravagance, but their climate discourages gardening, all too obviously in some places. But both the big employers in Valkeakoski offer prizes for the best-kept gardens, and many home-owners make ingenious and artistic use of the existing trees and boulders round their houses and grow a wealth of flowers that defies the climate.

Everyone, by and large, is happy with the housing scheme. The company naturally feels that home ownership gives an employee a sense of security and encourages him to stay where he is. The employee for his part, feels more independent when he owns his home than when he rents it; if he comes from a farm, he regards possession of his roof as normal. He has the best of both worlds in that he can sell his house if he leaves Valkeakoski or stay in it after he retires from the company.

The company takes care of its workpeople, if they so wish, from the age of fifteen until the end of their lives. In Valkeakoski it has a school where boys are trained for work in all its mills and factories in different parts of the country. It is usual in Finland for industrial concerns to provide the kind of training which would be given in technical schools in many other countries. Thirty-five schools are run by industry, in addition to less highly organized training given by smaller firms. United Paper Mills' residential school at Valkeakoski takes 120 boys (from three times as many applicants) and gives them two or three years' training between the ages of fifteen and eighteen. A third of their time goes on theoretical work, mainly Finnish, mathematics, physics and chemistry; the rest is spent in all departments in the factories. The boys get their tuition, board and lodging free, and a small regular wage, which is just a little more than pocket money. When they are working in the factory they receive a bigger wage, out of which they pay for their board and lodging. They are trained to become skilled workers, but the best of them often want to carry their studies further at a college of technology. In that case the company can only hope that they will eventually return – as some have done – to take up managerial positions.

For those at the other end of their careers, there is an old people's workshop, where employees can continue to work and supplement their pensions after they retire at sixty-five or sixty-six. In addition to the state retirement pension, the company gives a pension to all who have been employed fifteen years or more. They can work in the old people's workshop for thirty-five hours or as little as one hour a week, without any pressure, and with breaks for free coffee in the morning and afternoon. The women make paper sacks and the men do woodwork, such as making wastepaper baskets for the offices. Here the hourly rate is about half the average in the factory. The workshop does not cover its cost, but the company regards it as an important social contribution, and not a means of making money.

Both United Paper Mills and Säteri cater amply for leisure. They run numerous clubs, of which more than a score are devoted to different sports. United Paper Mills owns motor-boats which take employees on weekend cruises through the lakes; cottages which can be hired very cheaply for summer holidays; and another cottage in Lapland for winter sports holidays. Ski-ing is one of Säteri's great enthusiasms; it reckons that if the distances covered on skis by all its employees in a winter season were added together, Säteri would have ski-ed twice round the globe; those who have made the biggest contribution to the total are given an extra ski holiday free at a ski centre. Some fortunate employees, from both office and factory floor, are given free holidays in various parts of Europe to widen their horizons, and from time to time United Paper Mills sends a small group with a record of long and good service on a short visit to the United States.

United Paper Mills make special provision for its female staff and for the wives and mothers of employees. There are playgrounds where workers' children are looked after by girls employed by the company – the counterparts of the 'park aunts' of the big towns. It runs a domestic centre in the town where courses are held in dressmaking, cookery, weaving and other home crafts. Cookery classes for male employees are also arranged from time to time; and in the school summer holidays, there is a highly popular course in cookery and housework, lasting a month, for schoolboys and girls. (In the new Finnish society, husbands are expected to share the household chores with their wives; an Act of Parliament obliges schools to teach domestic subjects to boys as well as girls.) Because vegetables are an expensive item in Finland, the company grows tomatoes, cucumbers and lettuce on a big scale and sells them in three shops in the town, where employees can buy them at a ten per cent reduction; and it satisfies the Finnish love of flowers by growing masses of carnations and making them available in the same way.

United Paper Mills is perhaps a little more lavish than most in the benefits it showers on its workers, but it is by no means unique. The Finnish industrialist's sense of responsibility to his employees and to the community goes back more than a century (an elementary school was founded in 1861 by an old-established woodworking company for the community where one of its factories is situated). Industrial welfare began to develop before Finland became independent and at a time when the ideas of her Russian masters ran in a wholly opposite direction. It naturally acquired many of the features of paternalism which are criticized by the trade unions in other countries. Yet the personalized industrial welfare of Finland has always corresponded to the Finns' deeply felt need to be looked after when they find themselves in unfamiliar surroundings, and to their anxiety, which can sometimes become over-possessive, to look after others similarly placed. Industry is still an unfamiliar way of life for many Finns and a high proportion of its employees are first-generation industrial workers. For them the protection of a company that appears to care about them is precious, if sometimes abused. The workers at a big Helsinki factory once demanded that the management should purchase their weekly bottle of schnapps on their behalf, and so save them the journey to the State Liquor Shop; but the management, though benevolent, had the courage to refuse.

This protection was doubly needed immediately after the war, when reparations goods had to be so urgently produced for the U.S.S.R., and new workers had to be housed, trained and adjusted to the different life of industry. Employers at that time felt that they could combine the interests of the country and of their employees with their own aims and interests. They were, in those days, convinced that social welfare was a weapon against communism; but the experience of Valkeakoski suggests that it is not always an entirely successful one, although it may be an instrument of reconciliation. Employers also hoped that their own extensive welfare schemes would lead to a postponement of the introduction of state welfare projects. That hope has now faded; social benefits have gradually been made universally available by the State, and the disadvantages of lavish industrial welfare have become more apparent. It has considerably widened the gap between the rewards of the industrial worker and the small farmer; it has led to some competition between employers to provide more and more benefits, on a scale which must be reduced before long. The introduction of state schemes has added to the employers' costs, as the workers want state benefits and all the previous private benefits as before. There is a fear that the unions may demand the same level of welfare benefits from every firm, which could effectively put small concerns out of business. Moreover, this lavish welfare has developed during a period in which Finland has had a labour surplus. In a time of manpower shortage, the workers' demands and expectations could reach new peaks. But, in the meantime, the country owes a great deal to these enlightened employers who have eased the human transition from agriculture to industry, and in that way strengthened the foundations of the modern economy.

Valkeakoski and many similar communities represent the first stage of the transition from the agricultural to the industrial setting. They have developed in response to a situation which now hardly exists in Western Europe. But the planners of the town of Tapiola, six miles from Helsinki, have looked farther ahead than most of their peers in the West. Tapiola represents the rejection of the urban and industrial setting of Western Europe and the U.S.A., the reaction against living in cities as we know them. 'Present-day urban milieux, with their terrorizing traffic, persistent nervous tension, exhaust gases, soot and dust, are unfit for human life from all points of view.' This dictum of Heikki von Hertzen, the president and planning director of the Housing Foundation, which built Tapiola, is not particularly original or exceptional. But while city-dwellers all over the world regularly make similar statements, von Hertzen and his colleagues are among the few with the energy and the opportunities to do more than complain.

The idea of building Tapiola originated with the Finnish Family

Welfare League, with the aim of providing a proper setting for family life and leisure. Together with five other voluntary associations and trade-union organizations, they formed the Housing Foundation in 1951. This Foundation attacked the task with such vigour that by 1965 it had built a town for 16,000 people, of which the Professor of Urban Development at the University of California said: 'Tapiola is known all over the world as the most modern and beautiful new town built anywhere.'

Several different elements have combined to provoke the superlatives of this reputation. First and foremost, nature has provided Tapiola with a site of exceptional beauty, and the planners have jealously guarded it. To the south and east lies the Gulf of Finland with its pattern of islands, and to the north and west the forests from which Tapiola, 'the dwelling of the forest god', takes its name. The planners' fierce determination to preserve this setting arises in part, one surmises, from familiarity with some of the desolate and regimented new towns elsewhere in Scandinavia, where almost every blade of green has been banished from once-beautiful sites. In Tapiola nature dominates both town plan and architecture; it was insisted that streets and buildings should conform to the contours of the landscape, and that man-made plans should yield to the woodland. The planning director is still almost obsessional on this point. 'Once I was beaten,' he says. 'Early one morning at six o'clock, a beautiful little birch wood was cut down without my knowledge and against my clear orders. At that time the technicians won, but it was the last time that nature and man were forced to give way to technics.'

The sense that the natural setting has been preserved is accentuated by the absence of motor roads. All through-traffic skirts the town, and within it most of the roads are narrow and wooded, with houses or flats set well back among the trees, almost as near to ski-tracks and forest walks as they are to the macadamized road. There are, of course, exclusive residential districts elsewhere in the world with these same fortunate characteristics. But Tapiola is neither exclusive nor a suburb; it is a community of people from many walks of life, and this is the second major element in its success. It is only six miles and fifteen minutes by bus along a motorway from Helsinki, where many of its inhabitants work; it would have been easy to make it a beautiful dormitory, and oblige them to seek their amusements in the capital. But this was what the planners were determined to avoid, and they have succeeded so well that it is the people of Helsinki who go out to Tapiola to eat in the twelfth- and thirteenth-storey restaurants, with their excellent food and wide views over the archipelago. Tapiola's town centre includes, as well as offices and shops, a theatre, a concert hall, an art gallery, a municipal library, a church, a hotel, schools, a swimming bath and a public health centre. It can thus offer those who live in the town everything they need. Ultimately it is planned to provide work in Tapiola for between five and six thousand people; about two-thirds will work in the professions and the service trades, and about one-third in light and small-scale industries, situated in zones separated from the residential areas by green belts. Each of Tapiola's three neighbourhood units is also surrounded by green, and each is self-contained to the extent that it has its own essential foodshops. One of the basic planning principles was that no dwelling should be more than 250 yards from a foodshop.

Tapiola is also a community in the sense that its residents constitute a cross-section of the population, though not an average sample. Fifty-five per cent are 'white-collar workers' and the rest 'blue-collar workers'; their occupations include those of university professor and unskilled labourer. All the residents, however, live in the same environment and in housing of the same standard – the highest that could be reached. There was never any question of building large and expensive houses in one area and small cheap ones in another; all sizes and types of dwelling are to be found everywhere in the town. Size is the only thing that is determined by what the owner can afford. Over ninety per cent of houses and flats are owned, as the Housing Foundation is convinced of the social value of owner-occupation, and has found that even the lowest-paid workers are anxious to buy their homes with the help of state and other loans available for the purpose. This insistence on a uniformly high standard everywhere, and the encouragement to maintain it which is given by ownership, are further elements which distinguish Tapiola from many new towns in other countries.

Lastly, though perhaps most significantly, the distinction of Tapiola's architecture matches both the splendid conception of the planners and the beauty of the setting. The initial principle was that architecture must be subservient to nature, but Tapiola's architects have created a partnership between the buildings and their surroundings in which each nourishes the other. This is a relatively new achievement in Finland, and one largely inspired by Aalto and the generation of architects that has come to the fore since the war.

The pre-war architects often had difficulty in relating their buildings to the landscape, and a harmony similar to Tapiola's was only occasionally reached. Here, it has been reached without any attempt at uniformity or rigid overall planning. Several architects were given a more or less free hand to design limited areas, and their freedom to experiment gave Tapiola the name of 'the architects' playground'; but it resulted neither in flamboyant nor eccentric design, nor in disturbing clashes of style.

The design for the town centre was put up to competition, which was won by the distinguished architect Aarne Ervi. The whole plan is one of great spaciousness and brings nature right to the doorsteps of offices and shops. An old gravel pit has been turned into an ornamental lake, round which public buildings are set. Narrow green belts run between the centre and the neighbourhood units, and in the traffic-free centre itself, trees thrive and flowers bloom in masses. The types of dwellings range from detached houses for single families, with the maximum of five rooms, plus kitchen and bathroom, allowed by law, to a few tower blocks of flats. This variety gives Tapiola a welcome individuality and saves its inhabitants from the depression that comes of having been sacrificed to equality and tidy planning. There are none of the long rows of identical houses or uniform blocks so dear to developers elsewhere. There may be three or four similar blocks in one group; but within close sight there are also three or four short terraces of two-storey houses. The predominating type of housing is a three- or four-storey block without a lift, where flats of two, three or four rooms, plus kitchen and bathroom, are intended for families. The detached and terrace houses are naturally also for families. The high tower blocks consist mainly of one- or two-room flats, and are intended for couples without children or single people. All share the same high standard of interior equipment; and heating, hot water and electricity for the entire town come from a remote heating plant on the outskirts.

All the houses have their own gardens, and small plots can be rented by flat-dwellers. There are only a few garages attached to the houses, but several centrally-heated garages are provided in each neighbourhood unit; there are automatic laundries, saunas and clubrooms for the use of residents; and among the most valuable of amenities for the practical Finns are the 'hobby rooms' which give adults as well as young people space and facilities for activities such as carpentry, which are ill-suited to small flats.

Are these two towns, Valkeakoski and Tapiola, the prototypes, as it were, of future urban development in Finland? There are already many small industrial towns similar to Valkeakoski, and the incidence of civic pride in Finland suggests that the demand for a beautiful setting for working and living will become more and more general. It could, nevertheless, happen that some industrialists become hypnotized by the mere notion of size (a quality to which the Finns are already susceptible), and insist on the economic advantages of concentration at certain points as opposed to dispersal over a wide area. On the other hand, the international recognition given to Tapiola has strengthened the case of Heikki von Hertzen and the Housing Foundation. Already it has undertaken comparable projects elsewhere in Finland, with a firm determination to prevent the emergence of any more towns built on the pre-1950 pattern. von Hertzen said in 1965: 'Tapiola is not an isolated development. From it is evolving a national urban policy that will guide this traditionally rural nation of farmers, woodsmen and fishermen to the day, twenty-five years from now, when nine out of ten of us will be living in towns and cities.'

CHAPTER FIFTEEN

Designing for the World

When the Milan Triennale – which has been called the Olympic Games of design – was held in 1951, Finland won no less than six Grands Prix, seven gold medals and eight silver medals. The exhibits which won these prizes had a vitality and an originality which gave a new look to post-war design. Yet they were the products of Finland's lean years, when the country was preoccupied with the problems of making reparations deliveries to the Soviet Union and of rehousing her own citizens, and when beautiful things might have seemed a foolish extravagance. But there had been an artistic explosion in Finland. The isolation of the years of war and recovery had driven the Finns back to the sources of inspiration of their own land; the changed life of the post-war years and the need for simpler and more practical things had led to a massive redesigning of everyday objects; and the doubts of the outside world provoked the desire to assert the country's independence and indentity. The same need had been felt at the end of the nineteenth century, when the music of Sibelius had reminded the rest of Europe of Finland's struggle for existence. Now it was the glass and ceramics, hand-woven textiles and *ryiji* rugs, of which other countries knew little, that spoke for Finland abroad. Inside Finland, these years marked both an artistic peak and the beginning of the marriage of mass production and great design which was to lead eventually to the export all over the world of glass, china, furniture, textiles, clothes and jewellery marked 'Made in Finland'. In two subsequent Triennali, Finns won twenty-five per cent of the Grands Prix, and their average between 1951 and 1964 was about one-fifth of the total awarded. During that time Finland became a leader in design in a world that was left to wonder how a country which it had known as small, remote and even poor could reach such a position.

In Finland design is rooted in daily life, in history and in nature, and has at no time been severed from these roots. But it has evolved

PLATE IX. *Vuoksenniska Church, near Imatra, designed by Alvar Aalto* (1958)

PLATE X (left). *Finnish factories are often set in the midst of water and woodland.*
PLATE XI (above). *One of the great power stations of northern Finland, designed by Aarne Ervi (1949).*

PLATE XII (above). *One of the many houses in Valkeakoski built and owned by industrial workers, who also take great pride in their gardens.*
PLATE XIII (right). *A view of Tapiola town centre, and, beyond it, blocks of flats and a factory.*

PLATE XIV (above). *Top, the sculptor Väinö Aaltonen with his marble bust of Sibelius. Bottom, 'A la Russe', sculpture in welded metal by Eila Hiltunen.*
PLATE XV (right). *Top, damask table mats by Dora Jung. Bottom left, double decanter designed by Kaj Franck. Bottom right, the highly successful multi-purpose 'Kilta' oven-proof ware, also by Kaj Franck.*

and adapted itself to new circumstances and rarely been tempted to pay false homage to the past by returning to its precise forms. In the old days the poverty and remoteness of the country, and the isolation of so many of its inhabitants from shops and markets, forced the country-dwellers to provide for their own daily needs. From the Middle Ages the Finnish countryman grew accustomed to seeking in the forest all the material he needed for the implements of life and work. Wood was a simple and supple medium; it was rewarding to the novice, and the ease with which it could be fashioned into objects both useful and decorative gave the ordinary Finn, as well as the craftsman, a feeling of mastery over his material and confidence in the skill of his own hands. He was perhaps a natural whittler. Today it is still easy to picture him sitting in winter on the bench in his *tupa*, talking in summer with his cronies on the heath, knife and wood in his hands, and all the while working on something simple and beautiful. For even in their days of famine and poverty, the Finns were never obsessed by utility but easily gave way to the occasional extravagance or the charming fantasy which still appear today.

The countryman combined his own natural sense of form and line with ideas which were for the most part native and instinctive, and which he pursued without any sense of inferiority. There were no wealthy noblemen, no pretentious burghers for him to ape: the small manor-houses and the parsonages merely set a quiet standard which was within his own reach. While he worked in wood, the womenfolk spun and wove, with an eye for colour and design as instinctive as his own eye for form. By the time industry came to Finland these country crafts were too deeply rooted and widely enjoyed to be destroyed by the machine; and before it could invade the market the Finns had built up their defences against mass-production. They continued to defend their crafts until the early 1950s. Then hand and machine came to terms: industry took in some of the foremost designers, who for their part willingly agreed to design for the mass market.

Arts and crafts had long before acquired the dominating position they now hold in Finland. In 1875 the Finnish Society of Crafts and Design was founded; it was only the second organization of its kind in the world. (The corresponding Swedish society had been founded some thirty years earlier.) Its purpose was to further the development

PLATE XVI. *Top, Birger Kaipiainen's fanciful bird, made from multi-coloured ceramic beads. Bottom, 'Tiara', Nanny Still's cut crystal bowls.*

of Finnish design and to train artist-craftsmen in its school. But like so many of the organizations of that time, it also had the oblique political object of asserting the national identity through design, and perhaps of providing undercover opportunities for the discussion of nationalist aspirations. Shortly after, in 1879, the Friends of Finnish Handicrafts was formed to maintain the traditions of handwork – principally weaving, embroidery and rug-making. Its members were, however, determined to avoid the conservatism of tradition. They sought out the old designs of the different provinces, but simplified and modernized them and adapted them to twentieth-century purposes.

In the years after independence the Finns gradually began to break new ground. Aalto made his revolutionary bent plywood furniture, and the fact that his designs of the 'thirties are still being produced today is proof of their enduring quality. New designers of ceramics and glass came to the fore, and handwoven textiles developed and responded to modern trends. But it was after the war that the first partnership between design and industry began to bear fruit, and it was this partnership which contributed so much to Finland's success in the 1951 Triennale. Wärtsilä-Arabia, one of the largest china manufacturers in Europe, and the Wärtsilä-Nötsjö, Karhula-Iittala and Riihimäki glassworks had all taken groups of artist-designers into their employ; they were not necessarily to design for mass production, but were to be left free, in studios specially provided for them, to experiment and create whatever they wished, whether useful, simple or extravagant. They were not expected to earn their salaries in hard figures that would appear in the firms' books and to justify their employment, as it were. Both Arabia and the glass works were sufficiently realistic to know how much prestige would accrue to them as a result of this open-handed gesture to creative design; but they can hardly have hoped that they would reap these rewards as soon as 1951, when their designers won so many prizes at the IXth Triennale, as they did in those that followed.

By this time most of the distinctive characteristics of Finnish design had become clearly defined, and have remained so ever since. On the one hand, practicality and fitness for purpose are combined with beauty of form and colour – all part of the inheritance of the centuries. On the other a zest for experiment and an extravagant dedication to beauty for its own sake set Finnish design apart from the elegant yet sober work of the Swedes. The Finns probably owe their more extravagant gestures to the eastern influences which came to them by way of St Petersburg in the nineteenth century, and which today still give a byzantine look to some of their more fanciful creations. This eastern strain also helps to save them from lapses into impeccable good taste; though the Finns are, in any case, too full-blooded a people for their arts to suffer from a genteel anaemia. And always dominating the beautiful, the useful, the simple and the extravagant is the inspiration of the natural world, of its colours and shapes and forms.

In his notebooks Leonardo da Vinci counselled the painter to study 'the embers of the fire, or clouds, or mud, or other similar objects from which you will find most admirable ideas . . . because from a confusion of shapes the spirit is quickened to new inventions'. Many Finnish designers seem to have known instinctively the power of the confusion of shapes to stimulate new inventions, and they are fortunate that the shapes and patterns of their landscape change so constantly that the eye is quickened by their confusion and not staled or sated by their permanence. When the ice on the sea and the lakes breaks up in spring into thousands of different shapes, reflecting a thousand minute variations of light and colour, it provides the pattern for beautiful and unusual pieces of decorative glass. The bare birch branches thrown against the white sky of winter take on a more formal outline in woven damask or printed cotton. The sudden and dramatic colours of nature reappear in textiles, and in combinations which might be thought impossible by those who had not seen for themselves what the Finnish landscape could devise.

The cast of mind of the designers themselves adds to the individuality of their work. They have a versatility which enables them to work in several different media and styles, with a resulting constant process of cross-fertilization. The furniture of Alvar Aalto, architect and town-planner, is known everywhere; less known outside Finland are his designs for glass, textiles and lighting fitments. The sculptor Wäinö Aaltonen ranged from civic statuary to special pieces of silver and glass. This versatility has been steadily developed in the post-war years. Tapio Wirkkala, one of the foremost contemporary designers, works in glass and wood, designs cutlery and lighting fitments, and plans entire exhibitions. His wife, Rut Bryk, is equally at home designing fanciful and highly individual ceramic wall decorations, or simple patterns for machine-woven cottons. Timo Sarpaneva has worked as a graphic artist and in textiles; more recently he has become known for his purely decorative glass of great originality and his cast-iron casserole pans which are both elegant and practical – though the latter only if the cook has the muscle power in her arms which is needed to lift them. Kaj Franck, less spectacular than Wirkkala and Sarpaneva, has to his credit a wide range of glass and china which is both functional and beautiful. Some of his designs have been so often repeated and so widely sold all over the world that they have become almost universal and timeless.

But all their gifts of design would not have been sufficient to give the Finns their world-wide reputation had not two opposing currents converged in mid-twentieth century. The Finnish, and indeed the whole Scandinavian tradition, was one of poverty, simplicity and fitness for purpose. It had never served either aristocracy or wealth. It was untouched by the gorgeousness of the Renaissance or the vulgarity of the nineteenth century. During the twentieth century it shed some of the characteristics of poverty, but retained its simplicity. Meanwhile, in the West, with its decorative tradition stemming from the Renaissance, the current was gradually moving away from the elaborate and the superfluous and in the direction of simpler forms, amenable to mass production and in tune with a simpler mode of living. It found them in the design of Finland and of the other Scandinavian countries, and learnt that the practical and the beautiful need not exclude each other.

In Finland, happily, there were people who were determined that this great moment of opportunity for Finnish designers should not be lost, that design should be given a firmer and broader base both for its own sake and for the sake of exports. In the early 'fifties economists regarded design exports indulgently as a form of window-dressing, unlikely to bring in any worthwhile amounts of foreign currency. But in the mid-'sixties, these 'new exports' accounted for eight per cent of the total. This was partly due to the technical re-structuring of the furniture, textile and leather industries, but it would never have been possible without the enormous efforts of a handful of people convinced of the potentialities of Finnish design. Foremost among them was Olof Gummerus, the director of the Society of Crafts and Design. His deep understanding of the whole field of design ranged from the shape of a teapot spout to the economics of export, from sales and publicity methods to the philosophy of art, and made him the guiding spirit of a brilliant group of new and established designers. He and the artists with whom he worked aimed to make design serve the whole of industry and to persuade the Finnish consumer to recognize and demand the best. This needed a more vigorous attack than the outside world has often thought. The distinction and modernity of hand-made and artist-designed products was counterweighted by the old-fashioned ugliness of many factory-produced goods. Machine-made textiles, in particular, lagged behind some of the cheapest of Western fabrics. Some manufacturers willingly took designers on to their staffs, and the result was revolutionary; others bowed only after considerable persuasion and pressure. Even those in the van had their blind spots; a design that was rejected and shelved for several years in one of the pioneer firms became a repeated best-seller all over the world when at last it was given a trial.

At the same time, Finnish consumers received some intensive education and indoctrination; they could have anything they wanted as long as it was the best. Their national pride was stimulated by successes abroad, and they responded quickly by swinging to one of their characteristic extremes. The whole country became so design-conscious that almost every designer was elevated to a local Parnassus, and the cult of the signed piece was carried to the point where even decorative candles carried the designer's name. The English word 'design' was adopted everywhere as part of the signature, and now even the small girl who pastes up her own Christmas cards is likely to print 'Design Helena' in one corner. Beautiful and expensive glass appeared in the small shops in the backwoods. 'Yes, this is Kaj Franck's latest,' the owner of the village store would pontificate as she stretched out a hand through her stocks of weedkiller and long woollen underpants to pick up a vase. 'But in *my* opinion his new designs are not the equal of last year's.' One could only applaud the salesmanship that had persuaded her to stock art glass, and the knowledge she proudly displayed of her merchandise.

In another respect the Finns were a naturally receptive public. Throughout the North the love of the home is very marked, and the relative absence of the clubs, cafés and pubs of other countries makes the home the centre of social life. Thus the general interest in domestic design is correspondingly greater than in, for instance, the Mediterranean countries. Add the native gift for extravagance, and it is not difficult to credit the statement that the Finnish housewife owns, on an average, fifty coffee cups. She also takes an unusual interest in table-setting, experimenting endlessly with different arrangements and combinations of colour, china, table linen, flowers and candles. So glass, china and linen are not, for the Finns, necessities to be replaced when broken or worn, but objects to be collected for the pleasure they give, and the opportunities of creative expression they provide for their owner.

In the great period of expansion of design in the twenty years or so after the war, wave succeeded wave, and different media seemed outstanding at different times. Looking back to both the near and the distant past, textiles, in their broadest sense, emerge as the most distinctively Finnish achievement and the one in which Finland excels. The roots of this excellence go back hundreds of years to the days when most Finnish housewives not only spun their yarns and wove their fabrics, but also made the knotted wool rugs called *ryijy* in Finnish and *rya* in Swedish. *Ryijy* rugs were brought to Scandinavia from Morocco and Spain by the Vikings, and up to the fifteenth century they were made in Norway and Sweden as well as in Finland. But it is only in Finland that they have been maintained and developed as an art form, which has subsequently been taken up by other countries. The early *ryijy* rugs were utilitarian and intended to cover floors and beds, and to line sleighs. But soon the decorative crept in, and the Finns found a new use for their *ryijy* rugs – as wall hangings. While the barons of richer nations commissioned magnificent tapestries to adorn their halls, the Finns made their own rugs to clothe the bare walls of both castle and farmhouse. As the *ryijy* grew in beauty it acquired greater value and significance; it was often part of a dowry, and was handed down from mother to daughter. Still today most Finnish churches have a wedding *ryijy*, which is used only for the bridal couple to stand on during the ceremony.

There were many different types of *ryijy* rugs, with the traditions of different provinces behind them. Some depicted people, animals, scenes; others were designed simply, formally and geometrically;

some, more complicated, showed a strong oriental influence. All were alike in their lovely colourings, on which no present-day craftsman has been able to improve. The home-made vegetable dyes yielded soft blues, greens, yellows and delicate and subtle rose; the Finnish sheep yielded a silky fleece more apt for *ryijy* than any imported wools. The rich traditions of these rugs were not allowed to die before modern artist-craftsmen had begun to specialize in the designing of *ryijy* and hand-woven materials, developing old patterns and making bold and unexpected innovations. Modern *ryijy* have an intoxicating *élan*, an abstraction and a degree of fantasy difficult to associate with rugs. Many of them, particularly those by Kirsti Ilvessalo, can be described only as an explosion of form and colour. Among other designers who have made a great contribution to the development of the *ryijy* are Uhra Simberg-Ehrström and Eva Brummer. The artist-designed hand-made rugs, with their linen warp and woollen weft, and tufts up to two and a half inches long, are extremely highly priced. But inexpensive and less glowing machine-made versions are on sale in many countries; and it is whispered that some of the machine-made copies available in Finland have been manufactured in Britain.

At the farthest remove from the traditional *ryijy* rugs are the experimental and ultra-modern textiles designed by the dynamic Marjatta Metsovaara. She produces an original and colourful range of conventional fabrics; but she has gone far beyond the conventional in materials for screens, room dividers, wall coverings and table mats. Copper and linen threads, coarsely woven, make screens through which light can filter, copper and raffia make a woven wall covering, and plastic cord table mats. Some of the most beautiful of these fabrics have been designed for the plain glass windows of modern churches, where they are stretched tightly across the panes to decorate the glass rather than form a curtain.

Damasks, whether hand- or machine-woven, are outstanding among the more elaborate of conventional textiles, and here the most distinguished designer is Dora Jung, who has developed a number of unique techniques of her own. She is known particularly for her damask church tapestries and altar cloths, entirely in the modern manner and in keeping with the powerful simplicity of the new Finnish churches. Dora Jung has also done a number of beautiful designs for machine-made table linen. At the other end of the scale, though equally remarkable in their own way, are the home-made table-cloths to be seen in many remote farmhouses. These, the products of winter evenings and a loom shared with other housewives in the neighbourhood, are often more pleasing to the eye than some of their expensive machine-made counterparts in countries where textile arts are less highly regarded.

To the fabrics, cottons in particular, intended for ordinary daily use, artists have brought great originality of colour combinations, whether in simple woven checks and stripes or in bold and dramatic prints. How far these heady colours and patterns serve to brighten everyday life can be judged from the fact that they are used in a number of factories for female workers' overalls; they appear, more startlingly, in the endless corridors of the ministries, where trolleys are pushed round and coffee dispensed by young women dressed in the most exotic of print overalls. The Ministry for Foreign Affairs has been enlivened by an overall and matching headscarf in a futuristic black design on a brilliant emerald ground, which may either stimulate or disturb the perusal of files.

The Finns' other traditional craft, furniture, has not perhaps flowered in the modern world as fully as their textiles, nor as a land of forests deserves. There is not sufficient variety of local wood to stimulate invention; birch is the only cabinet-maker's wood available in large quantities, and pine, though now fairly widely used, does not lend itself to great originality of treatment. What the Finns have done has been good, but since Aalto produced his new designs in the 'thirties there has been little outstanding development. Some authorities say that designers are inhibited by the lasting excellence of Aalto's furniture, and because they cannot produce anything better or more original, turn their backs completely on furniture-designing. This is the general dilemma of designers in Finland. In so small a country they dare not appear to imitate each other, and sometimes have to strive too hard after novelty. Certainly wooden furniture has attracted only a few of Finland's designers, who are otherwise anxious to try their hands in several media. On the other hand, men like Ilmari Tapiovaara, Olli Mannermaa, Yrjö Kukkapuro and Antti Nurmesniemi have experimented fruitfully with furniture, often of metal and fabric, for public buildings, hotels, hospitals, theatres, schools, offices and ships. In this hitherto neglected field they have made enormous strides and moved farther ahead, in both appearance and suitability for purpose, than designers in most other European countries. The natural gift for the handling of wood itself is best expressed today on a smaller scale, and most notably in the original jewellery, buttons, candlesticks and small decorative objects made from natural and coloured wood by Kaija Aarikka.

In glass and ceramics the two contrasting elements of northern simplicity and practicality and eastern extravagance are particularly evident. Most of the outstanding designers have created ranges of simple and elegant table glass and china, often departing from conventional shapes but always keeping the practical purpose in view. But in the decorative they roam in total freedom, far from accepted shapes and forms, and into a borderland between applied and pure art. Often an elemental impulse produces a massive, almost primeval form, as in the heavy glass pieces named 'Iceblocks', or in the roughly sculptured bowls made by a new technique of glass-blowing, which gives them a knobbly surface and makes them refract the light in innumerable different ways. A characteristic of much of Finnish glass, whether it takes the form of a small bird or of a massive abstract block, is that it calls out to be handled, as if its designer had somehow communicated to it some of his own powerful feeling for his material. Sibelius once said of the great boulders which strew the landscape and seascape of Finland: 'When we see these granite rocks, we know why we are able to treat the orchestra as we do.' These boulders must also be the source of power of the glass designer, and one of the reasons why he can handle his material with such vigour and audacity.

Some ceramic artists have also expressed themselves in this rough and rugged style, but their imagination has more often led them eastwards to the byzantine. Rut Bryk's pictorial ceramic wall plaques, with their vitality and colour, suggest this inspiration. It is more evident still in the work of Birger Kaipiainen, whose enormous and colourful birds, made of small ceramic beads, each a work of art in itself, won him a Grand Prix at the 1960 Triennale.

The Finns came later than the Danes and the Swedes to modern jewellery, although they had a tradition of craftsmanship handed down from their forebears who had worked with the great Russian jewellers of St Petersburg. Their modern jewellery, however, owes nothing to elaborate eastern influences, but is simple, bold and without pretence. Jewellers, among whom Börje Rajalin and Björn Weckström are outstanding, use silver almost exclusively, combining it with native semi-precious stones such as Lapland garnets, tourmaline or jasper, or the distinctive black quartz. In table silver the Finns had almost no traditions behind them, but, led by Bertel Gardberg, they have produced many designs in silver and stainless steel which can easily stand comparisons with the work of silversmiths in the other Scandinavian countries with a longer tradition.

Early in the 'sixties the Finns broke into fashion design on an international scale – the most surprising development of all to those who had known their former dreary clothes and solid footwear. The success of their simple clothes derives chiefly from the imaginative use of the exuberant fabrics of their textile designers, and they have wisely concentrated on informal and leisure wear. Their boots have had a sensational success with the Paris couture houses, for they combine chic and dash with the resistance essential in Finland to the worst of winter weather.

How much further, one wonders, can the energetic Finnish designers go, as they invade field after field? The Finns themselves see no limit to their opportunities. Already many of their offices are furnished as well and as colourfully as their homes; they hold that design must extend eventually to the factory floor, that workers will come to expect machinery that is easy on the eye as well as functionally sound. They believe that Finnish machinery will be able to compete better in world markets if excellence of design is added to technical quality.

Closer at hand, there are still many pieces of household equipment to be redesigned. The Finns have already been most successful in reshaping some of the objects in daily use. Several designers have made their own new versions of the traditional copper coffee kettle, a permanent resident on the hob of Finnish farmhouses. Ordinary kitchen tools have been restyled with considerable elegance, and some gorgeous and colourful artist-designed shelf paper has made the conventional small checks and flower patterns look sadly ordinary.

The restyling of old and familiar objects is only a minor part of Finnish design, but it is perhaps the key to the attitude and success of the designers. They are able to blend nostalgia for the past with appetite for innovation in such a way that the best of the past is neither rejected nor slavishly copied. What was good yesterday can be preserved and improved today, to be enjoyed alongside new fantasies and new inventions. But there is an inevitable end to ideas drawn from natural and native sources, and at times one wonders how long they can continue to inspire the Finns. The development of design since the 'thirties has shown a certain repetitive pattern. New, original, often startling trends have appeared in one medium, as, for instance, in furniture in the 'thirties and in glass in the late 'forties and early 'fifties. Then there has been a period of consolidation, in which beautiful work has continued to be done, but which has come dangerously close to stagnation. During that period the designers who gave the original impetus have moved on to another medium, which has then come to the fore. As long as this cycle can be kept in revolution, always providing restless designers with stimulus and change, design will continue to prosper. But it is perhaps too much to hope that the vigour and momentum of the first two post-war decades can be maintained indefinitely.

CHAPTER SIXTEEN

Industry Today

Until 1939 the Finnish economy was constructed in a peculiarly one-legged and idiosyncratic way. There was only one large-scale industry – woodworking. It used exclusively domestic raw materials, but depended almost entirely on the export market. Most of the other pre-war industries, which were on a smaller scale, supplied the home market with goods which were manufactured from imported raw materials. The Finns believed that their only native raw materials were timber, the copper from a single large mine, and the nickel deposits near Petsamo, which they were to lose to the Soviet Union in 1940. War and the reparations demanded by the U.S.S.R. completely changed the character of the Finnish economy. They created a large metal and engineering industry where only a very small one had previously existed, and stimulated the search for other minerals within Finnish borders. Today, in spite of the continuing dominance of the forest industries, the economy rests firmly on two legs, one wooden and one metal. The metal leg may be shorter than the wooden one and it may be more difficult to manage, but it has removed the dangerous lopsidedness of the pre-war years. In addition, further diversity has been provided by other, though smaller, industries which have developed fast since 1952.

The share of wood and wood products in total production and exports has been reduced by these younger industries. But the forest industries, which had their birth in the manufacture of tar centuries ago and are now responsible for seventy per cent of all exports, have shaped Finland's economic life and must continue to do so. They have made Finland into a modern country, with an important contribution to make to the modern world in products ranging from matches to yachts, spools to prefabricated wooden houses, paper handkerchiefs to newsprint, as well as the numerous chemical by-products of the manufacture of pulp and paper. Beyond all this, they have influenced the whole national frame of mind and the scale of economic thought. The woodworking industries were geared to the export markets from the outset, and have given Finland links with distant parts of the world and the habit of looking outwards. The development of the paper and pulp industries gave larger dimensions to economic and industrial thinking generally. Pulp and paper are not products which can be made, in the beginning, in small quantities in a shed; they can be produced only on a large scale. Fortunately Finland had, among her small population, men bold enough to tackle and succeed in enterprises of world-wide scope. So, when the time came to build up the heavy engineering industry, there were other men ready to think in world-wide terms, and able to take in their stride undertakings such as the building in Latin America of a paper mill complete with all the necessary machinery. The paper industry cannot survive without constant modernization of processes and techniques, and this, in its turn, has stimulated a more up-to-date approach to industry in general. The reverse side of this wide and lively outlook is sometimes seen in the difficulty the Finns have in handling smaller transactions and in dealing with more detailed paperwork. Occasionally one suspects that few things are too big to ask of the Finnish industrial world, but a large number of things are too small. Challenge seems essential to its successful functioning.

The forest industries began to take on their more modern shape in the nineteenth century, when the export of raw timber developed on a sizable scale. Their oldest branch is the sawmill industry which still contributes about one-fifth of all forest exports. This century, however, has seen the rapid development of the wood-processing industries, whose main products are mechanical and chemical pulp, newsprint and other paper, kraftpaper, board and plywood. The loss of Karelia, and with it a significant proportion both of the best forest land and of the paper industry's means of production, was a severe setback, but the capacity of the paper and pulp industries was nevertheless enormously increased in the next two decades. By the mid-'sixties Finland had become the second largest exporter of newsprint in the world and one of the leading exporters of pulp, sawn timber and birch plywood. Today she boasts the largest paper mill in Europe, and the majority of her mills are bigger than those in Sweden and comparable in size to those of Canada and the U.S.A. All are highly automated, and in some mills the process of paper-making is controlled and corrected by computers.

Given these advanced production techniques and the world appetite for paper, Finland's economic future would appear assured, were it not for the limitations on the supply of raw material. The need to import raw timber may prevent the paper industry from expanding beyond a certain point in the next few years, although the energetic forest improvement programme now in hand will ensure better supplies at a later stage. However, even when some restriction of expansion is allowed for, the forest industries are bound to remain the main source of Finland's income and prosperity in the foreseeable future.

From the present standpoint of the economy as a whole, the forest industries have a defect which arises out of their modern and automated virtues: their manpower needs are very limited, and they cannot now absorb more than a small proportion of the labour which is being freed by the mechanization of agriculture. Thus the newer engineering industries have the added value that they provide employment in one of the last countries in Europe with a labour surplus, (although the possession of a reservoir of manpower has been an asset, as expansion has not been held up by labour shortages). For the Finns, no two industries could present sharper contrast than wood-processing and engineering. The one is a natural development of a pattern of life among forests and lakes, more easily related to the daily round than most of the great industries of the world. The other is an artificial importation, unrelated in the first place either to natural resources or natural inclinations. Before the war Finland was primarily an importer of machinery and capital equipment. The Soviet reparations demands turned her, in a single decade, into an exporter of those goods, able to compete on equal terms technically with countries with far longer tradition, and made the engineering industry the largest employer in the country.

The way the metal and engineering industries were built up during what one of its leaders has called 'the post-war purgatory' has already been described. After the reparations deliveries were completed, the Finns had to make up their minds what to do with the industry they had created. Although there was an enormous pent-up domestic demand to be satisfied, it clearly had to remain principally an export industry. The problem was how to compete with countries of longer experience and greater resources. They decided to specialize in the heavy equipment most closely related to their own needs and experience: that meant, in particular, icebreakers and paper-making machines. They did this with remarkable success. Finnish yards have turned out the biggest diesel-engined icebreakers constructed anywhere in the world, and exported them to the Soviet Union, Sweden and Western Germany. In addition, they have concentrated on other smaller vessels, since really large keels cannot be laid in the shallow Finnish coastal waters, and the skerry-pointed archipelagos make navigation difficult for large ships. Cable-laying vessels, car ferries and passenger ships up to 7,000 tons have been completed for both the home and export markets. Paper-making machines now account for three-quarters of total machine exports. A Finnish firm delivered in 1966 the largest kraftliner machine ever imported into the U.S.A.; and it is calculated about twelve per cent of the world's paper-making machines are now made in Finland. Whole factory complexes, complete with machinery have been delivered in Latin America and Turkey, and engineers from Finnish firms have gone to set them up.

The many other products of the metal and engineering industries include excavating machinery, locomotives, trains, aircraft, tractors and all the lighter equipment needed in agriculture and forestry at home. They also include zip fasteners for France, aluminium boats for Ghana and Greenland, and sporting rifles for the U.S.A., where every third imported rifle comes from Finland. On the constructional side, Finnish engineers have built hydro-electric plants and dams as far away as Iraq.

Impressive as are the achievements of this young industry, it is still faced with certain export problems. About half of all metal and engineering exports go to the U.S.S.R. and other Eastern European countries. The Finns learnt from the reparations programme exactly what the Soviet Union required, and the Soviet Union learnt to respect Finnish workmanship. So it is natural that this high, though decreasing, proportion of output should go eastwards. However, the amount that can be exported to Russia depends on the amount Finland is able to buy in return from the Soviet Union. Payment is made in inconvertible roubles, and the Finns have some difficulty in spending them to good advantage. On the other hand the Russian market has provided a basis for development, and the Finns hope that it will enable them, as the industry expands, to lower their prices and compete better in Western markets. By 1965 nearly forty per cent of metal products were going to Western Europe, principally to the E.F.T.A. group.

A competitive and successful metal and engineering industry presupposes an adequate supply of basic metals, and here the Finns have been more fortunate than they dreamt in the immediate post-war years. The mineral supply picture has been radically changed by an intensive prospecting drive, which began in the early 'fifties with magnetic flights at a height of 500 feet. Then, in 1954, Finland was one of the first countries to undertake electro-magnetic flights at a height of 1,200 feet. More recently the popular hero of mineral prospecting has become a handsome Alsatian dog which, after two years' training, learnt to detect sulphide-bearing rock beneath eight or nine inches of soil. It cannot distinguish between copper and iron ore, but if it begins to scratch and scrabble there is generally rock worth investigating in the vicinity. In spite of the blaze of TV and press publicity which has surrounded this dog, geologists take its achievements seriously. It cannot work without a man, but a man-plus-dog team is far more successful than a man alone. So the pioneer Alsatian is now both prospecting and training other dogs, and it probably earns every mark of the rumoured high salary which it receives from the State.

As well as copper, Finland now mines zinc, nickel, lead, iron, wolfram, vanadium, pyrites, chromium, selenium, cobalt and titanium. Production of copper, zinc and nickel is far in excess of domestic needs, and Finland has become the world's largest producer of vanadium, which is used in steel manufacture. But local supplies of lead are insufficient, and resources of iron, the most important raw material of the engineering industries, fall far short of requirements, so that the big new steel mills have to rely heavily on imports. However, in spite of this relative domestic lack of iron ore, the metal supply situation has changed sufficiently since the war to reorientate a large section of the economy. Before the war the state-owned mining and metal-working company, Outokumpu Oy, operated only one mine in Northern Karelia, which was the second largest copper mine in Europe. Now it has seven mines in different parts of the country, yielding zinc, lead, nickel, wolfram and pyrites, and is able to export half its production. The total Finnish mining output has increased more than tenfold since 1938.

Other industries have mushroomed since 1952. The big hydro-electric schemes which now supply power for the northern half of the country have made possible the development of industry in an area where it was lacking; and together with the programme of railway electrification, they have called into existence an expanding electro-technical industry. Further demands will be put on this relatively young industry by the plans now in hand to build a group of nuclear power stations in the south, where all other sources of power have now been tapped. The building industry has grown particularly fast and at times has employed a higher percentage of all workers than in any other country. The production of the chemical industry, which hardly existed before the war, doubled itself in six years; food-processing is another industry which has done well in foreign markets, particularly in the U.S.S.R.

Really large industrial firms are not numerous in Finland, although the average size is rather bigger than in the other Scandinavian countries, Sweden included. The giants have been made larger by diversification to provide a hedge against economic difficulties. Several of the wood-processing companies also have engineering works; one combines pulp and paper production, textile manufacture and engineering. These, in general, are the companies with sufficient capital to develop and modernize. Capital is one of the commodities in shortest supply in Finland, and much of the post-war industrial progress has been made possible by loans from the World Bank and from countries in Western Europe. Finland has never had substantial money resources, and those which are available have been absorbed by the rapid pace of development.

This shortage of capital is one of the principal reasons for the extent of state ownership in industry, and for the large size of several of the companies controlled by the State. There are more than thirty firms in which the State owns a majority of the shares, but they are, juridically, private enterprises and are administered and taxed as such. These state-owned companies include, not unexpectedly, the Finnish broadcasting organization, Finnish Airlines, and the State Alcohol Monopoly. (The last is a highly profitable enterprise, on which the state finances depend almost as heavily as the habitual drinker on the bottle.) Less expected are the firms which the State has acquired purely as a matter of expediency. The largest woodworking concern in the country, Enso-Gutzeit Oy, was bought in the early days of independence when its Norwegian owner wanted to sell, and the State purchased ninety per cent of the shares rather than let it fall into foreign hands. Outokumpu was bought for the same reason in 1932, when no one in Finland could invest sufficient capital to develop the mines. Valmet, a heavy engineering company, is a fusion of several small armaments firms which the State was obliged to take over at the end of the war when the armistice terms with the Soviet Union put a ceiling on Finnish arms production. Several of the other state companies have been founded since 1952 in response to postwar industrial needs; without them the rate of industrialization could not have been as rapid, as they have supplied the basic needs of industry. They include mining and metal-producing enterprises, a new oil refinery, and the electrical engineering companies created specifically to construct and administer the hydro-electric power plants in northern Finland. All in all, the value of the production of these state-owned or state-controlled enterprises amounts to seventeen per cent of the total for the country; one of them, Enso-Gutzeit, is the largest single exporting firm in Finland.

This state-ownership programme, which has grown gradually since Finland became independent, looks remarkably like socialism through the back door, but has been carried out largely by 'bourgeois' governments, often with the co-operation of private enterprise, whose politics are far removed from socialism. The majority of Finns of all parties are, in fact, anxious that politics should be kept right out of these state companies, which are run in exactly the same way as private firms. 'If any Prime Minister told me how to run my company,' says the managing director of a big state-owned firm, 'I should know exactly where to tell him to go!' A considerable amount of cross-investment also blurs the line of demarcation between state and private enterprise. The National Pension Fund may have, for instance, shares in a big private company which, in its turn, has invested fairly heavily in a state-controlled power company. But the heads of these state-owned firms know that, in small Finland, their performance will be scrutinized all the more closely and judged all the more severely by the tax-paying public because the State has a controlling interest.

The Finnish economy is heavily dependent on exports and highly sensitive to world trade cycles, as also to fluctuations in the growth rates of Finland's major customers. More than a quarter of the national income is earned by the export of goods and services, and industry cannot continue without imports of raw materials and fuel. The public as a whole has an above-average understanding of the need for exports, but it is not alone in enjoying inflation and its natural extravagance increases the demand for imports. However, in spite of set-backs and recessions, the record of production and exports is healthier than that of a number of other European countries. Wages have risen fairly steeply but they have been well out-paced by production, and exports were almost doubled in the decade 1954–64. The composition of exports has changed gradually, as the newer industries have secured a foothold in foreign markets. The share of the woodworking industries fell, in 1965, to below seventy per cent of the total, while the metal and engineering industries accounted for nearly eighteen per cent. Exports of textiles, furniture and consumer goods amounted to eight, agricultural products to four or five per cent.

In 1961 Finland became an associate member of E.F.T.A., and since then her trade with the countries in this group has increased steadily. One of the most notable features of this increase has been the growth of exports to Sweden, traditionally regarded as one of the most difficult and exigent markets to break into. In 1965 the share of the major trading groups in Finnish exports was: E.F.T.A., 34 per cent; E.E.C., 28 per cent; the Eastern bloc, 21 per cent. Western countries take the biggest proportion of the products of the woodworking industries, and of consumer goods; while the bulk of metal and engineering exports goes to the Eastern bloc. Although there is a slight variation from year to year, the United Kingdom is more often than not Finland's biggest single customer, and for that reason Britain's growth rate is closely watched in Finland.

The balance of payments situation in Finland is equally closely watched, and subject to considerable variation. In spite of checks on consumption and exhortations to 'buy Finnish', it has proved during several years impossible to avoid a trade deficit. Inflation has, at times, been even more rampant in Finland than elsewhere in Europe, and only the 38 per cent devaluation of 1957 (the third since the war) made prices sufficiently competitive for exports to increase steadily.

The economic future depends largely on a successful incomes policy which, in the past, has been difficult to maintain over a long period. If cost levels can be stabilized, economists consider that it should be possible to maintain an average growth rate of 3½ to 4 per cent a year in the future. The rate has been considerably higher in some years since 1952, but the period of major expansion may now be over.

However, there are certain hurdles peculiar to Finland, of which one is the supply of manpower. Finland is one of the few European countries where growth in production has not been hampered at some time by a labour shortage. On the contrary, general plus seasonal unemployment caused by the weather has frequently posed its own problems and sent Finns in their thousands to Sweden in search of work. Now the time is not far ahead when Finland will be able to absorb all her own manpower in the developing industries, and may also feel the lack of the Finnish workers who have gone to Sweden. Wages are not low in Finland, but they are higher in Sweden; this makes many Finnish exports more competitive but keeps labour in Sweden. The growth of Nordic co-operation has increased the obsession of all the other Northern countries with keeping up with the Swedes, the Joneses of Scandinavia. This means not only higher wages but also more extensive social services and social security payments. The development of the common labour market in Scandinavia will inevitably demand a more or less common standard of living in the Northern countries if one is not to thrive at the expense of another.

To achieve some sort of parity with Sweden, Finland will need to maintain and increase her growth rate, and also to accelerate the rationalization of agriculture, which has hitherto proceeded rather slowly. Sustained economic growth depends ultimately on the strength and unity of Finnish governments. The capacity for growth is there, but the political obstacles common to so many countries are particularly numerous in Finland. Both the frequent changes of government and the devotion of each of the several parties to their own sectional interests militate against long-term overall planning. Nevertheless, since 1965 a plan for growth, drawn up by an independent Economic Council, has existed; its implementation will inevitably depend both on the ability of successive governments to push it forward and on the economic situation at home and in the world as a whole.

Chapter Seventeen

The Nordic Family

One of the minor characteristics of the Northern countries is an attachment to flags which is childlike rather than chauvinistic. The flags, large and small, of all nations are produced and flown at the slightest provocation or pretext. In the precarious years after the war one frequently saw in Finland not the blue and white Finnish flag alone, but the flags of all five Nordic countries, Denmark, Finland, Iceland, Norway and Sweden, flying side by side. In those days of isolation it sometimes seemed a gesture both brave and pathetic, a hopeful demonstration of a solidarity which was not yet fully achieved. Then it was not easy to believe that the five flags heralded a time when the bonds between each country would grow firmer and stronger, and when the North would emerge as a distinct entity with its own part to play on the European and the world stage. It was still less easy to look ahead to the day when the cliché 'Finland between East and West' would be outworn, and Finland could be counted a full member of the Nordic family.

Now Finland must be viewed first and foremost as part of the North. In spite of her many differences from the Scandinavian peninsula and Denmark, her place in the modern world is with them. Today the North appears in a clearer light as a region with its own special character, at home in the twentieth century and in tune with its evolving mood. In the North the rest of the world can see on a small scale many of the things it seeks for itself: order and education, social democracy and a simple way of life. The world may not covet the dullness and absence of excitement which sometimes accompanies this 'middle way', but it envies the achievement of moderation. The Northmen of today have preserved the sense of law and order which the Vikings of a thousand years ago took, along with their fury, to the lands they explored, conquered or settled – lands as far apart as America and Sicily. But over the intervening millennium they have lost the aggressive instincts which took them so far afield. The fires of conquest burned themselves out when Sweden at last renounced aggression and power politics at the beginning of the nineteenth century, and the North became isolated and insignificant. When the men of the North left their homesteads again later in that century, it was not as warriors and explorers but as humble emigrants, seeking in the American continent the livelihood they could not harvest from their own lands, then agriculturally unrewarding and in part industrially retarded.

So the twentieth century has been, throughout the North, a time of reawakening and renewal after a long stretch of near-dormant years, removed from the turmoil of European politics. Since the Second World War the Nordic countries have assumed an international role far more important than their small size would warrant, and gained it for several reasons besides their known moderation. Geography, separating them from the great power blocs, gave them the initial opportunity to develop independence and detachment in an over-committed world. Even the suspicious did not suspect them of aggressive intentions. Their colonial past lay deep in history, out of danger of charges of imperialism from the most rabid of anti-imperialists. The world saw in the North a point of stability, from which it called two Secretaries-General of the United Nations, the Norwegian Trygve Lie and the Swede Dag Hammarskjöld, and two other outstanding men of peace, the Swede Folke Bernadotte and the Finn Sakari Tuomioja. These men came from a background of opinion strongly oriented to internationalism and peace by mediation and negotiation. The small countries of the North have often been lightly judged as provincial and even parochial, possibly because they have little gift for abstract thought systems of universal application. But in modern times the Nordic people, collectively and individually, have often displayed a far keener interest in world affairs than the inhabitants of larger and more powerful states. They are traditionally seafaring men; over the centuries they have habitually gone to other countries to study; in order to do business with the world they have had to travel and adapt themselves to other needs and customs. Today the citizens of the small countries of the North have become less isolated from world movements than many of the people of the great monolithic states.

For the Nordic countries, internationalism runs along two courses:

participation in world affairs, and co-operation among themselves and in the European context. The two interlock at various points because the five countries have acquired the habit of considering each other when formulating their respective foreign policies. This does not mean that they have been able to evolve a common policy, nor that individual policies are always entirely acceptable throughout the North. But it does mean that differences and divergencies are better understood and accepted because they have often been discussed in advance, and because they are believed to be genuinely unavoidable. It also means that when the Northern countries speak with one voice on international questions, as they frequently do, they carry a correspondingly greater weight. The development of Nordic co-operation is one of the great pragmatic successes of the post-war years, and has demonstrated the ability of the Northern countries to absorb the major political differences between them. They have in many respects achieved a greater and wider degree of integration than have the countries of the E.E.C., and they have done this in spite of differences of political position which would be intolerable to the E.E.C. Norway, a member of N.A.T.O., traditionally looks westward to the Atlantic; Denmark, also a member of N.A.T.O., has been more closely influenced by developments in Germany than have the other Nordic nations; Sweden, determinedly neutral, always keeps an eye turned towards the East as well as to the West; Finland has her special relationship with and treaty obligations towards the Soviet Union; and small and distant Iceland, formerly an outpost of Denmark, has her own particular problems of size and geography.

Successful co-operation, in these circumstances, could not have been reached without great flexibility and a determination not to be bound by the letter of the law. The Northern countries prize this flexibility highly; and much as they hope for eventual inclusion in a more closely integrated Europe, they would be reluctant to enter into arrangements so rigid that their own flexible co-operation was threatened. The form taken by Nordic co-operation, which has been considerably strengthened on the economic side by membership of or association with E.F.T.A., underlines the temperamental differences in the approach to unity between the pragmatic Nordic countries and Britain on the one hand, and the more theoretical Common Market countries on the other. It also underlines a certain regional detachment, a way of looking at Europe as if from the outside. To the Northern countries, as to Britain, 'the Continent' is another region, from which all except Denmark are separated by the sea.

A former Swedish minister, Professor Bertil Ohlin, has hopefully observed that 'from a general European point of view, the North may be suitable as a place of experiment for new ideas concerning international co-operation'. The experience of the Northern lands might well point the way to certain practical and limited forms of co-operation which could be adapted and adopted elsewhere. But the countries of the North, and in particular the neighbouring Denmark, Finland, Norway and Sweden, have long-standing affinities which have no parallel elsewhere in Europe, and which counterweight their divergent defence policies. They have many individual characteristics which they are anxious to retain; they have also many common characteristics which give them a basic similarity of outlook. They are all small countries in terms of population, and the numerical differences between them are not so great as to encourage inequality of respect or the development of a 'pecking order'. Only Iceland, with a population of 180,000, is so small and so distant as to require a special approach in some matters. Their smallness, though a seeming disadvantage in a world of power politics, has allowed them to develop on their own individual lines; and it has made them, in the twentieth century, better places to live in than many larger countries with a long tradition of world power and prestige. This has depended, in the first place, on the energy with which they have exploited their resources and achieved the above-average level of prosperity which, in its turn, has allowed them to enjoy their advantages. There are the advantages of space, of an open society, of individual personality as opposed to anonymity. There is the stimulus of more interesting and responsible work for a greater number of people, although there are, at the same time, less room and a smaller choice of jobs at the top. There is the stimulus of being able to innovate and achieve without having to throw off a burden of superfluous tradition. There is the absence of the oppressive obligation to sustain a great role in the world, and the corresponding possibility for each country to cultivate its own garden more profitably.

The Northern lands are individually all homogeneous countries, and there is a large degree of homogeneity between them. Their racial minorities are small; they are all Lutheran countries with only small religious minorities. All except Finland speak a related language, and there Swedish is an official language, the mother tongue of the minority and the second language of the majority. All have comparable social backgrounds in which the gaps between rich and poor, between those who govern and those who are governed, and between people following different occupations, are smaller than elsewhere in Europe. The monarchies of Denmark, Norway and Sweden have shed much of their pomp and circumstance, and today their existence irks only a small minority. The common ideal of the egalitarian society is pursued more conscientiously and relentlessly in some Scandinavian countries than in others, but everywhere it entails the same process of levelling upwards rather than downwards. The North wants to be an educated middle-class society; it rejects the cheap and the shoddy and does not deride such attributes as honesty, conscientiousness, good behaviour and good speech. These may not be universally achieved, but they are commonly accepted as constituting a desirable standard, and this makes the day-to-day operation of social democracy far easier and more relaxed.

The Northern countries have developed a common social philosophy, though the extent of social welfare and benefits is not equal everywhere. Denmark and Sweden in particular have regarded themselves as 'social laboratories', in which various experiments in community work have taken place. All consciously include an objective less clearly defined in the social policies of many other countries: the attainment of that intangible quality, 'contentment with life', as related to more material elements such as housing or working conditions.

All in all, the countries of the North share a basic set of values and a basic way of life, both more fundamental and enduring than their divergencies in foreign and defence policy. They have so much in common, and have had for hundreds of years, that one can be surprised at the late development of their co-operation. One of the reasons for this delay lies in another shared Northern characteristic – a national self-assertion which has demanded, particularly in Finland and Norway, a period of sharply-edged independence of their neighbours. Finland had to prove that she could stand alone after centuries as part of the kingdom of Sweden or as a Grand Duchy of Russia;

Norway had to assert her national character after the long era of subjection to either Denmark or Sweden which ended in 1905. Now, with their independence and sovereignty assured, the Northern countries can meet in a form of co-operation between independent equals which belongs only to the twentieth century, and in which the historical subordination of one to another is largely forgotten.

This, then, is the setting of Finland's present and future development. It brings to a close the isolation of the past and stabilizes her position in Europe and the world. It opens up possibilities of economic, cultural and social achievement greater than Finland, or any other one country of the group, could hope for single-handed. How far will it change the character of Finland and the Finns, whose sharp individuality has been strengthened in isolation and resistance? The Danes, the Norwegians and the Swedes are similar to each other both in heredity and in their man-made environment. The Finns are, as it were, half-brothers who bring a different genetic inheritance into an environment which is comparable, though modified by the duality of the marchland. Their eastern strain makes them more emotional and imaginative than the true Scandinavians, and they respond less happily to the calm order of the Nordic countries. They cannot summon up the disciplined acceptance of uniformity and equality shown in some matters by the Swedes, and they are often caught between conflicting desires to be like and unlike them. The centuries of subordinate relationship to Sweden have left the Finns with a still unsatisfied anxiety to prove that Finland can do as well as her more advanced and wealthy neighbour. Over the years, many Swedish developments have reached Finland, with a certain time-lag, and made a considerable contribution to the Finnish advance; but Finland sometimes risks overstraining her resources, or choosing less suitable policies, when emulating the Swedes.

In a world where regional groupings are becoming increasingly common, the smaller nations have much to gain – and something to lose – by co-operation with those around them. The Nordic countries, by reason of their natural mixability, could move faster along the road to fusion than many others. The process of breaking down internal regional differences is already gathering pace in Finland. Industrialization and consequent greater mobility have brought about in a couple of decades a greater social intermixture of Tavasts, Karelians and Swedish-speaking Finns than has existed at any time in Finland's history. The free movement of capital and labour throughout the Nordic countries will presumably lead to a greater intermixture of Danes, Finns, Norwegians and Swedes. Perhaps an even more closely knit North may eventually develop and many national differences may be submerged as all become Northmen.

Yet it is difficult to imagine a time when the Finns will become indistinguishable from the other Scandinavians. Today they are caught up in a whirlwind of change, after centuries in which change has been for them little more than a slow movement in the air. As the North influences and is influenced by the rest of Europe, the Finns may acquire some of the superficial features of both Northern and Western standardization. Beneath the surface, out of an instinctive tenacious reaction, they are likely to cling all the more closely to the traditions, the background, the language and the land which have contributed so much to their individuality. The Finns have above all one most individual characteristic – they are among the few peoples of Western Europe who are still in love with the world. If they should lose this zest and optimism they would lose themselves and they would no longer be Finns.

Bibliography

General

Facts about Finland 1963. 7th rev. ed. Helsinki, 1963.

Finland in Focus. Helsinki, 1964.

Introduction to Finland 1960. Ministry for Foreign Affairs, Helsinki.

Introduction to Finland 1963. Ministry for Foreign Affairs, Helsinki.

MEAD, W. R. *How People Live in Finland*. London, 1965.

The Northern Countries. Publ. by the Foreign Ministries of Denmark, Iceland, Norway and Sweden. Stockholm, 1952.

Geography

MEAD, W. R. *An Economic Geography of the Scandinavian States and Finland*. London, 1958.

MEAD, W. R., and SMEDS, HELMER. *Winter in Finland*. London, 1967.

MILLWARD, ROY. *Scandinavian Lands*. London, 1964.

History and Politics

ALENIUS, S. *Finland Between the Armistice and the Peace*. Helsinki, 1947.

ANDERSSON, INGVAR. *A History of Sweden*. London, 1956.

BURNHAM, R. E. *Who are the Finns?* London, 1946.

COLIN DU TERRAIL, HUGUES. *La Finlande et les Russes depuis les Croisades Suédoises*. Paris, 1963.

FRIETSCH, C. O. *Finlands Ödesår*. Stockholm, 1945.

GRIPENBERG, G. A. *Neutralitetstanken i Finlands Politik*. Stockholm, 1960.

JAAKKOLA, JALMARI (trans. JEAN-LOUIS PERRET). *Précis d'Histoire de la Finlande*. Lausanne, 1942.

JACKSON, J. HAMPDEN. *Finland*. London, 1940.

JAKOBSON, MAX. *The Diplomacy of the Winter War*. Cambridge, Mass., 1961.

JUTIKKALA, EINO, and PIRINEN, KAUKO. *A History of Finland*. London, 1962.

KASTARI, PAAVO. *Presidenterna och deras Ställning*. Stockholm, 1961.

KIVIKOSKI, ELLA. *Finlands Forntid*. Helsinki, 1965.

MAZOUR, A. *Finland between East and West*. New York, 1956.

MANNERHEIM, C. G. *The Memoirs of Marshal Mannerheim*. London, 1953.

Nordic Co-operation. Report of Conference organized by the Nordic Council for International Organizations in Europe, Stockholm, 1965.

NOUSIAINEN, JAAKO. *Finlands Politiska Partier.* Stockholm, 1964.

PARES, BERNARD. *A History of Russia.* London, 1926.

PASZKIEWICZ, HENRYK. *The Origins of Russia.* London, 1954.

The Scandinavian States and Finland: A Political and Economic Survey. Royal Institute of International Affairs, London, 1951.

TANNER, VÄINÖ. *The Winter War.* Stanford, California, 1957.

UPTON, A. F. *Finland in Crisis, 1940–1941.* London, 1964.

VILKUNA, KUSTAA. *När Kommo Ostersjöfinnarna till Baltikum?* Acta Ethnologica et Folkloristica Europaea, 1948–49, Stockholm. 1949.

WUORINEN, J. H. *Finland and the World War II 1939–1944.* New York, 1948.

WUORINEN, J. H. *A History of Finland.* New York, 1965.

ZILLIACUS, V., (ed.). *Bonde-Finland.* Stockholm, 1949.

SOCIAL AND ECONOMIC

COLLINDER, B. *The Lapps.* New York, 1949.

From Spruce to News. Finnish Paper Mills Association, Helsinki, 1964.

HEIKKILÄ, RAIMO. *Finland, the Land of Cooperatives.* Helsinki, 1963.

HUSTICH, ILMARI. *Land i Förvandling.* 2nd ed., Stockholm, 1964.

KARJALAINEN, AHTI. *A National Economy Based on Wood.* Helsinki, 1956.

KNOELLINGER, CARL ERIK. *Labor in Finland.* Cambridge, Mass., 1960.

KUUSI, PEKKA. *Social Policy for the Sixties: A Plan for Finland.* Helsinki, 1964.

LINNAMO, JUSSI. *Folkhushållet Finland.* Stockholm, 1964.

MEAD, W. R. *Farming in Finland.* London, 1953.

Social Legislation and Work in England. Publ. by the Ministry of Social Affairs. Helsinki, 1953.

WARIS, HEIKKI. *Samhället Finland.* Stockholm, 1961.

WESTERMARCK, NILS. *Finnish Agriculture.* Helsinki, 1964.

RELIGION AND EDUCATION

Finland and its Students. National Union of Students of Finland, 1962.

KALLIO, N. *Education in Finland.* 5th ed. Helsinki, 1961.

SENTZKE, G. *Finland, its Church and its People.* The Luther-Agricola Society, Helsinki, 1963.

LITERATURE AND THE ARTS

Literature and Language

COLLINDER, BJÖRN. *Finskan som Kulturspråk.* Stockholm, 1964.

HAVU, T. *An Introduction to Finnish Literature.* Helsinki, 1952.

MAGOUN, F. P., (trans.). *The Kalevala.* Cambridge, Mass., 1963.

TOMPURI, ELLI, (ed.). *Voices from Finland.* Helsinki, 1947.
TORNUDD, KLAUS. *Svenska Språkets Ställning i Finland.* Stockholm, 1960.

Music

ABRAHAM, G. *Sibelius: A Symposium.* London, 1947.
HELASVUO, V. *Sibelius and the Music of Finland.* 3rd ed. Helsinki, 1962.
JOHNSON, H. E. *Jean Sibelius.* New York, 1959.
KARILA, T. *Composers of Finland.* Helsinki, 1961.
PARMET, S. *The Symphonies of Sibelius: A Study in Musical Appreciation.* London, 1959.
RICHARDS, DENBY. *An Introduction to Contemporary Finnish Music.* London, 1967.
RINGBOM, NILS-ERIC. *Sibelius.* Stockholm, 1948.

Painting

SAARIKIVI, S., NIILONEN, K. and EKELUND, H. *Art in Finland.* Ed. J. Ukkonen. Helsinki, 1961.

Theatre

HEIKKILÄ, RITVA, (ed.). *The Finnish National Theatre.* Porvoo, 1962.

ARCHITECTURE AND DESIGN

Alvar Aalto. Ed. by H. Girsberger and K. Fleig. *Zürich,* 1963.
BECKER, H.-J., *and* SCHLOTE, W. *New Housing in Finland.* Stuttgart, 1964.
Designed in Finland. Published annually by the Finnish Foreign Trade Association, Helsinki.
Finland Builds Today. Finnish Foreign Trade Association. Helsinki, 1964.
HÅRD AF SEGERSTAD, ULF. *Scandinavian Design.* Helsinki, 1961.
HÅRD AF SEGERSTAD, ULF. *Sextio År Finsk Konstflit.* Stockholm, 1962.
HAYCRAFT, JOHN. *Finnish Jewellery and Silverware.* Helsinki, 1962.
RICHARDS, J. M. *A Guide to Finnish Architecture.* London, 1966.
SCHILDT, G., MOSSO, L., and OKSALA, T. *Alvar Aalto.* Jyväskylä, 1964.
TROUP, LOTTE. *Modern Finnish Textiles.* Helsinki, 1962.
WICKBERG, N. E. *Finnish Architecture.* Helsinki, 1962.

TRAVEL

Helsinki à la Carte. Ed. A. Goodrich. 3rd ed. Helsinki, 1961.
NICKELS, SYLVIE. *The Travellers' Guide to Finland.* London, 1965.
NICKELS, SYLVIE. *The Young Traveller in Finland.* London, 1962.

OFFICIAL AND PERIODICAL PUBLICATIONS

Bank of Finland Monthly Bulletin. Helsinki.
The Economic Review Quarterly. Helsinki, Kansallis-Osake-Pankki.

Economic Survey of Finland 1964. Ministry of Finance, Helsinki.

Finnish Trade Review. The Finnish Export Association, Helsinki.

National Budget for 1965. Ministry of Finance, Helsinki.

Report on Growth Policy in Finland. Helsinki, 1965.

Suomen tilastollinen vuosikirja – Statistik årsbork för Finland – Statistical Yearbook of Finland. Central Statistical Office, Helsinki.

Unitas. Quarterly review illustrating economic conditions in Finland. Helsinki, Pohjoismaiden Yhdyspankki.

MISCELLANEOUS

BENTON, P. *Finnish Food for your Table.* Oxford, 1960.

TOLVANEN, K. *Finnish Food.* A selection of Finnish recipes. 3rd ed. Helsinki, 1962.

VIHERJUURI, H. J. *Sauna, the Finnish Bath.* 4th ed. Helsinki, 1963.

Finnish and Swedish Place Names

In this book, Finnish names have been used for those localities which have corresponding Finnish and Swedish names. Since the Swedish names may sometimes be more familiar to the English reader, they are given in the following list.

FINNISH	SWEDISH
Suomi	Finland
Helsinki	Helsingfors
Hanko	Hangö
Hämeenlinna	Tavastehus
Hamina	Fredrikshamn
Hyvinkää	Hyvinge
Lappeenranta	Villmanstrand
Oulu	Uleåborg
Pori	Björneborg
Porvoo	Borgå
Suursaari	Hogland
Tammisaari	Ekenäs
Tampere	Tammerfors
Turku	Åbo
Ulvila	Ulvsby
Uusikaupunki	Nystad
Viipuri	Viborg

The Swedish *Åland*, however, has been employed in place of the Finnish *Ahvenanmaa*, as it has established itself in international usage.

A Note on Finnish Pronunciation

The pronunciation of Finnish follows certain clear and definite rules which, once grasped by the foreigner, enable him immediately to pronounce Finnish more easily than many languages.

The accent falls strongly and regularly on the first syllable of the word. Every letter is fully and equally voiced, whether it is a vowel or consonant. Every syllable, in pronunciation, begins with the consonant. Thus, for instance, 'Helsinki' is divided – Hel/sin/ki. Where vowels and consonants are doubled in spelling, they are also doubled in speech, and 'h' is fully aspirated, whether at the beginning or in the middle of a word.

An adequate guide to the pronunciation of Finnish can be given only by the use of international phonetic symbols; the approximate English equivalents of the vowel sounds are as follows:

a as in f*a*ther
ä as in h*a*nd
e as in l*e*nd
i as in s*ee*n
o as in h*o*t
ö as in b*u*rn
u as in t*oo*
y has no corresponding English sound; its nearest relative is the French u in *une*; but the lips are less rounded and the teeth more closed.

Index

Aalto, A., 32, 37 f, 42, 65, 157, 182; furniture, 186 f, 192
Aaltonen, V., 81, 187
Aarikka, Kaija, 193
Agrarian (Centre) Party, 121, 129, 141, 145, 156, 165
Agreement on Friendship, Co-operation and Mutual Assistance, 120 f, 126 ff, 135
Agricola, Michael (Bishop of Turku), 87
Agricultural Policy Committee, 166, 170
Agriculture, 151 ff, 160 ff, 204
 animal husbandry, 162 f
 co-operatives, 164
 dairy products, 162 ff
 land clearance, 162
 mechanization, 153
 production, 161 f
 specialist societies, 163
 subsidies, 162
A.I.V. fodder, 162
Åland Islands, 23, 33, 85
alcohol, consumption of, 48 f, 68 f
Alcohol Monopoly, State, 201
Alexander I, 35, 91, 96, 98 f, 117
Alexander II, 92, 100 f
Alexander III, 101 f
Arabia china works, *see* 'Wärtsilä-Arabia'
architecture, 30, 32, 35 ff, 39 f, 70, 125, 172, 181 ff
armed forces, 100, 102, 112, 131
armistice (1944), 116 f, 123
arts, patronage of, 81
Arwidsson, A., 100
Autere, H., 82

balance of payments, 203
Baltic Sea, 86, 96 ff, 101, 136
Bank of Finland, 101
Bergbom, Dr K., 76
Bernadotte, Folke, 206
birth-rate, 154
Bobrikov, N., 102 f
bolsheviks, 105, 142
bookshops, 72
Brahe, Count Per, 88
broadcasting organization, 201
Brummer, Eva, 191
Bryk, Rut, 188, 193
building construction, 30, 57 f
building industry, 201
Byzantine Empire, 85

'Calotte', 133, 136
Central Revolutionary Council, 106
Centre Party, *see* 'Agrarian Party'
ceramics, 186, 193
Charles X, 97
Charles XI, 89 f
chemical industry, 201
children, 58, 68 f, 177
Christianity, conversion of Finland to, 86
Christmas, 59
Church, social influence of, 69 ff; foundation in Finland, 86 f; Lutheran reformation, 87; Communists in, 143; Greek Orthodox Church, 172 f
Chydenius, Anders, 91
Civil War (1918), 64, 107, 143
climate, 16 f, 48, 160; spring, 26; summer, 26, 28, 40, 56, 59 ff; autumn, 27; winter, 27, 39 f, 56 ff

coastline, 22, 24
Collinder, Prof. B., 53
communications, *see* 'transport and communications'
Communism, 19, 109, 119, 125
Communist Party, formation in Finland, 108; driven underground, 110; resuscitation, 121; as People's Democratic Union, 122; supporters of, 139, 143 f; numbers and policy, 142 ff; made illegal, later reinstated, 143; coalition with Agrarians and Social Democrats, 144; inclusion in Government, 145 f
Compliants, 103
conscription law, 102
Conservative Party, 141, 145
Constitutionalists, 103
Continuation War (1944–5), 117, 155
copper mining, 196, 200
Crimean War, 101
customs union, proposed Scandinavian, 133 f
Czechoslovakia, 120 f

Danes, 210 f
decentralization, 155 f
Denmark, war with Sweden, 89; and Nordic co-operation, 131 f, 134, 136, 207
design, 184 ff
devaluation, 203
development areas, 155 f
Diet, 98 f, 100, 102
divorce, 68
Dutch in Baltic, 88

Eastern Europe, trade with, 126, 203
eastern Finland, 25, 44, 45, 67, 172
Economic Council, 204
education,
  schools, 65, 176 f
  universities, 41 f, 65, 88, 133, 156
  vocational training, 163 f, 176 f
E.E.C., 131, 137, 203, 207
E.F.T.A., 126, 128, 134, 137, 203, 207
Ehrenström, J.A., 35, 37
elections, 98, 103, 105, 108, 121 f, 139, 145
electro-technical industry, 201
Engel, C.L., 32, 35
engineering and metal industries, 122, 126, 196, 198, 202 f
Enso-Gutzeit Oy, 202
Erik, King, 86
Ervi, A., 182
Estates, Finnish, 98, 103, 138; Swedish, 16, 62 ff, 87 f, 138
Estonia, 14, 97 f, 101, 111
Estonians, 13 f
exports, 188 f, 196 f, 199 f, 203 f

Fagerholm, K.A., 130
Fallen Asleep While Young, 74
family life, 66 f, 69
Family Welfare League, 179 f
farmers, 155, 161, 165, 167, 170. *See also* 'Agriculture'
fashion design, 194
fauna, 28 f
Fennomanians, 93
Finland, on early trade routes, 85 as part of Sweden, 14, 16 f, 62 f, 85, 86 ff: absorption into Sweden, 86 f; under Gustavus Vasa, 87; founding, of Helsinki, 88; Swedish wars, 88 f; under Charles XI, 89; cession to Russia, 90, 96 as Grand Duchy of Russia, 16 f, 35, 73, 134, 138; occupation by Peter the Great, 97 f; under Alexander I, 98 f; under Nicholas I, 99 f; under Alexander II, 100 f; under Alexander III, 101 f; status of 'personal union' with Tsar, 102; under Nicholas II, 102 ff;

russification and repression, 102; temporary recovery of autonomy, 103; 'personal union' ended, 104; becomes part of Russian Empire, 104; Russian revolution, 105; Declaration of Independence, 105
See also 'eastern Finland, 'Sweden', 'Russia', etc.
Finnish Airlines, 159, 201
Finnish Artists' Association, 81
Finnish language, 13 ff, 18, 73, 87, 91 ff
Finnish Literature Society, 52, 73
Finno-Ugrians, 13, 14, 128
Finns, character, 15, 18, 20, 25, 43 ff, 46 ff, 75, 128, 138, 159, 211; origins, 13, 18, 43 f; 'pure' Finns, 44 ff, 63 f, 93, 95, 138; racial groups, 43 ff, 210; Swedo-Finns, 44, 45 f, 63 f, 93 ff, 138
First World War, 62, 104, 134
flora, 22 f, 28
food-processing industry, 201
forestry and timber, 167 ff, 196 ff; improvement programme, 169 f, 198.
See also 'Woodworking industries'.
Forestry Financing Committee, 169 f
forests, 22 f, 30 f, 161, 167 ff, 185
Form of Government Act, 108
France, 113
Franck, K., 188
Freudenthal, A.O., 93
Friedrich Karl of Hesse, Prince, 108
Friends of Finnish Handicrafts, 186
frontier, Finno-Russian, 17, 34, 45, 97, 11 ff, 116 f, 133
furniture design, 186, 192 f, 195

Gardberg, B., 194
geology and soil, 22, 160 f
Germany and Finland, 104 f, 107, 110 f, 113 ff, 117, 137, 155; and Russia, 104, 111, 113 ff, 121, 129
glassware, 186, 193, 195
governments, 139 f
Great Britain, 113 ff, 203, 207 f
Great Northern War, 34
'Great Wrath', 89, 97
Gulf of Finland, 96, 127
Gummerus, O., 189
Gustavus III, 90
Gustavus Adolphus, 89, 97
Gustavus Vasa, 33, 87 f

Hamina, 34; Peace of, 35
Hammarskjöld, Dag, 206
handicrafts, 185 f
Hanko (peninsula), 111, 113
Helsinki, 29, 32 ff, 156, 180 f; town plan, 31 f, 35, 37 f; architecture, 32 f, 35 ff, 39 f; music in, 79; as bilingual community, 94
founded, 33 f, 88; burnt down, 34 f; rebuilt, 35; becomes seat of government, 35; captured by Russia, 97; bombed, 112
Esplanade, 35 f; Great Church, 32, 35; islands, 39; market, 32 f; Orthodox Cathedral, 32; Parliament House, 36; Senate Square, 32, 35, 37, 101; Suomenlinna (Sveaborg), 34 f
Helsinki Convention, 132 f
Hiltunen, E., 82
Hitler, 111, 113 f, 117 f
home ownership, 175, 181
Honka, O., 129 f
housing, 175 f, 180 ff, 209
Housing Foundation, 179 f, 183
Hovi, M., 82
Hungarians, 13 f, 137
Hungary, 14, 120
hydro-electric schemes, 152, 155, 201 f

Ice Age, 22
Iceland, 131, 133, 207 f
Ilvessalo, Kirsti, 191
Imatra, 157
Imperial manifesto, 102
imports, 169, 198
income per head, 153 f
Independence, Declaration of, 64, 105
independence constitution, 146
independence movement, 15, 104
industrial welfare, 174 f, 176 ff, 209
industry, development of, 20 f, 30, 101; war reparations, 122 ff; post-war growth, 125; modernization, 152 ff, 156; location of industry, 154; automation, 156 f; social effects of industrialization, 210; Valkeakoski, 171 ff; mass production, 185; present situation 196 ff
inflation, 203
Ingermanland, 97
Institute of Arctic Medicine (Oulu), 133
Institute of Maritime Law (Oslo), 133
Institute for Theoretical Nuclear Physics (Copenhagen), 133
islands, 22 ff, 39, 108, 111, 154
Ivan the Terrible, 85, 97

Jaeger Battalion, 105 f
Jakobson, M., 97, 131
jewellery design, 193 f
Jung, Dora, 191
Jyväskylä, 156

Kaipiainen, B., 193
Kajanus, R., 78
Kalevala, 73 f
Karelia, 44, 97 f, 154; Eastern Karelia, 108, 110, 115, 165, 197; Karelian Isthmus, 112, 115 f
Karelian dialect, 54
Karelians, 43 ff, 46, 125, 172, 210
Karhula-Iittala glassworks, 186
Kekkonen, President, 21, 61, 129 ff, 135 f
Kemi River, 168
Kerensky, 105
Khrushchev, N., 129
Kilpinen, Y., 79
king, election of, 108
Kivi, A., 74
Kivimaa, A., 76
Kotka, 154
Kukkapuro, Y., 192
Kuopio, 156
Kuusamo, 112, 116
Kuusinen, O., 112
Kymi River, 168

Ladoga, Lake, 111
Lahti, 41, 154
lakes, 22 f
landscape, 22 ff
Liberal Party, 141, 145
Lie, Trygve, 206
Linna, V., 74
literature, 45, 72 ff, 87; folk poetry, 45, 73 f
Lithuania, 101, 111
Livonia, 97 f
Language Decree, 92, 100
language question, 14, 45 f, 52 ff, 63 f, 89 f, 91 ff, 100, 102, 104, 209. *See also* 'Finnish language' and 'Swedish language'.
Lapland, 24 ff, 29, 154 f, 160, 168
Laplanders, 54
Lappeenranta, 34
Lappish language, 14, 54
Lapps, 13, 43, 54 f
Latvia, 111
League of Nations, 110
legal system, 88, 91
Leino, Y., 121 f
Lenin, 104
Leningrad (St Petersburg), 97, 111, 113, 187, 193
Lönnrot, E., 73

Mannerheim, Marshal, 50, 100, 107, 111 f; appointed regent, 108; becomes President, 116; resignation, 118
Mannermaa, O., 192
manpower, 198, 204
Marshall Plan, 126
'Martha' organization, 166
meals, 58 f
Metsovaara, Marjatta, 191
midsummer celebration, 61
Milan Triennale (1951), 184, 186; (1960), 193
mineral resources, 153, 196, 200 f
Molotov, 113 f
monarchies, 209
monetary system, 101
music, 78 ff;
composers, 78 f;
singers, 79;
amateur music, 80

National Pension Fund, 202
nationalism, 72 f, 77, 90, 92, 100, 104, 138, 184, 186, 209
N.A.T.O., 132, 136, 207
neutrality, Finnish, 17, 111, 127, 129, 131 f, 134 ff
Nicholas I, 99 f
Nicholas II, 102 ff
Nordic co-operation, 20, 94, 125, 131 ff, 136, 204 f, 207 f
Nordic Council, 126, 128, 132 f
Nordic countries, common characteristics, 205 f, 208; internationale role, 206 ff
Norway, 131 ff, 136, 207 ff, 210 f
Novgorod, 85, 87
nuclear power, 201
nuclear-free zone, proposed, 136
Nurmesniemi, A., 192

Ohlin, Prof. B., 208
Opera, Finnish National, 79
'Operation Barbarossa', 114
'Oslo group', 110
Ostrobothnia, 25, 77, 154
Oulu, 41, 133, 156
Oulu River, 168
Outokumpu Oy, 200, 202

Paasikivi, President, 50, 70, 118 f, 121, 127, 129, 135
Paasio, R., 145
painting, 80 f
Palmgren, S., 79
pan-Slavism, 15, 101
paper industry, 196 ff
Parliament, 19, 103, 105, 107 f, 139 f, 147
parliamentary representation, 139, 144
Paszkiewicz, H., 128
peace treaty (1940), 112 f
Pekkala, M., 121
pensions, 177
People's Democratic Union, 122
Peter the Great, 85, 97 f, 117
Petsamo, 108, 116
Poland, 89
Poles, 101, 137
political system, 18 f, 138 ff
Pomerania, 97
population, 15, 29, 37, 40 f; movement of, 153 ff
Pori, 154
Porkkala, 117, 126 f
Porthan, H.G., 98
Porvoo, 34, 98
Power Law, 105
President, 19, 139; powers of, 141, 146 ff
presidential elections, 129 f
press, freedom of, 91
'professional' government, 140
proportional representation, 19, 139 f

Rajalin, B., 194
Rauma, 33
Red Guard, 106 f
refugees, 118, 125
religion, 31, 85 f, 91, 209. *See also* 'Christianity', 'Church'.

Renvall, B., 82
reparations, 20, 117 f, 122 ff, 125, 151, 178, 196
Richards, J.M., 35
Riihimäki glassworks, 186
Rovaniemi, 155
Rumania, 120
Runeberg, J.L., 74
Russia, Finno-Ugrians in, 13 f, 53, 128; ambitions in Baltic, 85, 97; workers' strike, 103; at war with Japan, 103; at war with Germany, 104; revolution, 105; Provisional Government, 105
Russia and Finland, 16 f, 64, 78, 96 ff; influence on Finland, 18, 109, 187; Russian occupation, 89, 97; annexation of Finland, 90, 96, 98; Finland as Grand Duchy of Russia, 16, 98 ff; end of Russian rule, 108
Russia and Sweden, 15 f, 88, 96 ff; Sweden and Novgorod, 87; wars with Sweden, (1741-3) 34; (1808-9) 35, 98
Russia, as Soviet Union
Soviet Union and Finland, 107, 109 ff, 119, 125 f, 127 ff, 135 ff, 207; trade with Finland, 134, 169, 199 f; recognition of Finland, 105, 108; troops in Finland, 107; Winter War, 112; Second War, 115 f; armistice terms, 116 f, 163, 135; reparations, 118, 122 ff, 125, 151, 196; Agreement on Friendship, Co-operation and Mutual Assistance, 120 f; trade treaties, 126; attitude to Finland in U.N., 130 f; attitude to Finnish political parties, 143, 146
Soviet and Germany, 111, 113, 114 ff, 121
Soviet Union and Scandinavia, 132 f, 136
Russian language, 92, 102, 194
Russians, Finnish affinities with, 128, 137
ryijy rugs, 190 f
Ryti, President, 115, 130

Saarinen, E., 36
Saimaa Canal, 127
St Lucia, Feast of, 58 f
St Petersburg, *see* 'Leningrad'
Sarpaneva, T., 188
Säteri Oy, 171, 175 ff
sauna, 60 f
Savo, 44; Savolaks, 44
Säynätsalo, 42
Scandinavian countries, *see* 'Nordic countries', 'Nordic co-operation'
sculpture, 81 f
Second War (1941), 115 f, 117, 155
Second World War, 17, 19, 44, 62, 110, 118, 131, 206
Seinäjoki, 42
Seven Brothers, 74
ship-building, 122 f
Sibelius, 25, 31, 50, 62, 65, 78ff, 184, 193
Sibelius Academy, 78
Sillanpää, F.E., 74
Simberg-Ehrström, Uhra, 191
Sinuhe the Egyptian, 74
Sirèn, J.S., 36
smallholdings, 161, 163, 165 f, 170
Snellman, J.V., 92, 100
Social-Democratic Party, 103, 105, 106 ff, 121, 122, 129 f, 142 f, 145 f, 165
social life, 40, 49 ff, 58 ff, 66
social services, 173, 209. *See also* 'Industrial welfare'.
social structure, 18, 62 ff, 64 ff, 209
Socialists, *see* Social-Democratic Party
Society of Crafts and Design, 185 f, 189
Soviet Union, *see* 'Russia'
sport, 39, 61, 177
Sprengtporten, G.M., 90, 98

Ståhlberg, Prof. K.J., 108
Stalin, 104, 107, 110, 113, 117 f, 125, 128
state ownership, 158 f, 167, 201 f
strikes, 103, 106
summer cottages, 49, 59 f
Suomenlinna (Sveaborg), 34 f, 39
Suursaari, 108, 111
Sveaborg, *see* 'Suomenlinna'
Svecomanians, 93
Sweden, ambitions in east, 85; under Gustavus Vasa, 87 f; wars, 88 f, 97 f; Thirty Years' War, 89; under Charles XI, 89; under Gustavus III, 90; waning of power, 98
Sweden and Finland, 89, 104; influence on Finns, 16 ff, 35, 86, 88, 91, 210; 'Northern Crusade', 85 f; relations in Middle Ages, 86 f; absorption of Finland, 86; Russia annexes Finland, 96; Sweden and Winter War, 112; Finns in Sweden, 95, 204; grain supplied to Finland, 116
Sweden and Nordic co-operation, 131 ff, 134, 136, 206 ff. *See also* 'Russia'.
Sweden-Finland, kingdom of, *see* 'Finland'
Swedes, 210 f
Swedish language, 14, 16, 63 f, 73, 88, 89 f, 91 ff, 209
Swedish Law, 91
Swedish Party, 141 f
Swedish-speaking Finns, 46, 75, 89 f, 92 f, 94, 138, 211
Swedo-Finns, *see* 'Finns'

Tacitus, 43
Tales of Ensign Stål, 74
talkoo, 175
Tallinn, 34, 88
Tammisaari, 34
Tampere, 41, 76, 154, 156
Tanner, V., 108, 129 f
Tapiola, 31, 51, 179 ff
Tapiovaara, I., 192
Tartu (Dorpat), Treaty of, 108, 111, 116, 118
Tavasts, 43 ff, 85, 210
television, 72, 77, 80, 133
textiles, 189 ff
theatre, 75 ff; amateur theatre, 77 f; Finnish National Theatre, 76; Tampere open-air theatre, 76
Thirty Years' War, 89
Thomas, Bishop, 86
Tilsit, Treaty of, 96
titles, 63, 65 f
Topelius, Z., 74
town-planning, 157, 171 ff, 179 ff
towns, 41 f
Toynbee, A.J., 15, 17
trade unions, 144, 179
transport and communications, 23, 29 f, 39, 55 f, 58, 151 f
  airlines, 55, 158 f, 201
  bus service, 36
  railways, 36, 56, 101, 158
  roads, 56, 58, 101, 158
  roads, 56, 58, 101, 158
  transport of timber, 167 ff
Tuomioja, Sakari, 131, 206
Turku, 34 f, 41, 86, 88, 97 f

Ulvila, 33
unemployment, 204
United Nations, 19, 126, 128, 130 ff, 206
United Paper Mills, 171, 174 ff
United States, 116, 136
universal franchise, 103
Unknown Soldier, 74
Uppsala, 86
Uppsala, Henry, Bishop of, 86
Uusikaupunki (Nystad), Peace of, 97
Uusimaa, 29, 154

Valamo Monastery, 173
Valio, 164

Valkeakoski, 171 ff; churches 172; social services, 173; industrial welfare, 174 f; housing, 175
Valmet, 202
Vantaa River, 34
Varangians, 85
Veps dialect, 54
Viipuri, 97 f, 112
Vikings, 15, 85, 205
villages, 29
Virtanen, Prof. A.I., 162
von Hertzen, Heikki, 179, 183

wages, 203
Walden, J., 171
Waltari, M., 74
Warsaw Pact, 136
Wärtsilä-Arabia china works, 186
Wärtsilä-Nötsjö glass works, 186
Weckström, B., 194
Western Europe, trade with, 200, 203
White Guard, 106 f
Winter War (1939-40), 47, 70, 97, 112, 117 f
Wirkkala, T., 187 f
women, 65, 67 f, 160, 163, 166
woodworking industries, 101, 152, 154 ff, 196 ff, 202 f
World Bank, 158, 201
Wrede, Baron, 171